"It'll require a feat of the loaves and fishes variety to better Mark McAvoy's comprehensive take on Cork's substantial contribution to rock music history. *Cork Rock: From Rory Gallagher To The Sultans Of Ping* is packed with facts and provocative anecdotes that weave the music into the culture of Cork and the world beyond. You've loved the music, now read the book." **Jackie Hayden – Hot Press**

"An excellent book" **Brian Boyd – The Irish Times**

"There's a hefty early focus on Rory Gallagher who's given an almost biographical going over. If you're into Cork music – or just want to learn more about it – you could hardly ask for a more quirky, fact-filled and well-written guide." **James Hendicott – State Magazine**

*Cork Rock: From Rory Gallagher To The Sultans Of Ping* was selected by Irish arts and culture website **OMG Entertainment** as one of their **'Best Eleven Books of 2009'**.

"A work of massive importance for Cork's cultural history and a hugely enjoyable read for anyone who has gigged, ligged or larked by the Lee." **Des O'Driscoll – Irish Examiner**

*Cork Rock: From Rory Gallagher To The Sultans Of Ping* was awarded the accolade of **Hot Press 'Music Book of The Fortnight'**.

"By the end of this colourful and deeply respectful book, a portrait of the city and the quirky talents it produces emerges, giving you a new found respect for the place and its distinctive inhabitants." **Irish Voice (New York City)**

"Opens with an excellent monograph of the truly talented Rory Gallagher" **Tom Widger – The Sunday Tribune**

"McAvoy vividly describes the growth and transformation of a music scene that both mirrored the trends of the time and produced a unique sound." **Aliah O'Neill – Irish America Magazine**

"An insightful and well-written book. Highly recommended!" **Ken Fallon – Cluas.com**

Finalist in the 2013 'Cork's Favourite Book' competition.

# CORK ROCK:
## FROM RORY GALLAGHER TO THE SULTANS OF PING

MARK MCAVOY

SOUTH BANK PRESS

First published in paperback only in 2009 by Mercier Press

First edition © Mark McAvoy, 2009

Second edition © Mark McAvoy, 2017

Published by South Bank Press, 3 South Bank, Crosses Green, Cork city, Ireland.

Contact the author on Twitter: @CorkRock

Mark McAvoy has asserted his moral right to be identified as the author of this work in accordance with the Copyright and Related Rights Act 2000.

ISBN 978-0-9956176-0-5

All rights reserved.

The material in this publication is protected by copyright law. Except as may be permitted by law, no part of the material may be reproduced (including by storage in a retrieval system) or transmitted in any form or by any means (electronic, mechanical, photocopying, recording or otherwise), adapted, rented or lent without the written permission of both the copyright owner and the publisher. Applications for permissions should be addressed to the publisher South Bank Press, 3 South Bank, Crosses Green, Cork city, Ireland.

# CONTENTS

Acknowledgements ................................................................. v

Foreword: Cork Rock: A Secret History? ............................. vii

Chapter 1: Going To My Hometown ....................................... 1

Chapter 2: What's Going On ................................................. 20

Chapter 3: There's A Fish On Top Of Shandon (Swears He's Elvis).... 45

Chapter 4: Town To Town ..................................................... 68

Chapter 5: Charlton Heston ................................................... 82

Chapter 6: Sugar Beet God .................................................... 96

Chapter 7: Singer's Hampstead Home ................................. 123

Chapter 8: Staring At The Sun ............................................. 150

Chapter 9: Where's Me Jumper? .......................................... 170

Chapter 10: After All ........................................................... 192

Chapter 11: How Can I Exist ............................................... 217

Chapter 12: Back In A Tracksuit ......................................... 252

Bibliography ........................................................................ 278

Useful Websites for Cork Rock Music Fans ....................... 280

Cork Rock and Related Acts ............................................... 282

# ACKNOWLEDGEMENTS

A very special thanks to the following who agreed to be interviewed or contributed photos and in so doing made a great contribution to this book. In no particular order they were: Dónal Gallagher, Skully, Ger O'Leary, Ciarán Ó Tuama, Jerry Buckley, Jack Lyons, Liam Heffernan, Mick Lynch, Kev Hopper, John McGuire, Oliver Tobin, Colm O'Callaghan, Joe O'Callaghan, Brian O'Reilly, Paud O'Reilly, Neil Hannon, Ann Redmond, Finny Corcoran, Paul Linehan, Ashley Keating, Katharina Walter, Kieran Kennedy, Giordaí Ua Laoghaire, John Byrne, Len de la Cour, Pat Egan, Graham Finn, Michael Crowley, Eric Kitteringham, Freddie White, Niall O'Flaherty, Morty McCarthy, Ian Olney, Pat O'Connell, Ricky Dineen, Cathal Coughlan, Sean O'Hagan, John O'Leary, Seán O'Neill, Alan MacFeely, Kieran MacFeely, Philomena Lynott, Rory Cobbe, Paul McDermott, Jim Morrish, Joe Philpott, John Spillane, Senator Dan Boyle, Marcus Connaughton, IRMA, Paul Fennelly, Mick Finnegan, Keith 'Smelly' O'Connell, Chris Ahern, Joseph O'Leary, Anne Kearney and the staff of the Irish Examiner, Leslie Ryan, Niall Connolly, Eoin 'Stan' O'Sullivan, Aimee Setter, Richard Coulthard, Nigel Farrelly, Dave Ahern, Ger Horgan, Hank Wedel, Barry McAuliffe, Ian O'Connell, Billy MacGill, Gary Sheehan, Eoin Aher, Paul and Grace Moriarty, the staff at Cork City Library and Sean 'Grasshopper' Mackowiak.

A huge thank you to Ciarán Ó Tuama for giving me so many unique photographs. A very special thank you to Morty McCarthy, Jim Morrish, Giordaí Ua Laoghaire, Paul McDermott and Eric Kitteringham for their assistance in proofreading this book and also to Brigitte 'Bibi' Lehmann for her support and advice. I would also like to thank my parents Joe and Sandra McAvoy for their support and encouragement.

Without all of you, it wouldn't have happened!

# FOREWORD

### Cork Rock
### A Secret History?

My primary purpose in writing this book was to document the history of Cork rock music and the culture that has sprung up alongside it. For a long time, Cork music fans have not had an accurate account of the bands and performers that helped keep rock music both alive and interesting in the Rebel County. With changes in musical styles and personal circumstances, the experiences and stories of previous generations are not necessarily passed on. I sincerely hope this book will go some way towards redressing this.

In conducting the various interviews for this book, I sought to highlight some of the many and ongoing achievements of Cork rock acts. I also wanted to identify some of the problems that local bands have encountered over the years. In some cases, these were recurring problems that each generation faced. I hope that bringing these issues to the fore will serve as a guide to those who follow in their footsteps and help them to avoid or overcome some of the pitfalls of life in the music industry.

Music can be seen as a celebration of the individual as well as something shared by wider groups. Songwriters write about a variety of topics such as love, death, politics and other areas of importance to them. The next step in this process takes the song out of the writer's control. The listener may attribute a different meaning to a song than the one intended by the writer. Music becomes a group affair when people identify something attractive in a song or an album or in the individual or band who plays it. The process moves a step further when fans gravitate towards each other and share the worldviews of the musicians who inspire them.

The rock music scene in Cork can be viewed as a collective subconscious, which adopts and discards influences from past acts and figures almost at random and veers in different directions determined by a range of factors including economics, popular international acts, visiting artists, fashion, technological advances, pop culture and nostalgia.

In Cork, there were certain focal points for different performers and generations of music fans. The Arcadia (known locally as The Arc) on the Lower Glanmire Road and Sir Henry's on South Main Street played central roles in a number of music eras. Other more short-lived venues also had an impact on the Cork rock music scene through different periods. Similarly, different figures were important in different time periods. Names such as Rory Gallagher, Finbarr Donnelly, Cathal Coughlan, Niall O'Flaherty and Paul Linehan all have their own unique places in the pantheon of Cork rock music.

Mark McAvoy<br>
April 2009

CHAPTER ONE

# GOING TO MY HOMETOWN

[Rory Gallagher]

Quirky. That word has frequently been used to describe Cork rock music and many other elements of the city's indigenous culture in areas ranging from architecture to literature: by-products of a city that has, in many ways, evolved in isolation - especially in relation to Dublin.

Aptly known as the 'Rebel County' due to its rebellious nature under British colonial rule, Cork has cultivated its own distinct identity through the years. This was exemplified in the eighteenth century when the city even appointed an ambassador to Dublin to maintain its voice in the capital. Today, many Corkonians describe the city as 'the real capital'. It therefore comes as no surprise that Cork has long been seen as a bastion of 'left field' thought.

Importantly, music has always been an integral part of the Corkonian psyche. Even though musical styles have changed throughout Cork city's history, generations of musicians and music lovers have continued to flourish in equal measure by the banks of the Lee. It has been suggested that this is in part thanks to the inspiring landscape that surrounds the greater Cork area. From the picturesque beauty of west Cork, to the banks of the River Lee and out to the sandy beaches of east Cork, the potential for inspiration is unrelenting.

Cork saw the power and vibrancy of music permanently etched into its soul with the establishment of the Cork School of Music in 1878, the first municipal school of music in Ireland and Great Britain. In the next century, Cork was the location where the acclaimed Irish composer Seán Ó Riada (1931-1971) perfected his art before going on to produce many impressive musical scores, most famously *Mise Éire* (1959) and *The Playboy of The Western World* (1962).

As highlighted by Vincent Power in his book *Send 'Em Home Sweatin'* (1990), the showband phenomenon was ushered in by Northern Irish band The Clipper Carlton, who by the mid-1950s were playing to full houses in Cork city. With this new musical scene, came social change that transformed youth culture. As high capacity ballrooms mushroomed across the country in the 1960s, massive crowds came from far and wide on specially organised buses and, with increasing prosperity, in cars. As Power points out, new courting habits began to flourish away from the prying eyes of the local parish. An added bonus of the new high capacity ballrooms was that they contributed to the removal of social barriers. For ballroom owners, managers and other entrepreneurially inclined individuals, the showband era was all about money. Vast sums were made on the back of well-attended gigs.

On Leeside, popular home-grown acts such as The Dixies (formed in 1954 and previously known as The Dixielanders) came to the fore, both as performers and as recording artists. Demand for showbands helped increase the number of venues across the city and county, some of which would also serve future generations of music fans and future music scenes. In Cork, The Arcadia Ballroom, owned by Dixies' manager Peter Prendergast, played a pivotal role in catering for showbands and their adoring fans. It was here that The Dixies took up a Saturday night residency as a relief band, warming up large audiences ahead of eagerly awaited visiting stars. With the kind of money to be made on the showband circuit, there were new possibilities for bands to go professional. Having been spotted by promoter Jim Aiken at a gig in Waterford in 1960, The Dixies decided to go full-time. They went on to have an accomplished recording career, which saw them release twenty-seven records, including their chart-topping *Little Arrows*, which graced the number one spot on September 7, 1968 and remained in the charts for twenty weeks.

Foundations laid during this time by builders (and brothers), Jerry and Murt Lucey, were also important for the future of music in Cork. They built two massively successful ballrooms. The first was at Redbarn in east Cork in 1957, and the second was the Majorca in the coastal town of Crosshaven in 1964. In 1968, the brothers opened The Stardust Ballroom on Grand Parade. Again, this proved to be a lucrative move and gave them an excellent bargaining hand when it came to attracting top class showbands, as they were able to offer them three consecutive live dates in County Cork. The Majestic in Mallow, built by Jack O'Rourke and Donie Collins, was another successful venue that was a popular destination for showbands. Opened in 1962, it even played host to luminaries such as Chubby Checker and Johnny Cash.

The huge interest in the showband phenomenon in Ireland was highlighted by the launch of a new publication devoted to this unique Irish musical movement. Regarded as the showband bible, *Spotlight* magazine was devised by Cork *Evening Echo* journalist John Coughlan and ballroom proprietor Murt Lucey. Originally based at Exchange Buildings on Cork's Princes Street, this pioneering pop magazine, partly financed by Lucey and edited by Coughlan, saw its first issue published by the Lee

Press on April 19, 1963. While early editions were sporadic, this unprecedented development in Irish music journalism quickly became a monthly publication. *Spotlight* secured much of its funding through advertisements and its revenue grew along with the popularity of the magazine. Printing later moved to the *Limerick Weekly Echo*, which had a greater printing capacity, as the magazine increased in size. Soon *Spotlight* adopted a national perspective in keeping with its increasing circulation. An important feature of *Spotlight* was its willingness to publish singles charts and polls, which acted as a barometer for the thriving showband circuit. *Spotlight* would later relocate to Dublin, where it was both edited and printed. The magazine did, however, maintain an accounts office on Leeside. In 1965, this publication was renamed *New Spotlight*.

With the added exposure afforded to showbands by publications like *Spotlight* (it wasn't the only one) and the increase in the live music audience, coupled with the growing number of live venues nationally, important infrastructure and concepts had developed that would later assist a far more long-lasting and creatively innovative live music scene - rock.

In terms of popular culture, the Showband era of the 1960s soon revealed the rare and unrivalled talent that was Rory Gallagher. One of the most iconic figures to emerge from Cork, it was Rory who put the city on the world stage with his distinctive abilities as a blues and rock guitarist.

The story of Rory's early years offers a unique insight into the Cork music scene of this period, though in telling it, it is necessary to step back a few years before the showbands' heyday. While there were many similarities with the current music scene, there were some important differences. Talent contests, parish hall variety shows and concerts offered young aspiring musicians the opportunity to perform.

# CORK ROCK

Rory's experiences and strong work ethic saw him play across the city and county, putting in the hard graft that most successful musicians have to go through. Rory was the first rock musician to capture the imagination of many Leesiders, as he lived out many a boyhood dream, rising from humble beginnings to take his place in the annals of rock history. Although Rory's music does not sit comfortably under the term 'quirky rock music', his own strong personal sense of identity would certainly be regarded as 'quirky' especially in the world of rock. Off stage, Rory went against the grain and defied the common perception of the personalities attracted to the rock star life. Quiet, polite, shy, respectful and always a gentleman, it is easy to see why he is still held in such high regard by those who knew him.

In Rory Gallagher, rock music fans found a guitar hero in the truest sense, a man of great vitality who lived for, and one could argue, died for his craft. Rory and his music possessed a purity, completely devoid of pretentiousness and his life is a testament to his great love of the blues.

It is worth noting that Cork became Rory's adopted home. He was born on March 2, 1948 in the aptly named Rock Hospital in Ballyshannon, County Donegal. He lived for a short period at East Port in Donegal, while his father Daniel Gallagher worked as a foreman on the construction of the hydroelectric scheme on the Erne River. As Rory's brother Dónal says, 'It is ironic that he was part of what delivered electricity to Ireland, as his son ended up playing electric guitar. If my father hadn't done that, there would have been no electricity for Rory's amps.'[1]

---

[1] I am extremely grateful to Dónal Gallagher (who was Rory's best friend and manager as well as his brother) for so generously sharing his memories of their childhood and Rory's musical influences. I quote him liberally because it would be impossible to find a more accurate, knowledgeable and important source.

Music was always at the core of Rory's life. A love of music ran strong in his family. Derryman Daniel Gallagher was an Ulster champion accordion player and had his own céilí dance band, the Inishowen Céilí Dance Orchestra, while Rory's mother Monica was an accomplished singer. Dónal was born a year after Rory. By then, the Erne scheme was finished and the family had moved to Derry. He remembers that, as a five-year-old, Rory wanted to be Roy Rogers, the guitar-wielding, singing cowboy. Rory's interest in blues music and rock 'n' roll was ignited at a very young age. His exposure to different musicians and styles came as a direct result of the American forces stationed in Derry at the time. Dónal has clear memories of this period in his family's history, memories that evoke some sense of the musical influences on Gallagher's generation. With the American navy stationed there in the post-war era, the American Forces Network (AFN) was like a local radio station. Dónal recalls:

> It had a number of programmes like *Jazz Hour*. Rory was intrigued with this. He managed to get the family radio and would surf it. He knew his own schedule, like the night Chris Barber would have a programme. Rory's taste in music was actually coming from a jazz background but, of course, Lonnie Donegan was the banjo player for Chris Barber's band, so Rory would get a little bit of the early skiffle. Then Lonnie Donegan broke out of that and started having hits in his own name. *Radio Luxembourg* started to devote programmes to the likes of Rambling Jack Elliot, Daryl Adams and guys who were kind of folky GIs. That whole post-war transition period brought American culture to Europe big time.

# CORK ROCK

In the mid-1950s, some time after Daniel Gallagher's work at the dam had finished, the Gallagher family relocated to Rory's mother's hometown of Cork. Here Rory's maternal grandparents owned a bar on MacCurtain Street. Originally known as The Modern Bar, it was later renamed Roche's Bar. Dónal recalls the reason behind the name change with amusement:

> I think the family members got a bit annoyed! It was a very traditional house and after all the 'Modern' Bar was fine in the fifties but, by the time of the sixties and seventies, she hadn't changed it. So the name Modern Bar was becoming a bit out of date. My mother's maiden side of the family was Roche, so it became Roche's Bar.

It was above Roche's Bar that the young Gallagher brothers lived: a central location, which provided both Rory and Dónal with a unique vantage point to gain an insight into life in Cork city. Dónal describes his grandmother's 'traditional bar', which from time to time played host to some of the city's most notable musical luminaries:

> When I say traditional, it was not a music bar. It was just a very good Irish bar. For instance, she was the last woman in the city to have proper wooden barrels. She was a great traditionalist like that. I remember as a very small boy people like Seán Ó Riada drinking in the bar because there would have been a connection as the Roches came from Cúil Aodha [Coolea] in Ballyvourney, so the families knew each other. But of course, I would say that the quality of the pint was an attraction.

At a surprisingly young age, inspired largely by the music he was listening to on the radio, Rory began asking his parents for a guitar. It was clear that he had already decided that he wanted to be a musician. Dónal explains:

> Even from the age of five or six, I remember him looking for a guitar. A guitar wasn't common by any manner or means. So he got a plastic one. You could either get the Lonnie Donegan model or the Elvis Presley model. I can't remember which one he got. I think he got the Elvis Presley model. Whatever Santa brought, you got! It was a four string, gut string ukulele type, but out of that he got chord structures. When we came to Cork, the bribe was: 'If you settle in the new school, we will get you a guitar.' So he would have been just nine at the time of his first proper six string acoustic guitar.

The roots of Rory's musical gift soon became apparent to Dónal:

> Rory had this ability to absorb and retain everything. He immersed himself in this culture of the blues. By the time we moved to Cork, it was far more difficult to get *Radio Luxembourg*. They played musicians like The Shadows and Joe Brown and musicians of that calibre who were coming up. Obviously, Elvis Presley had arrived on the scene, so that was bringing through people like Chuck Berry who we were getting to hear.

By nine years of age, Rory was teaching himself to play an acoustic guitar. During this period, he took his first tentative steps towards forming a band. As a youngster, his first foray into music came when he formed a skiffle band, on occasion roping in Dónal on tea-chest bass.[2] Such ventures gave him the confidence to enter local talent shows, at which he had some success. Despite the growing popularity of the showbands, Dónal recalls:

> He didn't want to go into a showband. He was actually trying to form a group. The kind of groups that were around then were Cliff Richard and The Shadows, Joe Brown and The Brothers and Marty Wilde and The Wildcats. Every singer had a band that would do some instrumental music. Rory was trying to form a group where he could do some Chuck Berry and some Elvis.

There were some problems forming a group if you were a pre-teen living in MacCurtain Street. Not that many kids were around because families had started to desert the city centre for new homes in the suburbs. The main thing in Rory's mind was to get up on stage as a four-piece. He did not mind if the others could not play their instruments. As Dónal says: 'You were a gang and Rory always felt he could carry it anyway. It didn't matter what noise it was! He was up in front and we were props more than anything else.'

Back then, as now, one way for a talented young musician to get himself on stage was to enter talent contests. By the age of twelve, Rory had developed enough confidence to enter and win one in Cork's City Hall. There is a famous shot in the *Cork Examiner* of him on that day in 1960 and legend has it that he put the prize money towards his first electric guitar, bought the same year.

---

[2] Little did the brothers know that in the future they would become good friends with skiffle legend Lonnie Donegan. In fact, Dónal Gallagher looked after Lonnie Donegan in his final years. He also helped him to trace his Cork ancestry: 'I did his ancestry with him and he is descended from John Donegan in north Cork from Ballydonegan who married a Mary Gallagher in 1850.'

Rory's victory may have been even sweeter because he won on the stage where, just weeks earlier, Chris Barber's Jazz and Blues Band had played a sell-out show. Rory had saved his pocket money for weeks in the hope of buying a ticket, but they sold-out before he could afford one.

Some of the talent contests in those days, however, were more about making money than discovering and rewarding newly emerging talent. Dónal Gallagher was ideally positioned to discover this and his recollections provide a unique insight into some unsavoury goings on within the Cork music scene of this period.

> Rory didn't win a guitar. There was no prize like that. It was only cash prizes then. A lot of these talent contests were actually bogus, because they would sort of imply the prize was one thousand pounds but the winner would only get a fiver. This was the case when Rory won one of the contests. A lot of them were unscrupulous people exploiting people in the city. There was one horrendous one where you were charged to enter the contest to win a prize that came from your money. It was rotten, especially when people had nothing.

Rory Gallagher was keen to perform and didn't restrict himself to playing talent contests. He played many places that even these days young musicians might feel are off limits. 'I would be called upon when he was doing lots of socials, church halls and the St. Anthony's Halls of this world,' Dónal remembers. 'Rory would play at the drop of a hat anywhere. He would go up and play what was the asylum up in Sunday's Well. He would play for patients when he was around twelve or thirteen.' Speaking of Rory's drive, Dónal suggests that his father's strong work ethic may have been in Rory's genes but that his focus was unique. The closest word Dónal finds to describe it is 'stage-struck', but he adds:

> No more than you see some football players who have to play every day while others can take it or leave it. Some guys just have to be on the pitch. They can't sit on the subs bench. He absorbed an awful lot about music. He read an awful lot about it, what he could from the papers. He had a burning ambition to get out there and tour with bands each year and go travelling and make it.

By the time Rory was fifteen going on sixteen, small clubs were beginning to spring up, the kind of places students went to. Too young to have made his reputation outside a very small circle, it was not long until Rory came to the harsh realisation that the best way to take to the stage was to join a showband, even though he was no fan of this type of band. Dónal recalls Rory's search for a place in one of these bands: 'He would check the *Evening Echo* and the *Cork Examiner* because there were always these newspapers in the bar and in the house. He went through the ads.'

The advertisement that caught Rory's eye was placed by two west Cork brothers, Oliver and Bernie Tobin from Drinagh. Oliver Tobin recounts how they quickly recognised Rory's special skills:

> When my brother put the ad in the paper, Rory Gallagher and a few others turned up. Rory played a couple of tunes and we knew straight away. He had only a solid seven guitar, which was the cheapest guitar you could buy, because he couldn't afford anything else.

It was while still at school that Rory began his career in earnest thanks to an apprenticeship with the Cork-based showband The Fontana. Alongside local musicians Bernie Tobin (trombone) and his brother Oliver (bass), were John Lehane (saxophone), Eamon O'Sullivan (drums) and Declan O'Keefe (vocals and rhythm guitar). One problem Rory could have faced was that, in theory at least, you were not allowed into dance halls until you were eighteen. Dónal Gallagher suggests that Rory got away with it partly because he looked older when he put on the showband suit and also because he played so well.

Lengthy live shows were part and parcel of life playing with a showband. Gruelling live sets of six hours plus were not uncommon. But this experience certainly benefited Rory and equipped him for later in his career. Oliver remarks that the young Rory began to develop his trademark onstage persona at this time:

> Rory came to play with us at fifteen years of age. What people don't know at all is that he was very introverted, shy, and he stood back in the corner [when on stage]. At fifteen, he could play guitar as well as someone who was twenty-five. He knew every Buddy Holly tune there was to know. His two biggest songs were Buddy Holly and Lonnie Donegan songs. He used to sing *Valley of Tears* [a Buddy Holly song].

Tobin recalls how at first Rory would stand in a corner at the back of the stage and that, although he had very long nails, the sound from the strings was perfect. 'He was an artist of unbelievable talent,' recalls Tobin. 'On stage he was able to bring that something special out in people who had it in here [gestures to his heart].' Tobin suggests that it was his brother Bernie who helped Rory gain confidence on stage, allowing the young musician to come out of himself:

## CORK ROCK

> Rory would be playing away down the back on stage and my brother would go in behind him and grab the neck of the guitar and drag Rory out the front and he would say, 'Go on Rory, go on Rory! It's like having a hard crap! You are constipated. Get them going!' And Rory would play guitar. My brother would be behind him while he was playing. So after a bit, Rory got into the swing of things and he was doing it on his own.

Dónal Gallagher also has fond memories of this important period in Rory's development. He says of an early show:

> I couldn't swear that I was at the first gig. I certainly remember one of the very first gigs they would have done. I did get allowed in! It was in Cobh, where cousins of ours had booked the band to play. I know he later did St. Colman's Hall in Douglas. He hadn't got the Stratocaster at the time and I remember the conversation going that he needed to get a better guitar.

And a better guitar, Rory soon got! In 1963, Rory discovered the 'battered Strat' electric guitar that would become his trademark: an event that has seeped into local music folklore. Over the next thirty-one years, this guitar would aid Rory in his quest to become an internationally renowned musician. Bought second-hand, the 1961 Sunburst Fender Stratocaster, reputed to be the first in Ireland, was purchased for one hundred pounds at T. Crowley and Son Limited, of Merchants Quay, Cork (in 1973 the firm moved to new premises on MacCurtain Street, a location previously used as a showroom for the Ford Motor Company). This store had also sold Rory his wooden acoustic and his Rosette Solid Seven electric guitars. Michael Crowley, who sold Rory his legendary guitar, has vivid memories of that day and of the origins of his famous Stratocaster:

> There were a lot of stories saying that it came from America, that it was the wrong guitar for somebody else and it should have been a different colour. It was bought second-hand and I sold it to him myself, so I know where it came from. It came as a trade-in from Jim Conlon who played with The Royal Showband. At that time, they were changing their band uniform and T.J. Byrne, their manager said: 'The guitars don't go with the new clobber; you'll have to change them!' They actually bought a salmon-pink colour [guitar] to go with the gear.

Michael Crowley remembers how determined Rory was to buy the guitar when he came into the shop with his mother, Monica:

> At the time, the guitar was £129.00 new and his mother kind of said to Rory that that was a lot of money and she didn't think they were that expensive. Rory was probably like all young fellas telling the mother they wanted something. Once you get them in the door, they know that their mother might feel embarrassed at not buying, but it didn't work. She went out the door with him afterwards. I can distinctly remember his face dropping and you could see the sadness on it. They went out the door and they stood outside and spoke for a while and then she popped back in and said: 'Is there any possibility you might come across a second-hand one?' At that stage, I would say we had only sold possibly two or three and I knew those who had them and I felt they were after buying these things as a lifetime instrument. So when the word came that

the boys in The Royal Showband wanted to change, I immediately thought, well, we'll keep that for Rory if it comes in. So the guitar came up and we sent the other guitar down by bus to Waterford for The Royal Showband. I came up to his grandmother's pub and said: 'Mrs Roche would you tell Rory when he comes home from school, that I've got a guitar in for him, if he's interested?' At that time, we closed for lunch from one to two o'clock and when we came back after lunch, Rory was there waiting outside the door. I took the guitar out of the case and he just looked at the body and the neck and said: 'Yeah, that's it!' He went out the door with his shoulders up and the head up. He walked with a kind of swagger and the shoulders were always up, so it appeared as if his head had been pushed down into the shoulders. He came back around 5.30 p.m. with his mother. She came in with a deposit and they took it away then.

Having long hair and being in a showband did not go down well with the powers that be in the North Monastery CBS, the school where Rory sat his Inter Cert. As Dónal Gallagher remembers it: 'The school could not understand why this guy was driven towards the devil and rock 'n' roll.' An incident that today would be recognised as physical abuse, led to Rory's moving to St. Kieran's College, a co-ed school on Cork's Camden Quay, to finish his education.[3] Dónal recalls the incident well: 'It's sad to say that he got a beating because it was found out that he was in a showband. He kept it very quiet.

---

[3] Other former St. Kieran's pupils include Mick 'Tana' O'Brien, a schoolfriend of Rory Gallagher, who later played with The Lee Valley String Band. Another past pupil was Corkman 'Irish' Jack Lyons noted for his long-running friendship with British rock band The Who.

He didn't tell anybody. I discovered this. Then my mother, God rest her, she found Rory's leg had gone septic.' By all accounts, the more liberal approach of St Kieran's suited Rory. His mother was forthright with the principal: 'My son is going to be a musician, that's his profession,' she said. 'He already knows it and he is working towards it. Some mornings he will be late coming in.'

The new school was accommodating. As long as Rory kept up with his studies, they did not put pressure on him. Dónal Gallagher says, 'Rory would do his homework in the back of a van going over to play places in Kerry like Cahersiveen and in those days there were no good roads. It was difficult, but he got his work done. He was a very good student.'

Rory was also a talented artist. Dónal reveals:

> He really could have gone in that direction. In addition to doing the showband, he did night classes at the School of Art, as it was known then, over next to Cork Opera House. In recent times, I have found the work that he did at the School of Art and I'm putting it together with art that he did on the road. So at some point, we'll do a little exhibition with all that.

In 1964, Rory toured Cork, Kerry and Limerick with The Fontana. He also toured Britain with the showband during Lent, when most of the Irish dance halls closed for this religious event. The opportunity to travel to Britain opened Rory up to an undercurrent of new musical influences that helped create the sound of the 'swinging sixties', which would influence him in the future.

At the beginning of 1965, however, one of the seminal forces in British rock 'n' roll came to Cork: The Rolling Stones. Rory was to witness this event that etched itself into the psyche of the local music scene for years to come. It was the classic Stones' line-up of Mick Jagger, Keith Richards, Brian Jones, Bill Wyman and Charlie Watts that played Cork's Savoy Theatre on January 8, 1965. Vincent Power noted that Rory thought Jones was a very skilled guitarist and that he was impressed with the way he used a slide guitar.[4]

Music fans and local musicians descended en masse for what was an eagerly anticipated opportunity to see a sensational live band rock Leeside. This sold-out gig would also serve to enhance the popularity of blues music in Cork. Among the local musicians there to see the Stones were Brian O'Reilly, who would later gain recognition with Fermoy-based folk-rock group Loudest Whisper, bass player Eric Kitteringham who would later become a band-mate of Rory's, and esteemed local drummer Len de la Cour. In the latter part of the 1960s, Len came to prominence in Cork music circles when he tried to break the European record for the longest drumming solo in local venue The Cavern Club.

Brian O'Reilly remembers the Stones delivered a stunning performance. He enthuses:

> It was one of the best gigs I was ever at in my life. The price of the tickets was eight shillings and six pence. It was 1965 and I went up to see the show and I said: 'Oh my God, this is it! This is absolutely amazing!' Hopping! The place was hopping! The venue was excellent. It was the old cinema at that stage but it could still fit over a thousand people. In 1965 the whole blues thing was happening. The Stones were very much blues and they opened our minds to a lot of blues music. They had a proper stage and everyone ended up going

---

[4] Vincent Power, *Send 'Em Home Sweatin'*, Kildanore Press, 1990, p.364.

down the front bopping and jumping around. It was one of the most amazing experiences in the 1960s that you could imagine.

While Rory and his good friend Tom O'Driscoll paid to see Mick Jagger and co. play The Savoy, Dónal Gallagher didn't manage to save enough money for a ticket. This was to prove no obstacle to the then fifteen-year-old, as luck was on his side. He recalls the remarkable incident that not only allowed him to see his heroes, but to get even closer to the stage than Rory:

> I was trying to save and I'd nearly got the price of the ticket. Then something distracted me and I spent the money. So Rory and Tom went off to The Savoy to see the Stones. I went down the back of Drawbridge Street [located behind The Savoy Theatre] and I thought, well at least I'll hear the gig through the doors, as I used to do for bands playing in The Arcadia when I couldn't get in. That is all you wanted to do - hear them. You couldn't see them but you could feel it! So, I was standing down by the back gate. There was a girl called Twinkle on the bill and this was just before the interval. She was supporting the Stones and she had a hit with a song called *Terry*. It was a whole British package. Then the back door down by the stage opened and this guy came out to have a cigarette. He looked like a Stone. I think it was Bill Wyman. But it could have been a roadie; they all looked groovy at the time! I was sort of huddled in because it was a chilly night. The door opened and I kind of fell out. He said: 'Are you going to the gig?' I said 'I haven't got a ticket,' and he said: 'If you want to go in, go in now! Quick guy!' They were sold-out, so they probably didn't care. So I went in and I found

# CORK ROCK

myself just down from the toilets. It was the interlude and people were going to the loos. This guy said to me: 'Are you the guy who broke in? Security are on their way down. Come into the toilet with me.' Then he said: 'Look! The seat next to me is empty. No one has come in for it. If you sit on it, they'll wait for the person who hasn't got a seat.' Security were standing there. So I walked up to the seat and found I was five rows in front of Rory. Rory's face! He was not happy. You know, here is a guy who kept his money and bought his ticket. I wasted my money, yet I ended up five rows ahead of him and closer to the stage. I was waving to him big time. Ha, ha, ha!

## CHAPTER TWO

## WHAT'S GOING ON

[Taste]

The 1960s were a revolutionary era that brought dramatic change to youth culture and to the world of music. In Cork, Rory Gallagher had begun a personal journey that would see him light the way for many future artists like Dublin's Thin Lizzy and U2.

Playing with The Fontana Showband opened doors for Rory allowing him to experience life on the road from a very early age, while also having the opportunity to get paid for honing his craft. Despite the fact that he was no fan of showbands, Rory still saw the benefits of participating in this scene and getting a foot on the ladder. As Dónal Gallagher explains: 'It satisfied him to a degree to get into a band and to get on a stage. They would play places around Cork like St. Anthony's Hall and St. Colman's Hall in Douglas and small gigs until they broke into The Arcadia Ballroom. That was the target, to get booked into The Arcadia. They were enthusiastic and determined.'

Once they made it into The Arcadia, The Fontana frequently delighted in trying to blow other showbands off the stage - even though, in those days, they were only the support act, also referred to as the 'relief band'. A mixture of their onstage personas, a willingness to play the more popular hits of the day, such as songs from the top ten, and their awareness and understanding of equipment such as the Binson echo chamber, meant The Fontana posed a real threat to established bands like

The Capitol, The Royal Showband and hometown group The Dixies.[5]

With a broadening of musical tastes and the emergence of the Irish beat scene (which was unfortunately confined to the cities), the mid-1960s saw The Fontana opt for a name change, restyling itself The Impact. During this period, Rory played music by the likes of Chuck Berry and other artists, which was seen as an avant-garde gesture for a showband. Dónal describes how this transitional period affected both The Fontana and Rory:

> With the beat style of music that was coming in at that time and legends that were coming back from Hamburg about The Beatles and the beat scene there, this had a huge influence on Rory. So The Fontana then evolved into The Impact and that was reflected in the change of style in the music and the clothes they wore.

This name change also facilitated a slight change in the group's line-up. Michael Lehane, brother of John Lehane, was drafted in on organ and Johnny Campbell would later become the drummer. After meeting Rory and discovering a shared taste in music, J. Philip Prendergast, younger brother of Peter Prendergast, the owner of The Arcadia, became the manager of The Impact.

The way the ballroom circuit was configured in Ireland at this time meant that ballroom managers and promoters frequently had their own showbands and would trade-off gigs, meaning that swapping bands for live dates was a regular occurrence. Prendergast's connection to The Arcadia Ballroom and the fact that his brother managed The Dixies were obvious benefits to The Impact.

---
[5] *Ibid.*, p. 358.

April 1965 saw another stage in the development of the Gallagher legend with an incident that unexpectedly exposed Irish audiences to rock 'n' roll. Rory demonstrated his true rebel spirit while appearing with The Impact on RTÉ's Saturday music TV show *Pickin' The Pops*, a half-hour show that featured a panel who listened to songs and predicted whether they would be hits. At the last minute, Rory and the band did not deliver the Buddy Holly track *Valley of Tears* that they were expected to play, a song Impact bass player Oliver Tobin recalls 'had the women going mad for Rory' when he sang it. Much to the shock of the show's panel of guests, who were used to reviewing the showband sound, Rory gave viewers a taste of the future and a rare glimpse of rock 'n' roll on Irish television. The studio audience was delighted with his performance of the Larry Williams R&B favourite *Slow Down*. Rory's brother Dónal, who was there, remembers that they were 'up and rocking'.[6] Rory's rejection of the 'safe' music of the day was a provocative act for someone making his first TV appearance.

Something else that added to Rory's notoriety that night was his hair. It was the first time that a showband musician with long hair had appeared on Irish TV. This was too much for some viewers in conservative Ireland. According to journalist Vincent Power, Rory's hair made him instantly recognisable and he took some stick from the public after the show, including people shouting at him in the street.[7]

Rory's ambitions, however, lay beyond Irish shores. As Dónal says:

Rory was keen that the band would get abroad. He felt

---

[6] *Ibid.*, p.357.
[7] *Ibid.*, p.359.

that it would become a one trick pony just going round and round the same places [if they stayed in Ireland]. The reason bands were getting to Hamburg was really as a consequence of post-war politics, as it was a port full of American naval personnel. All the ports at that time in West Germany like Kiel and Hamburg had clubs there to entertain the servicemen. The problem for Rory was: 'Hey, would these American people like my music? Could I entertain them?' So the very first trip that occurred was when they got booked to go to an American airbase in Alcalá de Henares, near Madrid. That was most likely thanks to Philip Prendergast's connections with agents in the UK.

By coincidence, The Beatles had their first Spanish gig in Madrid during the weeks in 1965 when The Impact had its residency at the nearby US Air Force base.

The gigs they played in that period were valuable for the Cork group in three ways. Firstly, they got a sense of what it was like to play to American music fans, but even more importantly, Rory learned that his blues sound could resonate with an audience that had grown up in the home country of blues music. Finally, by chatting to army entertainment officers, the band found out who to talk to to get bookings in US bases in Germany. Rory was on course and on his way. While this was the upside, there was one downside that particularly irked him. General Franco, the Fascist dictator, still ruled Spain. Conservative forces there remained suspicious of rock music culture and just as in Ireland; they saw long hair as a symbol of anarchy. Dónal remembers that:

> Rory had to get his hair cut to allow The Impact into Spain. He was disgusted, but he did it and there was a

picture in the *Cork Examiner*. He was seventeen and had literally finished his Leaving Cert that day. He took it a year early, so he could get on with his career as a musician. He was quite disgusted that people would see him with short locks!

The fact that the *Cork Examiner* published the photograph, which Dónal thinks was organised by Peter Prendergast, gives an idea of the splash the schoolboy musician had already made in his hometown.

In late 1965, The Impact returned to London. Bass player Oliver Tobin credits their time in London with giving Rory the chance to see some of the legendary 1960s acts who were very much a new force in music.

> Rory had a fierce advantage because when we lived in London we saw all the big bands. One of his favourite bands would have been The Pretty Things. We used to go and listen to Spencer Davis and Eric Clapton. Eric Clapton was his idol. When we first started as a three-piece, Rory used to put on his denim jacket and after playing numbers, like Eric Clapton, he would take it off again.

However, the British capital was to be the setting for a parting of ways for members of the Cork group. The Impact had a certain level of success in London playing on the same bill as bands such as The Byrds, but being abroad brought with it inevitable stresses and strains. A combination of bad luck and low morale was to lead to the demise of The Impact. Dónal assesses the various factors that brought about the split, including Rory's single-mindedness:

> They were starving, running out of money and

homesick. Some of the guys were not as committed as Rory and they might have been happier just having an ordinary job back in Cork. Rory had a vocation. There were no two ways about it. This was what Rory wanted to do. The band was beginning to disintegrate although Rory was trying to hold it together.

A friend of Rory's, eighteen-year-old Corkman Johnny Campbell, was drafted in to replace Eamonn O'Sullivan on drums. Dónal explains the history between Johnny and his older brother:

> Johnny's father and my father had been the best of friends in the military. So Rory knew Johnny who was a drummer with a band called The New Cadets, a showband sort of derivative. Johnny was brought out and he certainly had the same fire as Rory, the same enthusiasm for going and I think they persuaded Oliver to hang in there, even though his brother had gone back.

With bookings in Hamburg hanging over their heads, Gallagher, Campbell and Impact bass player Oliver Tobin decided to make the journey to Germany and perform as a trio. This was, however, easier said than done. Dónal recalls, 'I think by now all they had was a screwdriver for the ignition of the van and what was left of the equipment. The booking was for six or seven musicians. But they got themselves to Hamburg.'

After arriving in Germany, the group were forced to bluff their way out of the fact that The Impact was now just a three-piece, despite a booking to the contrary. Rory and his friends found 1960s Hamburg and its infamous Reeperbahn (focus of the city's red-light district) a real culture shock when compared to conservative Ireland, but their time in the city served as a rite of passage with its demanding schedules, long hours and challenging punters. It also gave the Cork musicians the opportunity to see great live acts, some of which were destined for the big time. Dónal says:

> Hamburg would have been a twenty-four-hour town, but it had the bonus for Rory that he could go and watch other bands playing. Intriguingly, because he then had a three-piece, he went along to see another band, Cream, featuring Eric Clapton. They had just emerged as a three-piece. That was the first time Rory met Jack Bruce. They were playing in The Star Club, so Rory would go along to see them and chat.

Oliver Tobin recalls an amusing event that took place while the group were in Germany watching the famous World Cup final in July of 1966:

> We watched the World Cup final, England and Germany, in a German girl's flat. She invited us up to watch it. When the match was over her father said something in German and threw us out. We said to the girl: 'What did your father say?' He said: 'How is it that these messers always win at war and football?'

Oliver has fond memories of what life was like for Rory and his fellow band members in Hamburg at this time. He enthuses:

> It was great because we used to go out to the pubs and clubs. You could be playing in Hamburg all night. Some fellas played for nothing. It was exciting to be there. We played in The Big Apple Club for three weeks. Anywhere we went, the women found Rory fierce attractive, even if he never played guitar. But

even when we were in Hamburg we used to go to mass.

It was not long until the trio returned to Cork, where a vibrant band and club scene was emerging. Dónal Gallagher had remained in Cork, while Rory had gigged in Hamburg, and was in a perfect position to see how the music scene in the city was evolving. He recalls:

> Probably the earlier part of that summer, before Rory and the guys had gone off, bands started up, like The Axills and The Martels. The Martels wouldn't have been what you would classify as rock. They would have been a mini showband in a way. They were excellent at playing The Hollies and the softer side of rock 'n' roll. They would have been able to play places like Dolphin Rugby Club, Shandon Boat Club and the dance hops that didn't have a stage big enough for a showband.

While Rory was getting international experience, another important event in Cork's rock music history was taking place on the northside of the city. On MacCurtain Street, an old army club was taken over by Tadhg Kidney and friends. They called it The Crypt and it was decorated in keeping with its name. Dónal Gallagher paints a vivid picture of what The Crypt was like:

> The Crypt, to give it authenticity, was a run-down premises that had been semi-abandoned by the military from nearby Collins Barracks. It was located on MacCurtain Street, right next to the Christian Brothers school, as it was then. I think you had O'Brien's ice-cream parlour nearby. Credit and blame went to Tadhg Kidney. To create atmosphere, the club had a coffin placed in front of its stage, which was dragged from the

undertaker, Forde's of South Gate Bridge. They thought they were going to get free advertising! It ended up in front of the stage. Part of the sport of the evening was to see what girls would dare lie in the coffin and, of course, the band would play in front of it and walk all over it.

In terms of the club's music policy, early rock and early beat club music was the order of the day. Jamming sessions would take place, with young bands playing there, at a time when there was nowhere else to play. It provided an important opportunity for young musicians to sharpen their skills. When asked was any money made out of this venue, Dónal responds:

> Not at all! There was nothing charged on the door because the guys got it free. There was no promoter behind it. It existed because there was really nowhere for kids to go. You were looking at some place that was just a teenage hop.

Despite the fact that The Crypt served an important dual role, as both an outlet for aspiring young Cork musicians and as a source of entertainment for music fans, its existence was brief. Dónal explains:

> Tadhg Kidney had it open for a few months until the Gardaí came one night. It was a short-lived thing because once the Gardaí heard the noise coming from The Crypt and the screaming and the roaring, they raided the place and that was the end of it. The Gardaí closed it and Tadhg was taken to court. He had to take the rap because he was the only one who was over sixteen and could be taken to court. [He ended up on the front page of the *Evening Echo*.]

By contrast, a venue that did gain relative longevity was The Cavern Club (later renamed The 006 Club), located at 25 Leitrim Street on the northside of the city. This venue was the brainchild of Corkman Billy Field. Field approached the young Dónal Gallagher, while Rory was away, with a view to recruiting him as a DJ for his new venue. Such a move appealed to Dónal:

> I had all Rory's records and I had a good lot of rock records as we were listening to DJs like John Peel, who was new at the time. That was very much the groove. I was trying to fashion myself as the Cork John Peel and play music like that. Knowing so many musicians on the scene, you kind of knew what was good, what was bad and what was fun. I had to make up the decks myself on a Thompson's cake crate. So the scene developed and the club, particularly at the weekends, would have bands like The Misfits from Belfast, which had John Wilson on drums [he later played with Rory Gallagher in Taste].

Interestingly, as this venue was more beat music centred, it could be hostile to members of the showband scene. With a strong sense of identity, The Cavern Club's clientele were not interested in what the showbands were offering. Not even a visit from Butch Moore, singer with The Capitol (he was also Ireland's first Eurovision entrant in 1965) could sway the punters. Dónal enthuses: 'The club developed. We were open, I think, every night of the week. Some nights we would just play records.' The showbands were terrified by what was happening in these clubs. 'The showband guys wanted to be hip and wanted to be seen and would come down to the club. I remember Butch Moore turned up and the crowd basically blanked him. It was like saying: "Hey! Go away!"'

As a live venue, The Cavern Club played host to acts such as hometown heroes Taste, as well as performers like John Mayall and Gary Moore. It could be argued that The Cavern Club was the first real alternative club or venue to challenge the status quo. While places like Sir Henry's and The Arc in its punk era would later follow, The Cavern Club set a precedent in Cork city. Describing the interior of the club, Dónal points out:

> It was the ideal set up for a club. I don't know what it had been formerly. It had all sorts of different levels and was a kind of wooden structure within a very cavernous place. Of course, there was all the usual luminous paint and they kept the place dark. God help you if you had capped teeth, they would look black. It had those ultraviolet lights.

By then, bands featuring people like Freddie White would drop into the club. Born into a musical family in 1951, in Cobh, County Cork, the young Freddie White, together with his band The Krux, would play regularly in The Cavern, especially on Friday nights. Freddie describes the venue as:

> A sort of coffee shop come nightclub. The Cavern was the real rock place, where all the beat club musicians came down from Dublin to play every week. There was no alcohol there in those days. It was just Coca-Cola you would buy and Don Gallagher was one of the resident DJs.

His early musical outings with The Krux offered Freddie an important release from unhappy school days:

It was a school band, a kind of blues group and we did it whenever we could steal away from being forced to go through this hell. I really thought school was hell. I had a horrible time. I went to Pres[8] in Cork and I thought it was a nightmare. It was like being in prison!

Musically, The Krux were influenced by the likes of Taste, Jimi Hendrix, Cream and Muddy Waters. Their live sets often featured cover versions of Jimi Hendrix, Fleetwood Mac, Cream and even The Monkees. However, Freddie makes it clear that he always looked up to Rory Gallagher. He recalls:

I saw him play in a club called The Shambles in Paul Street, which I think is now the Mainly Murder Bookstore. He played in there one night in the 1960s and I was literally three feet away from him with that sound! I was blown away! It was the first time I ever saw him. I suppose I would have been fourteen at the time. I escaped that night!

Freddie also remembers that by the time he was fifteen or sixteen, The Krux would: 'support Rory at various gigs around Cork, like school annual hops and concerts. We did a gig in The Savoy with him and I think he might have played in The Cavern when we were there.'

Another memorable Cork music event that the young Freddie White witnessed around this period was local drummer Len de la Cour's attempt to break a European drumming record in The Cavern Club. A native of Youghal in east Cork, Len garnered quite a bit of attention for his brave attempt. He recalls:

That was a moment of lunacy. I did the drumming thing

---
[8] 'Pres' is the colloquial term for Presentation Brothers College located in Cork city centre.

because I got peed off with the fact that nothing had happened with an audition that I had done. So I did it really as a publicity stunt. What I didn't realise was that when you are doing these things you have a five minute break every hour or an accumulation at the end of the day. I was trying to break the European record of something like forty-six and a half hours, so I played for fifty-two hours and twenty minutes without any break. When I wanted to go to the loo, a guy would take the snare drum and I would keep playing away on it with one hand, while I went for a pee. It was mad stuff really. If only I had known you could take a five minute break every hour!

De la Cour's drumming marathon did take a physical toll on him in the immediate aftermath as he concedes: 'I got off that chair and I actually couldn't stand up. There were people holding me up. I was wrecked, but you get into a rhythm of playing. The biggest problem was staying awake.'

Len would later go on to play with Cork band Sleepy Hollow, whose line-up also included Johnny Rice, Bill O'Brien and Paddy Madden. Sleepy Hollow supported Rory Gallagher in venues such as The National Stadium, The Savoy in Waterford, The Savoy in Limerick and Cork City Hall.

In the mid-1960s, The Axills were a well-respected and popular band in the Cork music scene. Formed in 1964, this four-piece was composed of bass player Eric Kitteringham, guitarist and keyboard player Peter Sanquest, drummer Norman Damery and guitarist and singer Derek 'Doc' Green. Eric Kitteringham reflects on their career:

> The Axills were the first Cork beat group to get anywhere. We used to do a lot of handy gigs like The

Shandon Boat Club and Cork Constitution Rugby Club. We played in Dublin and Limerick, but never outside Ireland.

Dónal Gallagher remembers:

> The Axills came from a scene where there had been a club started up. It was more like a basement under St. Luke's church, which was being used as a coffee house. They were aware of Rory. I remember we went up one night to check it out and Rory was delighted with it.

Later Rory went on to make occasional guest appearances playing guitar and singing with The Axills. However, according to Dónal, when Rory was invited to formally join the band, his response was pretty clear. He said: 'I'm not joining anybody's band!' After The Axills had broken up, Eric Kitteringham and Norman Damery called up to Rory's house. By then, The Impact had split. It was the beginning of a friendship between Eric, Norman and Rory.

## TASTE

The first incarnation of Rory's legendary three-piece, Taste, saw him link up with The Axills' former rhythm section, bass player Eric and drummer Norman. Eric Kitteringham recalls that their original band-name was The Taste, which was soon shortened to just Taste.[9] The group chose their name during a band meeting in The Hayloft upstairs in The Long Valley bar on Winthrop Street in Cork city centre. This meeting was also attended by their part-time manager Kevin Sanquest who

---

[9] According to bass player Eric Kitteringham, Taste was initially called 'The Taste'. This was quickly shortened to Taste as band members felt the original name sounded too similar to The Troggs and The Kinks. Eric also recalls that they took the name from a beer mat slogan: 'It's the taste that counts.'

had previously looked after The Axills. Dónal remembers the occasion:

> I was too young to go into the bar. They had the meeting and I remember Rory saying: 'The name is Taste!' I was trying to get my head around it. Like The Impact I could understand, but Taste!

Dónal believes Taste's first gig took place at The Imperial Hotel in front of a student audience. The early Taste played a three-way fusion of blues, rock 'n' roll and rhythm and blues. While they did write and play original material, their live sets also included cover versions. On occasion, the group were reported to have performed *My Generation* by The Who. Of course, this song resonated with another former St. Kieran's College pupil, Corkman and dedicated Who fan 'Irish' Jack Lyons, who befriended The Who's guitarist Pete Townsend in the 1960s. Taste also covered material from the likes of Chuck Berry and Booker T. & the MGs. The Cork trio were highly regarded for their performances at Shandon Boat Club, where they used to play for an hour non-stop, much to the delight of fans.

Life as a three-piece in those days was fraught with obstacles. Chief among these were the rules and regulations imposed by the Irish Federation of Musicians. Rory again displayed his rebellious spirit when his group came into conflict with the Federation when Taste had their first booking to play The Arcadia. A major bone of contention for the Federation was the number of band members in Taste. It was usual that the minimum number required for a band was seven or eight musicians. This rule protected the showband musicians of the day who felt threatened by emerging beat groups. The Federation routinely sent representatives to ballrooms and dance halls to inspect musician numbers on stage. One way of overcoming this obstacle was for smaller groups to recruit friends and pass them off as extra musicians, in an attempt to deter the wrath of the Federation. Taste were determined not to concede to the Federation's unfair demands. Vincent Power describes the battle of wills that took place between Rory and the Federation, who tried to force him to audition for permission to play. When Rory refused, supported by the venue's management, they had no option but to capitulate and let the gig go ahead. This marked a turning point in the Federation's influence over younger, more rock-orientated musicians.[10]

During this period, Rory had come to the realisation that he needed to break out of Cork, where his musical prospects were limited. Cork was a small city and there were only so many gigs that the band could play to a limited audience. 'The idea for Rory was to earn enough in the scene in Cork to move out. He had had enough of starving in the clubs and all that. Rory's attitude was Taste are professionals. He knew that he needed a van and a proper set of equipment,' says Dónal.

The first incarnation of Taste travelled to Hamburg in 1967 for a number of gruelling live dates. The Cork trio also played all over Ireland and, in Belfast, they gained a valuable residency at The Maritime Hotel, R&B club. When Dónal was asked why Rory chose Belfast over Dublin, he replied:

> Rory felt that Dublin was a soul town. It wasn't that they didn't quite get the blues. Obviously, the word was coming through from the likes of The Misfits and the Belfast bands that would come and visit Cork and they would say: 'Well there is a thriving scene.' Again the

---

[10] Power, *Send 'Em Home Sweatin'*, pp. 368-369.

port element in Belfast connected with Rory. There was Sammy Houston's Jazz Club and the Rhythm and Blues Club at The Maritime, which had been founded by Van Morrison. So they basically circumvented Dublin. In effect, it was like trying to build a circuit not dissimilar to what the showbands had.

Rory's love for the blues was shared by many in Belfast. Gerry Smyth suggests that the popularity of the blues was understandable in a city whose industrial culture contrasted with that of Cork: 'Belfast was an industrialised British city that had experienced an influx of American military personnel and their music during the war. African-American music was more than a hobby in Belfast...it was a passion.'[11]

Taste played their first Belfast show in 1966. The following year, the band came to the attention of Eddie Kennedy, manager of The Maritime Hotel's Club Rado, who offered to manage them - an offer that was duly accepted. Their earlier manager Kevin Sanquest remained in Cork, having only managed the band on a part-time basis. In 1967, Taste supported Eric Clapton's seminal trio Cream at Romano's Ballroom on Queen Street in Belfast. Taste also played the Woburn Abbey Festival on July 7, 1968, where by many accounts they upstaged an under-performing Jimi Hendrix who had played the previous evening.

Unfortunately, the original Taste line-up was not to last and Rory parted company with Eric Kitteringham and Norman Damery. Jean-Noël Coghe suggests that this decision was forced upon Rory by an A&R man from Polydor Records who offered Rory an album deal on one condition, that he replace his two highly accomplished and capable band members with

---

[11] Smyth, *Noisy Island*, pp. 31-32.

bassist Richard 'Charlie' McCracken and former drummer with Van Morrison's band Them, John Wilson.[12] In the end Rory reluctantly accepted. Questions later arose surrounding the involvement and motivations of manager Eddie Kennedy in this decision. According to Eric Kitteringham, the relationship between Taste and Kennedy was not particularly close and an air of suspicion had taken hold. Eric felt the fact that he and Norman Damery questioned many of Kennedy's decisions precipitated the change of line-up. Eric reflects:

> Norman, as he proved later, had a great head for business. He questioned everything and it drove Kennedy nuts. He questioned everything![13]

Taste's new line-up did achieve major success and toured extensively. The revamped group performed regularly in London at venues such as The Speakeasy nightclub and also acquired a residency at The Marquee on Wardour Street in 1968. At Cream's legendary farewell concert on November 26, 1968, at The Royal Albert Hall in London, Taste were selected as the support act. This was not surprising, as Clapton and Rory shared a mutual respect for each other, and it was this respect that led to the pair embarking on a tour of America together the following year.

Speaking about their relationship, Dónal Gallagher reveals:

> Rory loved Cream and was very fond of Eric. He had a huge and enormous respect for him and vice-versa. When Cream split up, Eric formed Blind Faith in 1969 and took Taste on as the support act for the tour to America and Canada. So that was six weeks spent

[12] Coghe, *Rory Gallagher: A Biography*, p.31.
[13] My sincere thanks to Eric Kitteringham for agreeing to be interviewed in 2012 and early 2013 and for helping to update the record of his memories of the Taste era for this book.

together on a bus because Eric wanted everybody to share the bus. Rory jammed in Chicago with Eric and they would have gone off to see Muddy Waters and people like that playing.

The year 1969 also saw a positive reception for Taste's eponymous debut album, which featured nine tracks including the excellent *Blister On The Moon* and *Catfish*. As Gerry McAvoy records, even John Lennon of The Beatles was impressed and cited Rory's guitar playing as an exciting new sound.[14]

Taste's second and final studio long-player entitled *On The Boards* was released in January 1970 to widespread critical acclaim and entered the Top 20 in the UK. Rory played saxophone as well as guitar on the record. The ten-track album featured the electric guitar driven blues-rock anthem *What's Going On*, while other tracks such as *It's Happened Before, It'll Happen Again* harboured a jazz influence. *What's Going On* was released as a single in Germany where it reached number 1.

Arguably the band's most memorable and triumphant performance took place at the Isle of Wight festival in August, 1970. Sharing a line-up that included The Who, Jimi Hendrix (who died three weeks later on September 18, 1970), The Doors and Miles Davis, Taste played a show regarded not only as a highlight of the band's career, but of the Isle of Wight festival that year. This fact is all the more remarkable as relations had soured within the group to the point that band members were reportedly not speaking. They did, however, enjoy a great rapport with festival-goers and their performance was considered so magnetic that they were called back for five encores. Taste's appearance was recorded and filmed. A six-

---

[14] McAvoy, & Chrisp, *Riding Shotgun*, p. 41.

track live album entitled *Taste Live at the Isle of Wight* was recorded from their set and released in 1971. A second six-track live album was released by Polydor in the form of *Live Taste*, recorded at the Montreux Casino in Switzerland, but this release did not occur until after Rory had pursued a solo career. Taste's last gig took place at Queen's University in Belfast on December 31, 1970. Following the band's split due to internal differences, bass player Richard McCracken and drummer John Wilson went on to form Stud. The circumstances surrounding the break up of Taste had a long-lasting negative effect on Rory.

## GOING SOLO

Following the demise of Taste, Rory embarked on what was to become a successful solo career. Having built-up a great reputation as a performer with Taste, Rory was able to recruit Belfast-born bass player Gerry McAvoy and drummer Wilgar Campbell to play as The Rory Gallagher Band. Both McAvoy and Campbell had played in Belfast four-piece Deep Joy and had supported Taste in the past. Rory was signed to Polydor, the same label that had looked after Taste.

The year 1971 was to be an important one for Rory: he released two albums, his debut long-player *Rory Gallagher* and sophomore release *Deuce*. This was also to be the year that he would play and record with one of his heroes, the great American blues player Muddy Waters. Rory played on the album *The London Muddy Waters Sessions*, which was released in 1972. Other musicians who played on this Chess Records' backed session included Hendrix's drummer Mitch Mitchell and Steve Winwood.

Rory's seminal record *Live! In Europe* was released in

1972. It entered the top ten album chart in the UK and became Rory's first gold certified long-player. The record featured one of his enduring anthems as its opening track, his cover of *Messin' With The Kid* (written by songwriter/producer Mel London). Another classic Gallagher track, *Going To My Hometown*, featured on this release. Referring directly to Cork, the place Rory called home, the lyrics of *Going To My Hometown* include: 'Got me a job from Henry Ford', a reference to the local Ford Motor factory. As Dónal Gallagher points out: 'Anytime you bought a car [in Cork], it had to be a Ford. It wasn't on the record, but live he would sing: "I don't want a Jenson, I don't want an MGBDT, I don't want an Aston Martin, just give me a Ford, it's fine for me!"'

During this period, Rory Gallagher was very much in demand playing various well-received gigs across Europe. His guitar skills were also receiving the attention that they so very much deserved. In 1972, he won the *Melody Maker* 'Musician of the Year' award. A change of line-up also took place within The Rory Gallagher Band. Rod de'Ath replaced Wilgar Campbell on drums and Lou Martin joined the group on piano duties.

In 1973, Rory released his albums *Blueprint*, and *Tattoo*, which included the classic Gallagher track *Tattoo'd Lady*. Also this year, Rory appeared as a guest musician on the Jerry Lee Lewis album *The Session*. The following year, British film-maker Tony Palmer made a documentary about Rory, *Rory Gallagher – Irish Tour '74*. This was premiered at the Cork Film Festival in 1974. Rory also released his live album *Irish Tour '74*, which had live tracks compiled from gigs at Belfast's Ulster Hall, Dublin's Carlton Cinema and Cork City Hall.

At the start of 1975, an event took place that really showed just how far Rory had come in the previous ten years. It was an event about which there has been much speculation, both at local level in Cork and internationally, and has become part of rock 'n' roll music lore. Rory Gallagher was approached by The Rolling Stones, who were eager to recruit his consummate abilities as a guitarist following the departure of Mick Taylor, the replacement for the late Brian Jones. At the time, the Stones were working on their album *Black and Blue* (1976).

Dónal Gallagher has the inside track on the Stones' offer as he answered the phone call at their mother's house in Douglas (a Cork suburb): 'What happened was by the end of 1974, Rory had his *Irish Tour '74* album so, going into 1975, he had finished the tour, and this would have been the third or fourth of January. Rory had gone to bed and it was certainly after midnight when, peculiarly, the phone rang.' Dónal explained that it was unusual to receive a call so late at night and also that getting a phone call through internationally was extremely difficult. He added that a late call could cause anxiety because of the security situation: 'Rory was quite a star at the time and because of the whole northern thing, there were fears about things like kidnapping etc.' Dónal answered the phone and heard an English accent asking: 'Can I speak to Rory Gallagher?'

To begin with Dónal was quite defensive with the caller. However, his attitude quickly changed when he realised who was calling:

> I asked him who was calling and the guy says, 'Ian Stewart'. I knew straight away who Ian Stewart was. He was the hidden Rolling Stone and one of the original founding members. I nearly blurted out: 'Oh, Ian Stewart of The Rolling Stones!' I was trying to be

very...you know...so instead I said: 'Oh, Ian Stewart of London?' And he said: 'That's right.' I went up to Rory and he thought it was a prank.

Stewart invited Rory Gallagher, on behalf of the Stones, to go to Rotterdam to do some recording and see how things would work out. He agreed to go and see what would happen, but then a problem arose over the dates he had been given. The Stones asked for a postponement, but Rory was opening a tour in Tokyo on January 30. Although the Stones had said the problem was due to the mobile unit not being ready, it seems that part of the problem may have been Keith Richards' poor health.

Rory was under time pressure because of the Japanese tour, but the Stones sessions were fitted in before he left. Dónal says he 'can't remember the exact date. But let's say he had to fly out on January 28 to be there for January 30. Eventually, he went over [to Holland] on, I think, January 24.' Rory was met at Rotterdam airport by Mick Jagger and they took a taxi to Hilversum, where the Stones had a deal with the concert hall for recording. They were staying at the Rotterdam Hilton hotel. Although Keith didn't show up for the first night and it seems to have been Mick Jagger and Ian Stewart who were pushing for Rory's recruitment, Keith had been very vocal about how much he liked Rory in an article written at the time of the founding of The Rolling Stones' label. When an *NME* journalist asked them who they would want to have on their label, Keith said: 'Rory Gallagher is my first signing.' So Keith liked what Rory was doing.

Dónal recalls what Rory told him about the experience:

On the first night, Mick said: 'Well Rory, let's start

jamming.' As I recall, what Rory told me was that Mick said: 'I've just written this song called *Start Me Up*, could you give me a riff?' Rory was writing his own song at the time, a blues number, and he gave Mick that riff. Keith came down the next night and the third night and the fourth.

At the time, the Stones were managed by Marshall Chess, the son of one of the men who co-founded Chess Records. He had said to Rory:

> 'Welcome to The Rolling Stones! Where is your manager?' Rory said: 'Well hang on! What are you saying to me?' And Marshall Chess said: 'We knew it would be you, but who do we have to talk to?' Rory replied that he thought it was just a jam session.

Rory, naïvely or otherwise, kept it like that. On his fourth night in Holland, Rory asked Mick what was going on. Mick replied: 'Hey, we would love to stay with you, but will you go up and have a chat with Keith? Keith wants to have a chat with you.' So Rory went up to Keith's suite. Although it was two in the morning, the door was wide open. Keith was comatose in the bed and while Rory went back a number of times during the night, he couldn't wake Keith. So in the morning, Rory caught his flight back to Heathrow as planned and left for Japan. Dónal recalls: 'He thought, well, okay, if they want me they can follow me.'

Years later, when Dónal asked Bill Wyman about what had happened, Bill said that he and Charlie Watts had had no say in the decision and added that Ronnie Wood, who did become the Stones' guitarist was Keith's mate. Interestingly, sometime afterwards, when Jagger was doing solo work, he got in touch because he wanted Rory on guitar. Dónal speculates that:

> What Jagger saw in Rory was the professionalism that they needed at that time. What's hard to say to people now is that Rory was probably selling more records in Europe than they were. He could get to Japan, but they couldn't because they were busted for drugs and couldn't get a visa in the early 1970s.

Later this same year, Rory would sign a new record deal with Chrysalis, after successfully completing his six-album record deal with Polydor. This marked yet another new era in his colourful career.

## CHAPTER THREE

# THERE'S A FISH ON TOP OF SHANDON (SWEARS HE'S ELVIS)

[Five Go Down To The Sea?]

The blues-rock explosion of the 1960s catapulted many rock acts to super-stardom and huge stadium concerts, but a backlash was inevitable. A new gritty, darker and more aggressive sound emerged in the late 1970s that had the establishment firmly in its sights. This was punk rock. 1977 saw acts like The Sex Pistols unleashed and a new spirit of 'Do It Yourself' enthusiasm took centre stage.

Rory Gallagher had captured the imagination of a generation of Cork rock fans and acted as a ray of hope as he showed just how far afield he could take his inspirational sound. His hometown gigs always retained a certain magnetism and a special significance for his faithful fans on Leeside, but for a new generation came new heroes.

While the showbands had flourished during Seán Lemass's reign as Taoiseach, punk rock would be the soundtrack to the uncertainty of the early Charles Haughey era. Just as one Northerner had rejected what, at the time, was seen as the musical establishment of the day, namely the showbands, another was set to mount a coup that would result in him influencing and inspiring Cork rock music for years to come. His name: Finbarr Donnelly.

Originally from Belfast, the Donnelly family had sought

out the more sedate environs of Cork instead of staying in the chaos and violence that had broken out in Northern Ireland. Initially, settling in the city's northside neighbourhood of The Glen, Finbarr would soon link-up with three young aspiring musicians from Churchfield to give birth to a musical monster that became known as Nun Attax.

A chance meeting in a city chip shop and a shared love of UFOs was the catalyst for a friendship and musical partnership that would transcend several bands. Guitarist with Nun Attax, Ricky Dineen, recalls how a mutual interest in the paranormal led to a meeting with his soon to be frontman.

> I was doing a bit of part-time work in a chipper on Shandon Street, while I was at school. There I met up with Finbarr Donnelly's brother Kevin. I was actually reading books about aliens and UFOs and - don't ask me why - Kevin spoke to me in this northern accent 'Aw my brother! He's into that.' He introduced me to Finbarr, and me and him kind of bonded from that. Donnelly was this alternative guy and he introduced me to punk rock and the joys of [listening to] John Peel. Eventually, we said we'd form a little band of our own and Donnelly was the obvious choice for a singer, if you've ever seen him.

The Sex Pistols may have sung about 'Anarchy', but Finbarr Donnelly had anarchy flowing through his veins. With a rather menacing appearance and a confrontational yet humorous persona, the Nun Attax lead singer would soon evolve from relative newcomer into one of the Cork rock scene's brightest talents.

When you hear the band name Nun Attax, it may conjure up images of a violent assault at the hands of a bride of Christ, but the actual name has its roots in geography. Dineen explains:

> I think Donnelly and a buddy of his came up with the name. Nun Attax is a geographical feature of some sort. Some sort of a secluded peak on a mountain, and they were thinking the punk rock way in school one day and they came up with Nun Attax. Everything ended with an X or a Z in those days, so it just sounded appropriate.

It was through Ricky Dineen that Finbarr met the percussion element of Nun Attax, drummer Keith 'Smelly' O'Connell and his bass-playing brother, Philip. An entertaining character, Smelly O'Connell, as he is known to this day, admits that the seeds of punk rock were sown in him before the arrival of the northerner. Smelly reflects on how, at the age of sixteen, he first caught the performing bug:

> It was at school with Ricky and Philip. I went to the Cork School of Commerce. We just formed a band for the Christmas concert at school and played Sex Pistols' songs to ruin it. I haven't a clue what the name of our band was. I don't even think it had one. We just dressed up as punk rockers and we couldn't even play as such.

Smelly's first impressions upon meeting Donnelly were of: 'A very knowledgeable bloke, very intelligent but a bit barmy.' A major source of inspiration for the aspiring rockers came from Finbarr's impressive record collection. 'We would be smoking joints and listening to music. Finbarr had a massive record collection. For the time, it was phenomenal and it was all new to us,' says O'Connell.

The first Nun Attax line-up was completed with the addition of Togher-based guitar player Mick Finnegan, who had been suggested to the band by mutual friend, Victor O'Callaghan.

They began rehearsing in Smelly's bedroom at his home in Churchfield. Nun Attax played their first ever gig on Valentine's Day 1978 in Mayfield Community School. Cover versions usually feature prominently in the setlists of young bands' that are just starting out and Nun Attax were no exception. Ricky reveals that: 'At that stage we were very young. We did punk rock covers and a few of our own. We would play The Sex Pistols; I think we did *Teenage Kicks* by The Undertones, and The Damned. We basically did stuff that was easy to play and easy to learn off.'

Nun Attax soon attracted the attention of future Cork rock luminaries such as Cathal Coughlan, who would later form Microdisney and go on to front Fatima Mansions, and Mick Lynch, who years later would famously grace the cover of *Melody Maker* as the frontman with Stump.

When asked were Nun Attax a major influence in his early days, Cathal Coughlan responds:

> Not musically, but definitely within the spirit of it. Yes! I thought they were pretty amazing. I can say hand on heart that I was always a lot more po-faced than they were. But with the same kind of approach of: 'Well nobody is going to like us anyway, so why not have a good time!' That attitude was definitely present but it was expressed differently.

While they could never be classed as stereotypical punks, Finbarr Donnelly assumed a pivotal role within Nun Attax, not just as the charismatic, animated frontman, but also as the exclusive lyricist. Quirky lyrics were Donnelly's speciality and this gave the group an edge, while also making them easily identifiable.

A fine example of Donnelly's peculiar lyrical style can

be found in the song *Elephants For Fun And Profit*, which he wrote for his later band Five Go Down To The Sea?. Lyrics such as these made his song-writing instantly recognisable:

> They just opened the hotel doors and filled my room with an elephant
>
> They just opened the hotel doors and filled my girl with an elephant

Discussing the Cork music scene at the time Nun Attax first emerged, Smelly O'Connell describes it as: 'Very tame! When we came along first, there was nothing like us around. It was all rock 'n' roll really and Hot Guitars and bands like that. There was nothing like what we were playing. It was just all rock 'n' roll and the long hair and the beards.'

Small venues did exist for eager music fans, such as The Subway on MacCurtain Street.[15] However, The Arcadia, a key venue during the showband era, became the chief focal point for Cork's punk rock generation. It is worth noting that no alcohol was sold there, but as Giordaí Ua Laoghaire, a local punk aficionado, says: 'The place was jointed on a good night![16] And young people at the time, oddly enough, were quite happy to have a good time listening to some really good bands.'

An important and prominent figure, who in 1977 began to run the more progressive nights at The Arc, was Thurles native and former UCC Student Entertainments Officer, Elvera Butler. To promote the student-friendly nature of her gigs, Elvera conjured up the name The Downtown Kampus.

Elvera cites the importance of developing a distinguishing

---

[15] The Subway was located below street level next to Crowley's Music Centre on MacCurtain Street. Open during the 1970s, it played host to acts such as The Boomtown Rats and is described by one former patron as 'a small, smoky little place, but not without charm!

[16] 'Jointed' is a commonly used Cork slang term meaning absolutely packed with people.

name. 'We didn't have the venue all week. We originally did a concert two nights a week, but the second night never really worked. Saturday night was this kind of scene night. So it was kind of a brand I suppose.'

The Arc formed the backdrop to many gigs featuring Finbarr Donnelly and his fellow punks. Mick Finnegan describes The Arc during this period as 'an amazing place'. He recalls one night that sums up the bizarreness and anarchy of the punk era and an early occasion when Nun Attax made a big visual impact:

> I remember once when we were playing down The Arc. We had a pig's head that we had put on a high hat stand and blood was pouring out of it. The spike was going into the pig's head and there was blood dripping down on to the stage. I'm not sure if that was the first time we played The Arc but it could have been. I remember the terror on Joe O'Herlihy's face when he used to see us. He was the sound engineer in The Arc. He used to hate us!

Mick's final gig with the band was to be an anti-nuclear concert at Carnsore Point in County Wexford in 1979. [17] He also played with a band called Antibodies that same day, but has clear memories of the chaos that soon engulfed the Nun Attax appearance. It was Mick's job to tune the Nun Attax guitars but he was, as he puts it, 'wasted'. The intonation on the first guitar was so impossible to tune, that he ended up working at it and the other guitars on stage, while an increasingly frustrated

---

[17] Carnsore Point in County Wexford, was the proposed location for a nuclear power plant in the 1970s. Free protest concerts took place at Carnsore Point in 1978 and 1979. Called *Get To The Point* and *Back To The Point*, they were a huge success, serving to highlight the entire question of nuclear power in Ireland and helping to ensure that the plan for the plant was shelved.

crowd began to roar and shout. With typical style, Donnelly retaliated and called them: 'A bunch of fuck-headed hippies!' Mick remembers the crowd's response was to pelt the band with anything at hand:

> We just had a laugh. It was an amazing day. Then towards the end, a nearly full can just whizzed past my head like a shell. I could hear the wind and everything. I was going on with Antibodies next, but I told them there was no way I was going back out. They were pleading with me to go on stage. I said I would if they could get me some protection. They got me a full-face motorbike helmet and I went back on and played the gig with the visor down.

Soon after the Carnsore Point concert, Mick Finnegan left Nun Attax, but continued to play with Antibodies. His leaving the Nun Attax ranks was for reasons that were not entirely obvious at the time, but Finnegan was beginning to explore other musical genres. He explains: 'I thought they were getting a small bit serious in a way. And I loved ska.[18] I'm playing ska now with a band called Pontius Pilate and the Naildrivers.'

Though he stopped turning up for Nun Attax rehearsals, Finnegan stayed on good terms with Finbarr Donnelly and the other band members. To this day, he has many colourful memories of Donnelly. He believes that one of the secrets behind Donnelly was his unique view of human behaviour:

> I liked him a lot actually. I got on great with him. He was a highly intelligent guy and had a completely exaggerated sense of the ridiculous. He was a fella who

---

[18] Popular music genre originating in Jamaica that saw a revival in Britain in the late 1970s.

could see the Matrix. He was Neo.[19] He could just see the games that people played with each other and he thought it was so funny.

During a chat with Donnelly, Finnegan suggested that Giordaí Ua Laoghaire's guitar skills would suit the group. 'I thought Giordaí suited them more. We all knew of Giordaí from around town,' says Mick.

Giordaí Ua Laoghaire's guitar playing was especially notable for his echo effects, and his distinctive hippie-like appearance was already familiar to Nun Attax members. Hailing from the Ovens area of Cork and a student of Coláiste an Spioraid Naoimh in Bishopstown, Giordaí admits that in those days Bishopstown was hardly a fertile breeding ground for punk rock enthusiasts.

> It was definitely a middle-class place. It didn't appreciate the punk rock thing. A lot of the guys there were definitely the kind of fellas who I would have hotly debated with about people like Jimi Hendrix and later on, believe it or not, we would debate The Velvet Underground and The Doors. Bishopstown was a place where people like Carlos Santana and Eric Clapton would have been idolised and Rory Gallagher would have been hugely loved. The Nun Attax would not have been appreciated at all, to my memory anyway.

Ua Laoghaire's first band grew out of jamming sessions in Bishopstown.

> I think we had about seven songs and it was stuff like Black Sabbath and Led Zeppelin. I've no idea what the name of the band was. It was a band that never gigged.

---

[19] Neo was the lead character in the 1999 film *The Matrix*.

Niall Marron was a member. He is still an active musician and plays a lot of Latin music and jazz.

The guitarist clearly recalls his first introduction as an eighteen or nineteen-year-old to the imposing figure that was Finbarr Donnelly. One Sunday in a rehearsal room early in 1979: 'Nun Attax walked in and there was Donnelly and I'd been avoiding him around town for ages because I was afraid of him.' Giordaí was surprised when the Nun Attax band members greeted him with: 'You were at XTC in The Arcadia!' It turned out they had been watching him during the gig because he didn't quite fit the punk aesthetic, with his longish hair, beard, a T-shirt that said something like 'Jethro Tull' on it, and as he says himself, doing his own 'spadgy' dance up at the front. They'd been saying: 'That guy is kind of a hippie guy. He looks like he should be playing Eric Clapton songs and he likes this?' Giordaí remembers a sort of meeting of minds that day and that they hounded him to play with them but, interestingly, Giordaí didn't join Nun Attax immediately.

Reflecting further on his first proper encounter with Finbarr Donnelly and the rest of Nun Attax, Giordaí remembers:

> They came in to jam on our gear with only a few instruments and no amps, and one of them could clearly play very well. That was Smelly O'Connell. He was a gifted drummer. There is no doubt about that. Philip and Ricky were at varying stages of learning their instruments but Smelly definitely had a natural gift. I was blown away by his sheer ability to muck in without any caring about technique or practicing. It just came naturally to him to get into the groove. I thought he powered Nun Attax ahead.

But I had a few years' guitar experience and I had a few tricks as well. I was a country boy and there was a certain difference of culture. I was living in Ovens and used to cycle in and jam with them. I liked a lot of different styles but I really loved new wave. They were great as well because records that were flying around the place at that time were the likes of The Residents, Captain Beefheart, XTC etc. I couldn't get enough of bizarre bands that were definitely from the left of centre of experimental rock music in the late 1970s. Nun Attax very much loved that. Stuff like The Mekons, The Ramones, Magazine etc. With all those influences, they were really into what became known in time as spadgy - that spadgy rhythm.[20] Cathal Coughlan wrote a great piece for me once called September Brings Spring To Spadgietown. It's about the idea of the spadgy event, the spadgy-looking fella, the fella with the odd gatch [meaning gait or way of walking], the music that is not really sexy and groovy but, like a lot of Nun Attax music, people would dance when they heard or saw it. As Donnelly used to say: 'It's time for me to do my sexy dance!'

As Mick Finnegan had departed the Nun Attax line-up, the Cork group needed a replacement. Giordaí seemed like the perfect choice given his notable skill as a guitarist. Ua Laoghaire explains the dynamic at play within the band that led to his joining:

>They didn't have a guitar player besides Ricky and he

[20] Author Morty McCarthy states that the Cork word 'spadgy' is used as an 'insulting term meaning idiot', while Seán Beecher records that it is derived from a term for a small bird such as a robin or a sparrow. See McCarthy, *Dowtcha Boy!*, p.65 and Beecher, *A Dictionary of Cork Slang*, p. 90.

didn't feel in control enough of what he did. They kept asking me to join and eventually I said yes. And then it became the most perfect band and I was saying: 'This is great'. But I had too much of a protestant work ethic for them. I liked jamming and working on things. They might turn up on speed like. But they were gifted. I used to love working things through and working on the music. They then recognised that in me and would slag me off about it. [Donnelly impression] 'Giordaí is very talented!'

Asked if he thought they saw him as a bit of a threat, because of his work ethic, Giordaí responds:

> I hate to get into their psyche now because I wouldn't be an expert on it. But having thought about it, the odd time, in the past, I would imagine that there was a whole suspicion of, how should I say it...they wouldn't have consciously said: 'Oh that's very middle-class.' But the middle-class thing, if you like, is the idea of ambitious people that are thinking in a linear way, going from A to B. Thinking I'll get this exam, then I'll get this exam, then I'll qualify for this, then I'll get this. That's a linear thing. And they were very un-linear. It was like each new day brought a different set of things to deal with. And then the next day was different. They also took the piss out of the business side of it. Philip O'Connell was the bass player and they used to refer to Philip as the 'businessst'. So after a gig, you didn't give money to them. You gave it to Philip because he was the 'businessst'. And they were very suspicious of anything to do with money or paying up for rehearsals or rehearsing. Everybody was eighteen or nineteen or twenty and we were having a laugh.

I came from that rural middle-class background where my parents worked to send us to college and things like that. They came from Gurranabraher, Churchfield and Blackpool, and they weren't aiming for college, even though they were bright guys and they could have gone there. Their cultural thing was different. So to me, rehearsing and getting better at the songs was a linear progression. But to them, it was like 'What?' Definitely our cultural backgrounds, for all of us, make a big difference to what we choose in life and how we approach life.

The organised chaos that was Nun Attax soon began rehearsing at a GAA hall out to the west of the city in a place called Ballinora. This unlikely setting was the backdrop for Donnelly and co. to harness their punk rock enthusiasm and galvanise it into songs. Giordaí played a key role in acquiring their new practice hall. The antics that took place here revealed an unusual aspect of Finbarr's genius. Ua Laoghaire enthuses:

> My old man knew a fella in the Cork County Council who knew someone in the GAA hall in Ballinora. That is how Nun Attax managed to get the hall. The committee walked in one night to see what this crowd were all about and I was on stage. When all these country guys walked in, Donnelly, of course, wound them up and they all filed back out again. He wasn't doing it to be antagonistic. Donnelly was a bit of a genius for finding out what would confuse you. And he would start doing that. He could be aggressive, but then anybody could be when they are nineteen or twenty and have taken enough alcohol. He usually found out what wound you up. In my case, he would find things that would wind

me up. But then, I would insist on doing them anyway, for the laugh - like playing Led Zeppelin's *Stairway To Heaven* - but he would enjoy it. Then I would insist on playing all of *Stairway To Heaven* and Donnelly would sing it and throw abuse at me at the same time. However, he was quite the influential character. In fact, I would say he was probably the most influential young man in that generation in terms of being the very first person to sing in a Cork accent within the area of rock music. He used to go from the Cork accent to the northern accent as he performed.

Giordaí fully recognised the band's achievements. 'They made some really great records. *The Glee Club* is one of the best that I think ever came out of anybody associated with Cork: "We are the Glee Club, we are ever so sad."' He is also insightful about Finbarr Donnelly's character. He suggests that Donnelly maybe secretly wanted to make it, but that the whole idea of letting people know he wanted this did not appeal to him.

It should be emphasised, even at this early stage, that Nun Attax were already becoming quite influential. In effect, they showed budding Cork musicians what they could achieve through their mix of entertaining live shows and their amazing frontman. Their Ballinora practice sessions were attended by future Cork rock luminaries Cathal Coughlan and Sean O'Hagan.

Originally from Luton, Sean O'Hagan explains what drew him to Cork:

> My parents came from Dundalk and Drogheda and they decided they wanted to get back to Ireland. They didn't want to go back to County Louth, so they thought Cork was an option. I think way back in my family there is a

kind of connection to Cork but it wasn't recent. It was basically said: 'We are going to Cork!' and I got there when I was a fourteen or fifteen-year-old kid.

Arriving in Cork, O'Hagan found it strange in comparison to life in Luton. His impressions capture a sense of the city at this time.

> Luton was an anonymous experience, an anonymous town. Coming from suburban England, Cork was bizarre. Cork back then was much stranger than it is now. It had a whole sense of its own. It was very isolated and surreal, full of character and strangeness. It wasn't plugged into the world in those days. That's why all those good musical things happened, because it wasn't plugged in. You actually did meet people from different backgrounds, even though it was small and a provincial society. It operated on loads of different levels. There seemed to be quite a lot of fairly open and lateral thinking and a lot of talk about politics and art, which didn't occur when I was in Luton.

While O'Hagan lived at Lotabeg in Mayfield on Cork's northside, punk rock was happening and the attitude and spirit of DIY music that stemmed from punk was becoming rife in the city. It was at a university party on New Year's Eve 1980 that Sean met his future musical collaborator, Cathal Coughlan, and began a partnership that would see the pair join forces to form The Constant Reminders and seminal Cork band Microdisney.

Sean recalls that on the night he met a bunch of people at a party where he asked:

> Have you heard of these guys The Mekons? Have you heard of these guys Gang of Four? Somebody said:

'I've heard of Gang of Four!' I said: 'Oh, you know about The Mekons etc.' Literally, I was so excited that I think we said we have to meet up. I told him I had a Telecaster and that I knew how to make those slashy chords, those slashy sounds on the guitar. Cathal was writing some brilliant, brilliant poetry and lyrics at the time. We just wanted to get together and literally share a creative moment.

Cathal also recalls meeting Sean:

> I met him at a party in some medical family's house. We just got talking about music and there were not many people who had heard of the kind of thing I was interested in really. I had already met Finbarr Donnelly. The Nun Attax used to practice in Philip and Smelly's mother's place. So when I met Sean, I kind of knew how things could be done in a kind of way that didn't involve having proper facilities and things like that.

Cathal hailed from Glounthaune just outside Cork city. He is eager to clear up any ambiguity that may surround his origins:

> I should point out that I am not from the bright shinny houses on the hill, but from a rather drafty place beside the water in the village, which is across from the church. One of my complexes going through life was that whenever you told people you were from Glounthaune, they immediately thought you were posh, which we weren't.

It was not long until Cathal and Sean united with Mick Lynch to form The Constant Reminders. Cathal explains how the group came together and who was in the band.

I met Mick through a mutual friend. He seemed like the epitome of a libertine in our little world. He was someone who would go off to London and work on a building site and live in squats in the summertime, which seemed adventurous to us. He was quite a charismatic figure in his own right. So it was the three of us that decided to do something together. Then we didn't know what it was really. But Mick had a lot of words and Sean had a guitar and a proper amp and we started practicing. It started as the three of us but, within a few weeks, we had a rhythm section. Jackie Walsh was the bass player and Dave Galvin was the drummer.

Sean O'Hagan cites the fact that Nun Attax had already shown what could be done, as the primary motivating factor behind the formation of The Constant Reminders:

> The Nun Attax had been formed for quite a while and the whole impetus and point of forming a band was that Nun Attax already existed. The reason why we rehearsed out in Ovens was because Giordaí was playing with Nun Attax at the time. That is how we ended up in there. We all went out and watched the Nun Attax rehearsal. In the old days in 1980, we all piled on a bus at Parnell Place and headed out to the country with our guitars - there must have been amps out there - and rehearsed and then had big long walks home through the country. You would have to wait for the bus to get back.

Singer with The Constant Reminders, Mick Lynch remarks on how Nun Attax focused his mind through their magnetic live shows. Mick recalls:

> I got a job sweeping up the coffee place and doing stuff down in The Arc. That is where I saw Nun Attax, well before I met Donnelly and Ricky and all them. Basically, the first time I went to see them, I was inspired! Of course, there was the energy and the humour as well. They were doing the punk thing and there was no posing, like all the Dublin bands that were coming down and pretending to be Elvis Costello. Donnelly used to always say: 'There are a thousand bands in Dublin and they all sound the same!'

Counting The Fall and The Residents among their key influences, The Constant Reminders played gigs around Cork, performing songs such as *The Underpants Song*. Their first gig took place at the UCC College Bar. Mick explains the dynamic at work in the band. 'It was Cathal and myself. Two frontmen and two big egos. Cathal would be the frontman for his songs and I would be the frontman for my songs. We would share the songs, but we would do backing vocals for each other.'

'It was all about trying to make a racket and rant over the top of it,' says Cathal. However, the band only lasted three months. Lynch wryly recalls the events that led to the demise of the band:

> We only did three or four gigs and had a huge blow-out. We got really pissed one night. We were supporting DC Nein in Sir Henry's. DC Nein were playing the Saturday night in The Arc and we were playing the Sunday afternoon...We played a really good gig, so Jimmy O'Hara [manager of Sir Henry's] said: 'Go back on and do another gig at nine. Free bar!' So, about

eight snake bites later, we went back up on stage. I was langers drunk like and I fell into the drum kit and couldn't remember the words. Then we had a big row and, basically, I was shoved out of the band.

Mick Lynch then went on to join Mean Features, which also featured guitarist Liam Heffernan (who went on to star in *Glenroe* playing the role of Blackie Connors), American-born drummer Steve O'Donoghue (who later joined the US Marines) and bassist Pat 'The Hat' Kelleher. Mean Features also briefly featured guitarist Kenneth Carr who only played one gig with the band.

In such a vibrant scene, it is the nature of the beast that musicians move from band to band and new bands emerge. After nine months with Nun Attax, during which the group had supported the young U2 in The Arcadia, guitarist Giordaí Ua Laoghaire as he puts it 'went over to the opposition' and joined Cathal Coughlan and Sean O'Hagan in what had evolved into Microdisney.[21] 'They were completely different. They definitely had a very linear idea about getting a manager and they were much more interested in trying to make it,' Giordaí explains.

Cathal says Microdisney got its distinctive name from word association in his head:

> It didn't really mean anything. By that time, I was scribbling all the time, but I had been doing that since I was a teenager anyway. You could never get away with a name like Microdisney now. I know that the Disney Corporation have actually copyrighted the whole thing.

---

[21] During their early Cork-based incarnation, Microdisney were known locally as Micro Disney *(two words)*. However, this was changed to Microdisney as the group evolved.

# CORK ROCK

It happened since we finished, which is a long time ago. At the same time as punk was spawning a wave of new bands in Cork, other musicians, inspired by local and international guitar legend Rory Gallagher, were also active in this thriving live scene. An accomplished musician who is nowadays more associated with the world of folk and traditional music, award-winning musician John Spillane is a man with a past in the local rock scene.

Like Giordaí Ua Laoghaire, John Spillane was a student at Coláiste an Spioraid Naoimh in Bishopstown. Spillane credits a teacher at his secondary school with influencing his direction during his formative years. John enthuses that:

> A very inspiring teacher there called Tony Doherty had a rock musical every year. He used to bring a lot of Cork rock musicians in to play. Freddie White played in the band a couple of years. Freddie played in the pit for the musical. He was the main guy and we were very impressed that he was there. Dan Dan Fitzgerald [who later managed Freddie White] played drums in the band. We were just kids in school, but they were the band that came in to play the rock musical. It was like *Joseph and the Amazing Technicolor Dreamcoat* and it was a big rock show.

Spillane credits Tony Doherty with encouraging many young students to pursue their music:

> I think an awful lot of musicians of my age group came out of Coláiste an Spioraid Naoimh at that time. As well as myself and the guys that were in my band, Tony Buckley, Dave Murphy and Niall Marron on drums, there was Paul Tiernan, who went on to play

with Interference and also perform as a solo artist. There was Kieran Kennedy, who later went on to be in the Hothouse Flowers. He was also in The Black Velvet Band. There was Victor Coughlan, who was the bass player with a lot of those bands at the time. There was Jerry Fehily, who was the drummer with the Hothouse Flowers. He was from Bishopstown and he was in those shows as well. So there were a lot of musicians!

Reflecting on his early musical outings, John recalls the band scene in Coláiste an Spioraid Naoimh in those days:

> We had a band at school called Bootlace and we later changed the name to Sabre. There was another band the year ahead of us called Asylum, which was Paul Tiernan's band. On drums they had Sammy Sullivan from Fair Hill on the northside. He is now U2's drum roadie and has been for many years. They also had Christy O'Connell on guitar, who was supposed to be the next Rory Gallagher and was a lightening guitar player. John O'Sullivan was on bass.

Sabre became a regular feature on the Cork live circuit of the day. In complete contrast to the punk scene, Sabre covered Rory Gallagher favourites such as *Messin' With The Kid*, *Calling Card* and *Bullfrog Blues*. While The Arc was the focus of Cork's punk and post-punk community, Sir Henry's was the hub of activity for the young John Spillane and his friends. Spillane affectionately remembers:

> Henry's was our place! We lived in Sir Henry's! We were school kids hanging around in Henry's. I would have started going in there in 1978. It was a pub and

there were bands playing there. Small Change had a residency there every Monday night. That was Mick Daly's band. Mick and Tom Stevens were on guitar, Art Lorrigan on drums and Pat Crowley on keyboards. Pat Crowley was a great rock 'n' roll keyboard player. He plays trad now. Then Sabre played in Sir Henry's every Wednesday night, around 1979/80. In my book, one of the big bands around Cork at that time was Southpaw. Johnny Campbell was in that band and Jimmy MacCarthy was the main singer with Southpaw. Declan Sinnott was the main man you could say, the guitar player. There was also a guy called Davy Whyte on drums and an American Jerry McConnell or 'Jerry the Yank' as he was called on keyboards.

During this period, it could be argued that the Cork rock music scene was split into two very different musical camps, punk and rock, each taking their influences from different styles, which at times created friction between the rival groups. John offers his own insight into this phenomenon:

> When new wave hit, we were old wave. We were half and half, original material and covers. Our covers would have been things like Neil Young, The Beatles, Bob Dylan and Rory Gallagher. We started off with our sets being half and half but, eventually, we had a fully original set.

Soon Sir Henry's began to feel the winds of change, with a marked difference in the musical nature of the crowds it was drawing. John explains that:

> In Sir Henry's there was a corner called 'the hall of fame' and we used to hang out there. It was called

that because it was where all the stars and the musos hung out. It was just the back corner of the bar. Jimmy MacCarthy was a big hero to me at that time and he used to be there. Declan Sinnott was a hero of mine as well. They were the guys that we admired who could really play very well. But the punks came in around that time and they would have been a couple of years younger than us. They were completely different and they came in, in fairness, like a breath of fresh air and they took the place by storm. Generally, they couldn't play but they had a following and they were wild! They used to play in The Arcadia. Back then, we played support gigs in The Arcadia. We would have been playing support to most of the more mainstream rock bands that would have come there.

Another important Cork music figure who started busking around 1981, but who would go on to become a regular feature of the Cork live circuit, was Hank Wedel. Having moved from New York City to the rural north Cork town of Mallow in 1974 at the age of eleven, Wedel would later form the band Princes Street. Hank recalls his early days in Cork and the origins of Princes Street:

All of a sudden Mallow was like Long Island and Cork city was like Manhattan. I came to Cork first to play basketball. I was in UCC for four years from 1981 to 1985. During that time, I started busking on the street. Cork has those pedestrian streets between Patrick Street and Oliver Plunkett Street; Winthrop Street and Princes Street in particular were great for busking. We were first a busking band. It was 1984, St. Patrick's Day, when we got together and that was Princes Street.

## CORK ROCK

It was the first time we busked all together.

Hank has a great ability to intellectualise about Cork rock music, while also taking a detached view. He offers a very interesting thought on Rory Gallagher and his relations with the punk rock movement of the late 1970s and early 1980s in Cork. He remarks:

> I think the punks loved Rory Gallagher because there was no compromise. It was complete hard rock. I think the whole thing about punk rock that was appealing was that it was immediate and direct, and anyone could actually do it. That is how rock 'n' roll started off. But just like in early rock 'n' roll, there was a lot of shit. There was a lot of shit in punk as well. I mean there were a lot of people chancing their fucking arm! But I think because of the way it was here in Cork, with Ford's closing down, there was a lot of alienation. I think that appealed to that sort of artistic mindset. UCC back then was not the bastion of conservatism that it is now. And as well as that, in the 1970s and the 1980s, socialistic and communistic ideas still had currency here. The nihilism of punk rock really hit hard.

CHAPTER FOUR

# TOWN TO TOWN

[Microdisney]

While punk rock and the culture that sprang from it had become rooted in the Cork music scene, many of the local figureheads had plans to take their music to an even greater audience. Chief among those intending to break out of Cork was Cathal Coughlan.

Coughlan's group Microdisney now included accomplished local guitarist Giordaí Ua Laoghaire. Reflecting on the situation after Giordaí joined, Cathal admits:

> We were floundering, but we had a bit more structure. Chris McCarthy was playing bass and he played better than the previous guy. Sean O'Hagan was doing everything really. He was organising the music and Giordaí was a wild card and for a time that really worked. But we are not talking about a very long period. That phase was over within about two years.

The Arc had given young Cork punk and post-punk bands both an outlet to play and the confidence to perform in front of a like-minded audience. However, nothing lasts forever and in the early 1980s the punk era at The Arc drew to a close. Elvera Butler, the chief architect behind The Downtown Kampus explains what happened:

> I think it kept going for about four and a half years. I finished at the end of May 1981. I had started back

in November 1977. We lost The Arc! The regulations changed dramatically in terms of the capacity of venues and insurance premiums. So it became totally impossible to run it after that. We tried to keep going but I think people were probably more apprehensive about going to venues for a while afterwards...because of the new policies. The place didn't really work unless you had a good crowd there. I then tried to do the same thing in The Savoy, the following autumn/winter, but we just lost our shirts doing it.

Before leaving The Arc, Elvera organised the recording of an EP, which helped a number of young Cork bands gain some well-deserved airplay on national radio. Called *Kaught At The Kampus* (1981), it was recorded during a live show on August 30, 1980. Elvera recalls the bands that featured on the record:

> That came out in February 1981. Microdisney, Nun Attax, Mean Features with Mick Lynch and Urban Blitz were on it. I would have had a more motherly relationship with Nun Attax and Microdisney, as I used to get them gigs outside of Cork and do things with them.

*Kaught At The Kampus* featured six tracks. These were the Nun Attax songs *White Cortina*, *Reekus Sunfare* and *Eyeballs* as well as *Summer Holidays* by Mean Features, *Breakaway* by Urban Blitz and *National Anthem* by Microdisney.

Discussing the benefits of the record for the bands, Elvera discloses:

> It would have got a lot of airplay. Dave Fanning and people like that championed it, but obviously it was very raw. It got a lot of press and it got a fair bit of

attention. Then, because the groups were playing support to visiting bands, they got openings out of that. Microdisney were touring with U2 at one stage and U2 were starting to make it. So it opened a few doors.

Nowadays, Elvera Butler runs Reekus Records, her own label and publishing company based in Dublin. However, the name of her company has subversive Cork roots. She admits:

> We did *Kaught At The Kampus* and that is where Reekus comes from, because of one of Donnelly's songs on it [*Reekus Sunfare*]. It wasn't a thing that was consciously set up. A lot of the bands wanted to put out their songs, so we just did a record. And you do one record and then someone else approaches you.

While Elvera had played a crucial role in nurturing Cork's rock music scene, tough times were ahead. The negative economic conditions strangling Cork during the early 1980s began to affect groups such as Microdisney. With the demise of a number of major employers in the city and the job losses that stemmed from this, people had less money to go out to live shows. Cathal Coughlan reveals:

> When we started playing with Giordaí, it was kind of monotonous. We were trying to be hypnotic and then we decided to do something that was more, I hate to say it, but sort of funky! It wasn't really. It was about as funky as a half-paralysed dog. We tried that for a while, but that really failed badly. It was just to keep our own interest more than anything else. By that point, The Arcadia was gone, so there was nowhere to play regularly, and with Ford and Dunlop's closing down and the economy becoming a joke in every respect,

there was nobody going out to live shows. Everybody lost interest except me and Sean, and we were kind of in two minds about going on, but we did!

A lack of suitable venues in the city is something that different generations of Cork musicians and fans have often cited. But during this period, things certainly looked bleak. Asked what was his favourite venue to play while Microdisney were still in Cork, Coughlan responds:

> After The Arcadia closed there really wasn't one. The Musicians' Federation were running something in a pub that isn't there anymore called The Bodega, on Oliver Plunkett Street. Now and again you could maybe do Sir Henry's. But it was all dependent on their mood really and what else was happening. They were as badly affected by the economy being shagged as anybody else. Their hesitance was understandable.
>
> One time we just rented a function room in the Metropole Hotel and somebody told them it was a Sunday night disco. So you had all these people with mohicans [hairstyles] walking into the Metropole. I know they have dance music nights and everything there now, but then it was as straight-laced as the Arbutus Lodge [renowned local restaurant and hotel]. It was just crazy. They were trying to get us to stop and we couldn't and it was real keystone cops stuff.

A friend of Cathal's and Sean O'Hagan's at the time was musician and music fan Fergal Keane. Keane would later go on to become a renowned RTÉ journalist. O'Hagan remembers Fergal during this musical era:

> We would see Fergal for a drink up in Sir Henry's and we used to spend a lot of time chatting about music and he was a great talker. Fergal was a big tall guy and he was always very stylish. He always had that kind of slightly mod thing about him. He would always wear a pair of big Levi 501s, Dr. Martens, a Harrington jacket and he was very dogmatic about his ideas. He was a wonderful guy. Fergal played guitar and sang lead vocals in his own band. In the scene, everybody knew each other and everybody went to Heaphy's and then The Phoenix bar and The Long Valley, etc.[22]

Coughlan witnessed Keane playing in a number of local bands: 'He would play bass mostly. I think he was the bass player in Prague Over Here and I think Chris Leahy played guitar with them.'

In an article entitled *A Great Day To Be A Cork Man*, which appeared in *Village* magazine in 2005, Fergal wrote: 'The Cork of the early 1980s could only have ever been European capital of despair, unemployment and emigration. The only thing it had to offer young people was a great music scene.'

As a Cork-based five-piece, Microdisney attempted to break into the Dublin gig circuit. They also saw band members come and go. Sean reveals:

> I think at one stage Rob McKahey, who later played with Stump, played in the five-piece band on drums. He joined the band and was with us for about five minutes. Jackie, the old bass player only lasted about two gigs. Then Chris McCarthy joined Microdisney, by which time the band rehearsed in a room over a pub right across the road from the Beamish and Crawford

---

[22] Heaphy's Bar, on the corner of Union Quay, later became The Lobby Bar.

Brewery called The Malt Shovel.[23] In the band then was Giordaí, Chris, Me, Cathal and Dave Galvin. That was when we started travelling up to Dublin playing The Magnet Bar. After we did *Kaught At The Kampus* (1981), we started travelling to Dublin. We did the Magnet shows and then we started opening for people in Dublin like Siouxsie and the Banshees. It was amazing! We were just these kids playing on the same bill as The Banshees.

There has always been a strong tradition of flamboyant dress associated with the music world, especially when you consider the glam rock and punk fashions of the 1970s and the new romantic fashions of the 1980s. But interestingly, Microdisney steered well clear of any form of pretentious dress. O'Hagan confesses:

> The one thing we always insisted on was that we never dressed up. We always dressed down and that was a big, big thing that people noticed. 'They're not punk rockers! They're dressing down! They look more like The Fall than The Sex Pistols, but their music sounds more like mutant funk than anything else!' And you know that was pretty cool.

Microdisney's five-piece adventure soon drew to a close. However, the group did record a demo called *Let's Get Married/Mr Fun* at a little studio in Tivoli. They also managed to record a radio session for the *Dave Fanning Show*, which featured additional tracks such as *Victory*, *Leper*, *Kackhand* and *Mitchelstown*. Eager to pursue a successful recording career, O'Hagan and Coughlan reverted to being a two-piece.

---

[23] The Malt Shovel on South Main Street is now called An Spailpín Fánach.

Discussing life as a duo in Cork, Sean says:

> Microdisney sort of imploded and Cathal and I started making music on our own. Cathal bought an SK10 keyboard, a little organ and I had a guitar and we developed this way of writing songs where there was a very simple organ sound. I played a finger style guitar and we had a drum machine. As a two-piece, we could create what we regarded as a big sound. But it was an empty sound actually, a vocal, a guitar, an organ and a drum machine. That is when we started making records. Up to then, writing songs was slashing away at guitars with the idea of actually writing in a very traditional way but with quite odd chord progressions. We rented a flat over a bakery on Daunt's Square. We put our gear in there and we met every day. We wrote songs every single day. Literally! We wrote a whole set and again we had this fairly anarchic thing about us even though we were writing soft tunes and small melodies.

Listening to the likes of Scott Walker, John Barry, Steve Young and Alex Chilton, Microdisney began to write songs that would eventually end up on their first album *Everybody's Fantastic* (1984). Before O'Hagan and Coughlan set about recording their debut long-player, they recorded two singles that would be released on Kabuki Records. Aided by Dave Clifford, who ran a music and visual arts magazine called *Vox* in Dublin, the two musicians went into the recording studio. Microdisney recorded *Hello Rascals* and its b-side *The Helicopter Of The Holy Ghost*. Engineering duties for this single fell to Terry Cromer. Luckily these tracks, released in 1982, caught the ear of legendary DJ John Peel and he began to play their single on his radio show. As a consequence, the talented Cork outfit were offered the opportunity to record for the famous Peel Sessions. Sean discusses their second single, which they recorded in advance of playing the Peel Sessions. It was released in 1983:

> The second single, before we did the Peel Session was *Pink Skinned Man*. That was recorded in the Eamonn Andrews studio in the Television Club in Dublin and it was mixed in a monastery. I don't know about this thing with studios and monasteries, but we utilised them and again it was engineered by Terry Cromer.

It was not long until Sean and Cathal decided to take a chance and pursue their dream of making music as a career, by moving to London in the hope of winning new fans.

> After we made these two singles the band seemed to be a happening thing. *Sounds*[24] magazine in London sent over two reporters and did a huge piece on Cork and the music that was happening there. I think *Pink Skinned Man* had become 'Single Of The Week' in *Sounds*. Then *Sounds* started writing about us and, of course, we thought that was amazing. Not too long after that we got the boat and went to London. Ricky Dineen from Nun Attax came with us and helped us carry our amps.

Reflecting on this important career decision, Cathal describes their reasoning in moving to London:

> We were mainly pissed off that there were no facilities for doing anything in Cork. By that time, we knew Dublin well enough to know that we didn't want to be based there. Right from the beginning, Dublin had

---

[24] *Sounds* was a British-based weekly music paper, which ran from 1970 until 1991.

always been great for us to go and play in. One of the first gigs we ever played was in Dublin. People were very friendly and appreciative and we made a lot of friends who are still friends today.

It just seemed as hard to get on in Dublin as it was in Cork. So there seemed to be no point in going there. So we were this two-piece thing, which was kind of semi-voluntary, semi-involuntary. It was an ambivalent kind of thing and we managed to make some records and put out a couple of singles, which John Peel played. It was a major wish to be told not only was he playing us, but he was playing us a couple of nights a week. We got to do sessions. So we just decided to grab it while it was going.

While Microdisney evolved into a duo, one of Cork's seminal bands was set to morph into a more successful performing unit. In the early 1980s, Nun Attax parted ways. However, most of the band members soon reunited to form Five Go Down To The Sea?. Nun Attax guitarist Ricky Dineen explains how Five Go Down To The Sea? came about:

Nun Attax split up after a gig in Dublin. We just had a bit of an argument with each other. We finished up for a while. It would have been around 1981 approximately. Later, we came across Mick Stack who was a very, very talented musician. He was very off the wall, which was exactly what we wanted. So we started jamming with him and started playing again. Mick Stack played the guitar and I played the guitar. We weren't sure what to do then, until we discovered a cello player at a play. She was actually playing in a play that Mick Lynch was in. Her name was Úna Ní Chanainn. We saw her playing and we got this idea that we would ask her to play in our punk rock band. We thought she would say 'piss off' straight away. But she actually said yes. One day, we were practising and she turned up. So we had two guitars and a cello and it worked very well. When Philip went his own way, myself, Smelly and Finbarr were toying with ideas all the time. Then Stack came along and then we got Úna in and that was the next stage.

The group soon evolved into Five Go Down To The Sea?. One striking feature of the band's name is that it included a question mark. This made the name even more distinctive and served to reinforce the quirky tendencies of the group. When asked who came up with the band name, Ricky reveals that it was Donnelly's idea: 'I think Five Go Down To The Sea? must have been another Donnelly idea. It was the name of a song we had previously as Nun Attax, and we decided we would call the band that.'

An interesting aspect of Nun Attax and Five Go Down To The Sea? was that neither outfit was influenced by Cork rock music. Keith 'Smelly' O'Connell who played drums in both groups concedes that they 'were influenced by nothing local at all. We had no interest in Rory Gallagher whatsoever. I remember seeing Rory Gallagher play in The Arc, but I had no interest. We were punk rockers! It was just a different thing. It's only in later years that I realised how talented the man was.'

There was another factor that set this bunch of young mavericks apart from many other Cork rock acts of the day. While many rock fans flocked to Sir Henry's, Donnelly and co's relationship with the venue was approaching combative.

No doubt this added to their subversive image. Discussing what Sir Henry's meant to him and his fellow band members, Smelly admits:

> I don't think we played one gig in Sir Henry's. We never played [there]! I think a couple of us were barred ... and that was why we never played there. We weren't able to play there. We were barred for being punk rockers and being too drunk. I remember one instance, we were drinking during happy hour and we were there for about four hours. We got slaughtered. We went away to another pub and came back and your man barred the lot of us. So we said: 'Fuck 'em! We wouldn't play there anyway!'

Smelly adds that: 'Microdisney played there but we didn't. It was a mutual thing as well. Not being big-headed or anything, but we could have played gigs anywhere in Cork at the time if we wanted to!'

While Sir Henry's at times may have been off limits for the members of Nun Attax, the band did gravitate towards The Phoenix on Union Quay. Smelly singles out Tom Dineen who owned The Phoenix in those days for particular praise as he was a source of great assistance to the band:

> The Phoenix was our pub and we got loads of help from the owner Tom Dineen. What records we did make were always thanks to him. He gave us money for instruments. We often made demos out in his house with a couple of the lads that later fell in with U2, people like Tom Mullally and John O'Sullivan. So if we wanted to play a gig in The Phoenix, it was never for money. We just played in The Phoenix instead of Sir Henry's and we jammed the place.

Smelly paints a distinctive picture of what you could expect to find when you entered The Phoenix in those days:

> You had all the hairies downstairs, the didley yadas, and upstairs was solely alternative punk rockers. Tom was ahead of his time. There was a bit of rivalry between the two groups in the pub, but Tom Dineen helped everyone.

Smelly recalls one particular instance during their Nun Attax incarnation when Dineen went out of his way to help Donnelly and his fellow punks secure a bank loan to help them further their musical career:

> He actually brought us into the Allied Irish Bank to sign a loan for us. The bank manager told him not to do it after one look at the heads on us. But we were all working at the time. So Tom just said: 'Look give them the money!' That was it. He just wanted to help and that was unusual at the time. We actually did buy equipment. We didn't drink the money. I remember we bought a brand new H&H amp, a brand new bass and there might have been something else as well.

Like Microdisney, Five Go Down To The Sea? took their music to England. This period also saw the Donnelly-led group record and release material; though they never managed to release an album, they did release three EPs. The first, produced in 1983, was their 7-inch *Knot A Fish* EP on Kabuki Records.[25] Produced by John O'Sullivan, it featured the tracks: *Fishes For Compliments, Elephants For Fun And Profit, There's A Fish On Top Of Shandon (Swears He's Elvis)* and *Why Wait*

[25] Around the time that Five Go Down To The Sea? recorded the *Knot A Fish* EP, they also recorded the track *Knocknaheeney Shuffle* in Sulán Studios in Ballyvourney, County Cork. However, this track was never released.

*Until April.* The second was the 1984 12-inch *The Glee Club* EP on Abstract Records. It featured the tracks: *The Glee Club, Jumping Joley, Often, Boon For Travellists* and *What Happened Your Leg?.* The final Five Go Down To The Sea? release was a 12-inch EP on Creation Records.[26] Called *Singing In Braille,* it was released in August 1985 and featured the tracks: *Singing In Braille, Aunt Nelly* and *Silk Brain Worm Women.*

Looking back now at his tenure with Five Go Down To The Sea?, I ask guitarist Ricky Dineen what is his favourite memory of this period. He responds:

> It has to be Donnelly. All the things we used to get up to weren't premeditated at all and they weren't to impress anybody. They weren't done in a rock 'n' roll way to impress journalists. It sometimes used to get violent. It seemed to come out completely spontaneously. His party piece in pubs and even on stage was to take the full side of a pint glass into his mouth, holding the glass through his mouth.

Asked what qualities Donnelly possessed as the frontman of Five Go Down To The Sea?, Ricky enthuses:

> I think he was what most people came to see. He was totally wild in a very natural kind of way. He used to speak with a mixture of a Cork and a Belfast accent. He didn't know which one was his own. In the end, it became more Cork than Belfast. But the things he used to come up with on the stage! Over in England, he used to say 'Fuck the Queen!' and things like that. Not because of anything political, but just to see what they

---

[26] This seminal British independent label was founded by Alan McGee in 1983 and was responsible for signing acts like Oasis, My Bloody Valentine and Primal Scream. Creation Records wound down in 1999.

would say and what way people would react. Some of them would love it.

Microdisney's Cathal Coughlan believes that Five Go Down To The Sea? had what it took to become a major success in their own right. However, things didn't work out for them in the long run. Cathal states:

> The thing about those guys was, I think as a kind of self-defence mechanism, everything had to be wrapped up in impenetrable code. People like me and Sean were more confident and hence probably more prone to making asses of ourselves. We would go out on a limb to communicate with people who we didn't know. The others were a bit of a closed shop and it stayed closed and that was really unfortunate because I think Nun Attax and Five Go Down To The Sea? could have been as big as Echo And The Bunnymen, if things had just gone a little bit differently.

CHAPTER FIVE

# CHARLTON HESTON

[Stump]

In November 1984, another veteran of the Cork rock music scene made his way to England. Although Mick Lynch was hoping to attend acting school, a year after he arrived in London he reunited with drummer and fellow Corkman Rob McKahey in a four-piece band called Stump.

Hailing from Douglas on the southside of Cork city, Mick Lynch was very active in the local rock music scene. Having been a member of The Constant Reminders and outright frontman in local punk band Mean Features, Lynch also worked in T.N.T. Records in Paul Street and for five years in Sir Henry's. This gave Mick a unique insight into not only the development of Sir Henry's as a live venue, but also the development of popular music in Cork at the time.

Taking its name from the late Cork baker and former Lord Mayor of Cork, Sir Henry O'Shea (1858-1926), Sir Henry's first opened in 1978. Mick recalls his introduction to Sir Henry's and how he came to discover the now famous venue during its earliest incarnation:

> I was in the School of Art in Cork and next thing I heard: 'Oh God! There is this great new bar and they do music with a live band on Monday nights!' So there were tentative steps made to get in there. Then it just became a hangout and an essential part of Cork life.

When they opened up the concert hall [they had sliding doors there] that meant bigger bands were coming down.

Naming bars after local Cork characters seems to have been the forte of the owners of the Grand Parade Hotel and Sir Henry's. The bar located downstairs in the hotel was named after the colourful and eccentric Cork character Klondyke.[27]

An important fact about the early days of Sir Henry's was that it was never intended as a live venue. Certainly, no role as a focal point for the city's youth culture was envisaged at that stage. Instead, the inspiration behind this new entrepreneurial development stemmed more from the Hard Rock Café style of operation, i.e. a bar that served food and played rock 'n' roll. Lynch explains:

> It started off as a posh café. Jerry Lucey [the then owner of the Grand Parade Hotel and Sir Henry's] had all these antiques in there and the idea was that all the solicitors would come up from the South Mall and have their lunch. The food in there was actually quite good. They used to have burgers and food like that... Jimmy O'Hara [manager of Sir Henry's] came back from America with this idea to turn it into Sir Henry's hard rock and roll café. I worked there for five years. I started off doing the bottles and ended up not quite being head barman but one of the more experienced barmen in there.

Asked about the clientele that frequented the venue when he worked there, Mick admits that: 'Sir Henry's was the first bar

---

[27] Klondyke's real name was Jeremiah Healy. He was also referred to as 'Doctor', having been christened this by supporters at UCC. He was elected to Cork Corporation in 1942 following his calls for a ladies toilet on Merchants Quay.

that played good music. It was more a biker's bar than anything else. But there was a gang of us punks that started drinking in there and we got on really well with the bikers. So it became a kind of a punk/biker pub.'

One band Mick says played regularly in Sir Henry's around the time that he started working there was Cork rock 'n' roll group Hot Guitars. They still play an active role on the Cork live circuit today. Formed in 1977, Hot Guitars released their only single, *Nasty People*, in 1978. With influences including Elvis, The Rolling Stones, Ray Charles and harmonica player Paul Butterfield, Hot Guitars have seen quite a few personnel changes over the years since their early days in Sir Henry's.

Joe O'Callaghan of Hot Guitars reflects on their regular line-up changes and their period in Sir Henry's:

> We had about sixty different line-ups and about forty different people passed through the band. But Sir Henry's is where we started. We played there for a good while. When that place opened, we were more or less the resident band for a good couple of years. We would have played half original and half cover sets. The covers we did were bluesy kind of punk, like with an R&B feel.

Among the musicians who performed with Hot Guitars was the young Kieran Kennedy from Fuller's Road in Cork. While he has, over the years, played with many acts, he has fond memories of his days with Hot Guitars. Kieran recalls: 'I was about sixteen and they very nicely gave me my first gig every Monday night in Sir Henry's. We used to do a cover of *Gino* by Dexy's Midnight Runners and I used to sing it. I had a high voice at that time.'

Kieran played with a host of acts after his tenure with Hot

Guitars ended. These included: Impact, T & T, Earthquake and punk band Romeo Butcher alongside Aidan McCarthy, son of Dixies' drummer Joe McCarthy. Aidan had also played drums in Cork punk act Berserk, regarded by many as Leeside's first punk band. Tragically, in 1981 Aidan McCarthy died in a car accident at the age of twenty. Later, Kieran Kennedy formed the rock band 1990 with John O'Sullivan and Wayne Sheehy, who had been the drummer in Cork band The Banditz. It was after meeting his future wife Maria Doyle at a U2 concert in Dublin's Croke Park, that Kieran Kennedy formed The Black Velvet Band, in which Maria was a singer. Having played with the Hothouse Flowers and performed as a solo artist, Kieran today produces other artists and collaborates musically with his wife, as well as running Maria's record label, Mermaid Records.

While Hot Guitars entertained the masses in Sir Henry's, the attention of many young music fans still focused on punk. But as Mick Lynch explains, Cork punk rock fans didn't buy into the same punk ideals as those professed by Malcolm McClaren and The Sex Pistols. Mick states:

> We weren't stupid! The whole Malcolm McClaren thing and the whole rock 'n' roll swindle was boring really. It had just gone away from its roots. Punk to me was ideological. We didn't have mohicans [hairstyles] and we didn't have needles. We used to just go to second-hand shops and buy incongruous clothes that didn't fit. That was our rebellion – that way.

While The Sex Pistols may not have been as popular in Cork as they were in Britain, one band that was a hit with local rock music fans was The Residents.[28] When asked was he a fan of

[28] A feature of this experimental US band/collective is that its members were and remain anonymous.

this avant-garde American band, a smile beams across Mick's face.

> Oh yeah! One good thing about Cork was that one person would get a record and it would do the rounds and get taped and that, because it was such a small group of people as such.

One important figure, who witnessed many a great gig in Cork and also knew Mick quite well during this period, was Jack Lyons. Lyons (known locally as Jackie 'The Bell', having worked as a bus conductor from 1968 – 1975) worked in Sir Henry's alongside Jimmy O'Hara running and promoting gigs. In his ever funny and entertaining way, Jack explains part of his role in the venue:

> I did all the promoting. That was about 1983, 1984 and 1985. I booked some of the bands but not all of them. You could say that my boss was Jimmy O'Hara and if the gig went down well Jimmy had organised it and if the gig was a bit of a bummer, then Jackie 'The Bell' had fucking organised it!

Being in the role that he was in, Jack witnessed Mick Lynch performing in Sir Henry's and remembers that he possessed an uncanny stage presence that was hard to beat: 'When Mick came on stage, he was a good stage person. He is tall and the stage likes him. It doesn't like everyone, but the stage likes Mick Lynch.'

Mick's distinctive onstage persona has proved a major asset to the various groups he has performed with. Mean Features certainly made an impression on music fans at Carnsore Point in Wexford when they played the anti-nuclear concert performing alongside Cork punk legends Nun Attax. However, unlike Nun

Attax, the gig did have a certain political significance for Mick Lynch, as he was a member of the anti-nuclear movement. He recalls an article he read by DJ Tom Dunne in which Dunne explained that the Carnsore Point gig marked a personal turning point for him. Mick explains:

> I read an article Tom Dunne wrote in the *Sunday Times* and it was about how he got into music. He said he was sixteen or seventeen and he was down at Carnsore Point and next thing there was a band up on stage, four fellas with black T-shirts and skinheads singing songs about Roches Stores' bags. Suddenly, he realised that music could be about anything. It didn't have to be about California or the clichés.

Lynch's Mean Features band-mate Liam Heffernan adds to the story by saying:

> I read an article by Tom Dunne where he talked about the first band that he saw at Carnsore Point, that rocked his head off and it was us. He was quoting lyrics in this article, like twenty-five years later. I eventually met him. A friend of mine had a party in Dublin one summer and Tom Dunne was thrilled to meet a Mean Feature!

In Cork, Lynch was instrumental in the formation and running of the Cork Music Collective. After The Arc closed its doors, many bands had trouble getting gigs and a lot of young musicians grew increasingly uneasy about the lack of suitable venues. The establishment of the Cork Music Collective was seen as an honest attempt to alleviate this problem. Its main aim was to put on live shows. Mick reflects on his experience with the Collective:

> We formed the Cork Music Collective and we were down in the old Bodega [which is now Kelly's Restaurant on Oliver Plunkett Street] and out the back there we used to run gigs on a Friday and Saturday night. I ended up doing the door and booking the bands because, as usual, collectives don't work and somebody has to do the job. That would have been about 1981/1982. It started off as great fun. We would have really eclectic nights with a big mix but then the traditional rock people got fed up and the punks and their bands got fed up with it. So we split it up a bit. We had good nights and we had bad nights. We started running a mod night and they fucked it up for everyone because they totally trashed the toilets one night. Every bowl, every mirror etc. After that the Bodega had had enough.

Mick, like many of his contemporaries, made the decision to move to London. Asked what prompted him to relocate, he says: 'I moved in November 1984. I had split up with my girlfriend and there was fuck all work in Ireland anyway.'

After Lynch moved to England, he was tracked down by talented Cork drummer Rob McKahey, whom he had met previously through the Cork music scene. For a brief period, Rob had been a member of Microdisney and was well-known in the Cork rock music community for his musical exploits. It was McKahey who played a key role in recruiting Mick for what was to be his most successful band – Stump. Mick recalls:

> Rob heard I was over and sent a postcard. He was already over there. He said: 'I'm in this great band and we are looking for a singer. Come down!' I ignored the first one. Then I got another one. So I said it to the [new] girlfriend and she said: 'Sure go down and

have a look!' So I did. I met Rob down the Old Kent Road [London] and I was introduced to the two lads - Chris Salmon, the guitarist and Kevin Hopper, the bass player. We went round to Kevin's house and down into the basement and this amazing music happened. They had maybe seven or eight tunes with no words to them. It was just all those polyrhythms and all the weird things that Kevin does with his bass.

This was to be the beginning of a very colourful period for both Mick Lynch and Rob McKahey. The group's influences included Captain Beefheart, Frank Zappa and XTC, and they became known as a particularly powerful live unit.

When asked how, as frontman of this four-piece, Mick would describe their live shows, he responds:

Well I've never seen us! Most of our gigs were good. Visually we were very entertaining. I could go on a bit between songs but I always got a good rapport with the audience. Because of the nature of the music, it had to be tight yet intricate.

Stump's first 12-inch EP, *Mud On A Colon* (1986), was a low budget recording that featured four tracks: *Orgasm Way*, *Ice The Levant*, *Grab Hands* and *55-0-55*. Released on Ron Johnson Music, the title of the EP came from a line in one of the songs.

This was followed up with the wonderfully titled *Quirk Out* (1986). This 12-inch mini-album, released on Stuff Records, featured six tracks: *Tupperware Stripper*, *Our Fathers*, *Kitchen Table*, *Buffalo*, *Everything In Its Place* and *Bit Part Actor*. While Lynch admits the title did suit the music, there was a downside. 'Unfortunately, we became a quirky band. So instead of a freak-out or a rock-out band, we were known as a quirk-out band. Rob McKahey came up with the title *Quirk Out*.'

Speaking about the reception meted out to *Quirk Out* from music fans and the press, Mick says:

> John Peel had started playing us. Then we brought out *Quirk Out* and that went to number two in the indie charts. We were kept off number one by *Bedtime For Democracy* [by Dead Kennedys], which was one of my proudest moments. Obviously, with the success of that, we were getting crazy press. Crazy press! There was a bit of a, I won't say bidding war, but there were various people interested. Chrysalis got it. But it was a mistake really, because then we were out of the indie league and we should have just stayed in the indie league for another while.

*Quirk Out* included a very distinctive track in the form of *Buffalo*, the video of which can be viewed on YouTube. However, the title owes more to Buffalo, New York, than the four-legged animal. Mick explains what the song was about and what inspired it:

> It's about American tourists. I had this theory that American tourists were reincarnations of buffalos. Their big arse, ambling along, pretty stupid! I got a lot of the lyrics from listening to Americans when I worked in a bar in central London. It was just the stupid things you would hear. I heard Yanks saying: 'Does the fish have chips? How much is the fish? Does the fish have chips?' That then crept into the lyrics.

*A Fierce Pancake* (1988) was to be Stump's first and only full album. However, the recording and production of this album was plagued with problems. German samplist Holger Hiller was recruited to produce the album, while engineering duties were to fall to Stephen Street (who had worked with The Smiths and would later work with Blur). Stump chose Hansa Studios in Berlin to record most of their debut long-player. Mick confesses:

> Trying to find a producer for it was a bit of a chore. Stephen Street was the engineer. He hadn't become a producer at that stage. But we jumped with him because he had been Morrissey's engineer and had a brilliant reputation. We had three weeks in Berlin, which was great and the [Berlin] wall was still up as well. We were within spitting distance of it. I think that was about 1986.

Asked why his group relocated from London to Berlin, and if it had anything to do with German producer Holger Hiller, Mick replies:

> Well Holger Hiller would have been part of it. We didn't want your typical studio, where you are stuck in this airless box looking at a little screen. So the recording room was a huge banqueting hall with big windows and oak panelling. It was the Lord Mayor of Berlin's entertainment complex. It was a brothel during the Second World War and was one of the few buildings that survived.

Working relations with Hiller soon became strained and members of the band were not satisfied by the mixing stage of the songs. Lynch elaborates:

> When we started mixing down with him, some of us weren't too happy with it. It was too polished. There was a bit of a split there. At one stage, we were offered Steve Albini who was getting a name from doing The Pixies and stuff like that. But the guitarists didn't like it because they heard that he spends all his time on drum sounds and then only a small bit of time on guitars.

Since Steve Albini is now a renowned producer, does Mick think things might have gone differently if they had got him on board? Lynch takes a deep sigh:

> Oh God! Aw Man! That would have been great like! It would have been a different record. But it was too big a change from *Quirk Out*. We wanted to prove that we weren't just this quirky band. There are a few tracks on it like *Living It Down* and stuff like that, that are more classic rock. I don't like that term. What word do you use instead of rock? More epic sounding!

Eventually Hugh Jones, who Stump had worked with previously, was brought in to finish the record and mix the Hansa Studios recordings. However, Mick believes the album veered too far away from their live performances and this was a problem.

One notable feature of *A Fierce Pancake* is that it is dedicated to Flann O'Brien and Wilhelm Reich. Lynch explains that: 'Flann O'Brien would have been essential reading for the whole band. We were all big fans and I suppose his sense of the absurd appealed to us. Wilhelm Reich was a hero of the bass player.'

Stump's album contained one song in particular that seems forever associated with the band and is probably their most popular song – *Charlton Heston*. Mick recalls how the song first came about:

> When we were in Berlin, we had a loose idea of linking one song to another and maybe having short pieces in-between that would almost make it seamless. So the songs would seep into one another. I had laid down all the vocal tracks and then I had a week off, while the lads did all their stuff. Then at breakfast one morning I had this line in my head: 'Charlton Heston put his vest on!' And the lads cracked up. There was: 'Michael Jackson put his cacks on.' There were all sorts of things. Then I wrote the first verse and it just became a song. So we had an extra song. It's just about Charlton Heston being really macho and Kev Hopper was experimenting with samplers at the time. He had this backing track that we called 'Fighting Gnomes'. That was the name of the *Charlton Heston* backing track. He was plumping for that to be one of the pieces we would use and they both just fitted. That song was probably the fastest song we ever wrote.

During his time as frontman with Stump, Mick graced the cover of respected British music magazine *Melody Maker*. He remembers the experience.

> We knew it was going to happen. But I didn't like the picture, but then you never do. It was quite weird walking into WH Smith and seeing your face on the cover of a music magazine. It was taken in a photo studio somewhere. Oh God! We were fed up with being in the photo studio. I think it would have been just after the album. When the album, *A Fierce Pancake*,

was being released, the record company pushed for interviews etc. It came through the record company's press department. Again there were weeks of interviews and telephone interviews.

*Chaos* and *Charlton Heston* were both released as singles in support of *A Fierce Pancake*. *Charlton Heston* peaked at number 72 in the UK singles chart in August 1988. However, it was not long until Stump split. Mick reflects on how their demise came about:

> We were in the difficult second album sort of mindset. Then we released *Buffalo* as a single, which was really a retrograde start. Then the press and the backlash started happening. I came home for Christmas and Rob came home for Christmas and then the band just imploded really. It didn't explode. It just imploded. We had always said in interviews that when the fun goes out of it and it becomes a job that would be it for us.

After Stump went their separate ways in 1988, Mick continued to be involved in music, but with limited success:

> I auditioned for the Inspiral Carpets. It didn't work. Then, as part of the payoff, I got the midi stuff and tried to do home recordings, but I'm not a technical person. I was complaining because Rob had two drum kits and Chris had four guitars and Kev had two bass guitars and I had a couple of T-shirts. So the record company gave me money on condition that I buy musical equipment.
>
> I was in two other bands. One was just a bunch of friends that never really got anywhere. Then I started working in the Royal Opera House as a stagehand. I

met Donal Boyle who was from Antrim, and he and his girlfriend had been in bands together since they were twelve, and their friend Niall who was a drummer. I went for guitar lessons and we ended up writing songs. The band was called Bernard. That was an excellent little band. That band was London-based and lasted about a year. We tried! We did demos and sent them off to people and tried to get signed and all that. Then Niall moved to Japan. Bernard actually played The Village [venue under Sir Henry's] around 1990.

Mick moved back to Cork in 1995. In recent times, he has made a welcome return to the live circuit on Leeside performing very distinctive, tongue-in-cheek style shows under the moniker of Don For Chickens. As Don For Chickens, Lynch supported English post-punk band The Fall in The Spiegeltent in Cork on July 3, 2008, as part of the Cork Midsummer Festival. Mick explains where this bizarre name came from:

> I do a one-man act called Don For Chickens. You know the card game, Don. I was up in a pub on the northside [of Cork] and there was a girl who wasn't very clever but she wasn't from Cork. There was a poster up on the wall that said: 'Don For Chickens Saturday €3.00' and she said: 'Oh God, I've never heard of them!' I needed a name, so that is how I got it.

With both Mick Lynch and Rob McKahey living in the Cork area, and Chris Salmon and Kevin Hopper based in London, it seems unlikely that Stump will re-form. However, with the release of *Stump: The Complete Anthology* (2008), a new generation of music fans now have the chance to hear just what all the fuss was about.

CHAPTER SIX

# SUGAR BEET GOD

[Cypress, Mine!]

When people think of Cork rock bands active in the 1980s, names such as Microdisney, Nun Attax and Five Go Down To The Sea? often come to mind. However, other talented groups and musicians emerged from the local rock scene during this period. While many Cork acts made their way to England in search of better prospects, others chose to stay on Leeside. Two important figures in the Cork rock scene, who were active in those days, albeit in different capacities, were Ger O'Leary and Dave Sullivan, the latter better known to music fans as Skully.

During punks' heyday at The Arc, Ger O'Leary was the in-house DJ, spinning all the underground hits of the day to revellers eager to see a good live show. Skully was a native of the Sunday's Well area of the city and his father, Victor Sullivan, had played in a local group called The Bluebell Quartet. In 1976, Skully formed and fronted a distinctive Cork-based trio by the name of Real Mayonnaize.

This band lasted for over six years and it was certainly a very enjoyable experience for Skully. Together with his band-mates, bass player Jerry Buckley, who was a neighbour of Skully's, and drummer Dave Rudd, from Douglas, Real Mayonnaize played across the city in venues, many of which no longer exist.

Both Ger and Skully have provided many valuable insights into the vibrant and open-minded music scene of the day and have the experience to offer analyses of the bands and music coming out of Cork during this time.

With clearly fond memories, Skully reflects on the hard slog that was the early days of Real Mayonnaize:

> We started gigging at all the little venues. We used to gig in Cobh and we would gig anywhere. We got little gigs and we would be lugging this big organ up and down the stairs of venues. I mean, the day we were going to make it was the day we played The Arc as a support band. That was what we were aspiring to! We played Sir Henry's and we used to pack Sir Henry's solid every time we played.

Bass player Jerry Buckley describes the Real Mayonnaize sound:

> We had a sort of punky sound as well as a keyboard sound. I actually played the cello as well. I'd fire up the cello and play it live and have guys with spiky hair coming up to me saying: 'Jesus, I love the sound of the cello: that was brilliant!'

The Underground was another Cork venue where Real Mayonnaize graced the stage.[29] This lively atmospheric venue was short-lived, but it played host to many local acts during its short lifespan. Ger O'Leary recalls the origins of The Underground and describes what it was like:

> The Underground would now probably be located in the children's department of Roches Stores [now

---

[29] The Underground was located on Fisher's Lane. This street, along with a number of others, such as Thomas Street and Merchant Street (formerly Fish Street), was demolished to make way for the Merchants Quay Shopping Centre, which opened in February 1989.

Debenhams] on Patrick Street. Thompson's used to have a cake shop and that whole block was getting ready to be condemned. A guy called Hugh Gloucester, who had loads of clothes shops around town at the time, decided he would open a pub, probably because he was getting the place for half nothing. He opened a pub and the closest way to equate it to anything now, would be the same kind of philosophy as somewhere like Fred Zeppelin's on Parliament Street: they could have any band in to play, but there was always a band in there, no matter when you went in. There were a lot of bands around at the time. Size-wise, it was about the size of An Crúiscín Lán on Douglas Street, but just buzzing! Anybody who was involved in music used to go in there.

Skully vividly remembers Real Mayonnaize playing this old venue: 'There was sweat pouring down the walls. The keyboard was soaking wet, with the whole stage rocking and the people crammed up against each other.'

Reflecting on the general musical atmosphere of Cork in this period, both Skully and Ger agree that the live circuit was extremely buoyant and colourful with many dedicated young music fans determined to see lots of new and interesting live bands. Skully points out that:

> The difference between now and back then is that there was a gig every single night you went into town. You had a place like The Arc. You just went there every single weekend. You would see The Chromosomes playing there and you wouldn't have a clue who they were or what they played, or anything! You went and what's more you queued.

Ger remembers some of the acts from out of town that would play The Arc, entertaining a generation of young Cork rock fans.

> In those days, you used to have a queue four people wide going right up to the gate of Kent Station, trying to get into The Arc: Thursday night, Friday night and Saturday night, any and every weekend, it didn't matter. The reason for that was that all the bands that were playing there were huge. I did all the discos before the first U2 gigs. I used to be the in-house DJ in The Arc, playing music like Graham Parker and The Rumour. One band that has to be mentioned is The Cimarons.[30] They were a reggae band. I don't know were they big anywhere else in the world, but when they came to Cork, the whole fucking city stopped. They were a monstrous band!

While playing well-attended live shows is all well and good, radio airplay has always been an important avenue for bands hoping to make it to the big time. Real Mayonnaize succeeded in getting on to the airwaves. Skully reveals:

> We became famous because we started getting played by *Cork City Local Radio*.[31] We were on the way to becoming mega gods when we were interviewed by Luke Ward on *Radio City*, which was based in Parnell Place. I remember it because I got a phone call after the interview. They were playing our cassette demo tapes,

---

[30] The Cimarons were a British-based reggae band that supported Rory Gallagher when he played the Macroom Mountain Dew Festival in June 1978. They were reportedly the first reggae band to play in Ireland.

[31] *Cork City Local Radio* (*CCLR*) was a pirate radio station based at 2A French Church Street in Cork city centre.

that were recorded at home, and someone said to me: 'Jesus Christ! Mr O'Leary is on the phone.' And I went 'Who is that like?' The reply was 'It's Mr O'Leary. Jesus Christ! He wants to talk to you.' I took the phone and the band stood around me and this guy was on the phone saying: 'I like your stuff. I like what you are doing. I'd be interested in meeting up and seeing if we could do a bit of recording.' And that was it. We were ready to sell off our lives!

Amusingly, Ger recalls: 'I was Mr O'Leary and I was probably seventeen at the time.' Skully adds that they 'met up and then that was where [they] started doing real recordings with real mixing desks and things like that...That was around 1978-1979.' Soon Real Mayonnaize, with Ger O'Leary on production duties, released their one and only single *Framework*, which was accompanied by the reggae influenced b-side *Breakfast Man*.

In 1985, Elm Tree Studios opened on the Mardyke. It was founded and owned by Ger O'Leary. He acted as both sound engineer and manager. These studios had a dramatic effect on the Cork music scene. Ger confesses: 'It was the main hub around which everything in the Cork scene rotated until it closed, around 1991.'

Asked how he would define the music that was coming out of Leeside during this era, Ger responds:

> I would say everybody was mad! I think everything that was coming out of Cork at the time was very quirky, real and had a bit of a twist to it. It is something that has been a pattern of Cork bands down through the years. It is just that Cork thing: We are mad! Fuck ya! I think it is part of our rebellion ...we are not Dublin, we are

not London and we'll do what we want to do. There is a band called Jezery starting to do it now. They're young guys and there is the same quirkiness, but they are also keeping their eyes on whether this will work. It is quirky, but we have to have something to offer besides the quirkiness.

While much has been made of Microdisney's achievements in taking their music outside of Cork, both Ger and Skully saw them first emerge from the Cork live circuit. Ger admits to knowing Cathal in the very early days: 'At the time, Microdisney were ... I wouldn't say quirky, but very unusual.' Skully agrees and says:

> Their timing was good too because it was the punk era and they were the best of our local punk bands. So their timing was excellent. They were amazing guys. I mean, they used to bring their gear around on the bus, on a double-decker bus. They used to fit the amps, the speakers and wires and everything on and go off and do a gig. At least, we had a horsebox!

When questioned as to whether Real Mayonnaize ever shared the bill with the young misfits that were Microdisney, Skully replies: 'Oh Jesus Christ! They were the enemy. Oh fucking hell! There was a different vibe back then. I remember the local band Max Von Rap going to see us live and they all stood at the front like this [gestures arms folded] and didn't dance and didn't move.'

Max Von Rap was centred around Cork musician Pat O'Connell, who was the bass player and singer. The group's line-up also included Pat's German girlfriend Ulli Hoffman on keyboards, Mick Finnegan, who had previously played guitar with Nun Attax, and a succession of drummers, one of whom was Rob McKahey, who later played with Stump. The group self-released a single in the mid-1980s entitled *Wish I Had A Kawasaki*, which they recorded in London. The single garnered radio airplay from DJ Larry Gogan and a number of other popular radio personalities.

Ger insists:

> Max Von Rap would have been an extreme. I mean that was the nature of Max Von Rap. You wouldn't have had that animosity between, say, Real Mayonnaize and a local band like Belsonic Sound, who would have been kind of contemporaries. Nowadays, you hear the guitarist from one band playing with another band, guesting on a demo, or someone like Annette Buckley guesting on everybody's demo. No way did that happen back then!

While there was a certain level of animosity between rival bands, the arrival of Elm Tree Studios in 1985 played a role in combating this admittedly pointless hostility between some groups. Ger reflects:

> It changed during the Elm Tree days, because you had a focal point where all the bands were coming to and a lot of bands started to get to know each other from hanging around the studio. However, there was one big problem. When Elm Tree opened up, it was the first time that bands were actually getting proper demos recorded, so they were sounding great. You then had a little circle, amongst all the bands, where they were all heroes in that circle. There was no kind of ambition or aspiration to go further than that. It was very parochial.

There were only two bands who were taking it outside of Cork. One was Belsonic Sound, who took it outside big time. In fairness, they were playing everywhere. They were superb live: one of the best live bands that I've ever seen come out of Cork. The other was Real Mayonnaize, who weren't doing so much on the live side. They were doing it on TV and radio outside of Cork. Then you had other bands in the city who were really good at that time, who were happy to say: 'We are doing it here!' A fabulous band called Without The were doing fabulous recordings and pushing limits at the time, but they never took it outside of Cork. They were just happy to play away and, eventually, just faded off into day jobs and things.

Sadly, tragedy was to strike Real Mayonnaize with the untimely death of their drummer Dave Rudd. This was an event that the Cork group would never recover from. Looking back at this tragic episode, Skully recalls the circumstances surrounding the death of his friend and band-mate:

> He was in Saudi Arabia and was doing some kind of apprenticeship course. His parents said he had to get a qualification before he went off touring with the band, but he took around six months off and went and got killed. It was all very mysterious and nobody ever really knew what happened. After that, the dynamics of Real Mayonnaize never really gelled. It was such a loss!

Following the demise of Real Mayonnaize, Skully decided to form a new band with talented local singer Ann Redmond. Redmond had been the frontwoman in Ireland's first all-girl rock act Porcelyn Tears. Hailing from Mayfield in Cork, this four-piece formed in 1983. They were all in their late teens and had just left school. The band featured Grace O'Sullivan on drums, Kay Creedon on Keyboards, Gerlyn Ryan on bass and Ann was the lead singer and songwriter. Later in their career, Gerlyn would leave the band to be replaced by a girl called Kamla Das from Jamaica. Interestingly, there was no guitarist in Porcelyn Tears. Recalling her unique band, Ann enthuses:

> We played our own instruments and we were self-taught as well. So it wasn't like any of us could even play when we started. We were sort of electronic and a band having no lead guitar had never been heard of at the time. We were actually Ireland's first all-girl rock band. We knew that at the time. We had write-ups in *Hot Press*. We had TV appearances on all the programmes that were out then like *TV Gaga* and *Anything Goes*. We did Dave Fanning's show about three times.

Porcelyn Tears were a post-punk band whose sound was influenced by groups such as The Cure, The Psychedelic Furs and Siouxsie and The Banshees. They played local venues such as The Underground, Sir Henry's, The Arcadia, and The Bodega on Oliver Plunkett Street. While the group did enter the studio, they never released any records. 'We recorded [tracks] in Windmill Lane and Joe O'Herlihy, who was our soundman, helped that along, but we didn't release any of them,' Ann reveals. 'We just used them for getting gigs and reviews and stuff like that.'

Being an all-girl rock act in those days was not without its problems. Ann explains:

> It was tough because we were girls. It was like: 'Girls

are doing the headlining in Sir Henry's tonight!' I suppose people would think because we were girls maybe there was a bit of favouritism, but it was quite the opposite. You had to prove yourself twice as much. Promoters were wary. They would say: 'Send us a lot of demos, send us some pictures and tell us if you are playing somewhere.' They were kind of afraid to take a risk because we were new. We were such a new thing.

Like many other Cork acts, Porcelyn Tears found Dublin a difficult music scene to crack, due in part to a certain closed-minded nature that was prevalent there at the time. Ann admits:

Dublin was hard to get into. You were always known as an outsider. You were a culchie band. It was a closed shop. It was like all the best bands came from Dublin and anybody outside that: No! But we did get in. I remember the first gig we played there. We had so much interest. We had Adam Clayton from U2; he came down to see us. People like him and people from the industry came down because they were curious.

A band that shared the bill on more than one occasion with Porcelyn Tears was Cork group Kryteria. The group featured frontman Paul Moriarty, guitarist Paul O'Brien, drummer John O'Flynn and bass player Pat Kiernan (later of Corcadorca theatre company fame). Another veteran of The Downtown Kampus, Moriarty, together with his band-mates recorded a track at Elm Tree Studios entitled *Arabian Nights*, which got played on the Dave Fanning radio show. While Moriarty had founded Kryteria in his late teens, the group's life cycle was only two or three years at most. Soon, he turned his attention towards the management side of music, managing, amongst others, a Cork band bizarrely named If. He later went on to marry Porcelyn Tears' drummer Grace O'Sullivan.

Despite being a ground-breaking band, Porcelyn Tears broke up in 1986 having become a little discouraged. However, Ann and her band-mates did have many highlights of their time together. Ann speaks candidly about their experience:

> It was very hard in those days if you were an all-female band and we were the only [Irish] one. I think the only other band that was on the circuit at that time was Bananarama. They were the only other all-female band. It was really, really hard to get taken up by a record company back then because we wrote all our own stuff. We played support to U2 at The Lark By The Lee in 1985. We knew U2 were coming even though they were only announced at the last minute, but we kept it to ourselves. We also did the Irish leg of a tour with New Order.

Ann reveals the circumstances that contributed to the demise of Porcelyn Tears:

> I think what made us become despondent was [the situation with] a guy called Fachtna O'Kelly, who managed Bananarama at the time. I think he came to see us in Sir Henry's. He was also involved with The Boomtown Rats. He was trying to sign us to either WEA or Polydor at the time and someone put a sort of embargo on it, saying: 'No, no, you are already handling one band!' We got that close and that was a major let-down, because it would have definitely put us on the map and got us over to London. It was hard and it was a tough one because that was what we were striving to

do - get management. Everyone did that at the time. You didn't get a record contract, you got management and then management got you the contract.

When Skully from Real Mayonnaize decided to form The Chapter House with Ann, he crossed a boundary. Today, it may seem ridiculous, but there was a form of extreme tribalism at play in the local rock scene during the 1980s. Elm Tree Studios boss, Ger O'Leary, explains this phenomenon:

> Skully had been in Real Mayonnaize. Ann Redmond who became the vocalist in The Chapter House had been with Porcelyn Tears, who were quite good and had done quite well. You had these two groups who had both been on the same level but had never spoken to one another. They had come out of the same little town but for her to join him and form a band together was like 'What are they doing?'

Skully experienced this phenomenon first hand: 'I remember when Real Mayonnaize split up, going down to meet Ann and it was like I was a traitor. Jesus! I had people not talking to me and everything because of it, because I met Ann and spoke to her.' The desertion by fans of his previous band proved an early obstacle for Skully when he embarked on the next stage of his musical career:

> As soon as Ann and myself set up The Chapter House, which was a much better band and far more professional, all the fans that I had before, with Real Mayonnaize, were gone. Maybe, they weren't interested ...because the new band was too big for them and they wanted a more obscure band to follow. I think that is what probably happens when there is this little parochial

group of bands fighting for the top position. You also have the mentality that only one band is going to make it, that only one band is ever going to get a record deal, so you don't tell anybody that they are good.

After Real Mayonnaize called it a day, bassist Jerry Buckley played with The Chapter House for a while. He also played in a band called Denis and the Dinmakers. This was a punk band named after Denis the Menace's band in *The Beano*. The line-up also included Ruth Beecher and Dave O'Connell. From this group, Jerry went on to play with the fantastically titled The 3355409s. Formed in 1987, this group lasted until 1989. Jerry explains how their bizarre name came about:

> I wanted to call it the 409s because the Beach Boys had a song, that I was actually listening to at the time, called *409*. The song starts off: 'She's real fine my 409'. There was a load of other names bandied around, like Elephant F and there were really ridiculous names. Somebody wanted to call it a bunch of numbers, so someone said 3355409 and then it just stuck. Everybody said we should put in our phone number and get gigs that way.

This band also featured members of two renowned Cork rock acts of the future: Morty McCarthy from The Sultans of Ping and Paul Linehan, who would later front The Frank And Walters. Jerry names the various musicians who made up The 3355409s:

> Dave O'Connell, who is now in Australia, was on guitar, Stephanie Vink, who is now in Holland, was on backing vocals, Ruth Beecher was the main singer, I played bass and Anne O'Halloran, who is now an established photographer, played drums. Later, Morty

McCarthy played drums with us for a while. He came in after Anne left to pursue her photography. Stephanie left to go back to Holland. Then there was myself, Dave, Morty and Ruth. When I left, Dave's girlfriend Caroline Parr, an Australian, played bass for a while. Then Paul Linehan of the Franks played bass.

Discussing their musical sound, Jerry Buckley considers:

> It had a rockabilly or a psychobilly feel to it. We did a couple of covers that were covered also by The Cramps. Basically, they were two-minute songs, 1 2 3 4 bang and they were over. At the time, it was a bit new. We used to use feedback in the studio to add intros and outros for songs and also a hard guitar overdrive sound and catchy or punchy bass lines. Mostly, it was very up-tempo and new wave sounding.

When questioned as to the themes encapsulated in his band's songs, Jerry enthuses:

> I suppose we did have girl/boy songs. We had one song called *Fast Friends* that we entered into a Dave Fanning video competition. Some guy from the Crawford School of Art did the video for us. The song and video turned out to be about six minutes long. We only found out afterwards that the limit was three minutes. The video was entered in the Cork Film Festival under a local category and won first prize. We were chuffed with that. We were legendary for a song called *Celebrity Blackout*, which we developed into a game. The game was that whoever could drink the most and fell down won *Celebrity Blackout*. So we used to go to parties and we would say: "Okay *Celebrity Blackout* time!" You

just drank and whoever passed out first was the winner. The song was very popular when we played gigs. Ruth Beecher wrote ninety percent of the lyrics and it was only after the band broke up, when we reflected on the lyrics, we realised that she was actually writing about us. I can see some of the words were pointing towards me because she was kind of saying she had friends who had steady jobs and I had a steady job. At the time, we didn't realise that she was writing about the rest of us and the way we lived our lives in comparison to the way she wanted to live her life. But we had great craic and fabulous fun gigs.

One chaotic live show in particular is etched in Jerry's memory:

> We played a very famous gig in Trinity College Dublin. Joe O'Herlihy, U2's sound engineer was looking for a pet band and he contacted us and said: 'I believe you're playing Trinity College. I'm going to come down and have a look at you!' So we arrived up and we got The Gorehounds' [very fast rockabilly band from Dublin] equipment. The Trinity gig finished us off. We went up there and Fürstenberg was just on the market. They made it very, very potent. The Dublin guys said to us: 'You'll never handle a few pints of this and play!' We did and we played and we made a mess of it. Anne fell off the stage. She was hammering the drums and the drums were seen to move back and back and off she went. Now, what Joe O'Herlihy said to us was: 'The music was fabulous but what a laugh, you're actors! Go away and get acting lessons.' It was one of those experiences. You just had to go through it. It was brilliant!

## CORK ROCK

The 3355409s marked Jerry Buckley's last rock 'n' roll adventure.

A very popular group that would have been active at the same time as The 3355409s was Belsonic Sound. This group had its roots in an earlier band called Belsen, which was founded by Finny Corcoran. Nowadays, he is a highly regarded sound engineer who for many years ran BPM Studios in Douglas in Cork.

Hailing from the Turner's Cross area of Cork city, Finny was still in his mid-teens and inspired by the new wave punk music of the day, when he formed a school band called Belsen. He recalls how this band first came together:

> I was about fifteen at the time. So it would have been about 1980/81. I was on guitar, my school friend Gene Russell, from the Lough, was on bass, a guy called Con O'Donovan was playing drums and we had a singer called Paul Mealy who had been in other Cork bands.

Their band rehearsed in the Quay Co-op. Musically, Belsen gravitated more towards the extreme end of punk rock, a point reinforced by their name, which was taken from the Nazi concentration camp Bergen-Belsen. Finny says:

> We had a big punk kind of phase. We were a hardcore kind of punk band. I think the name came from the punk thing: the shock value. Immediately after we called ourselves Belsen, we had second thoughts. We tried to distance ourselves from it after a while. That's why originally we had an 'e' in the name and then we changed it to an 'o'. We got hassled by Microdisney as well at one stage when we started. They didn't like the sound of it at all. They thought there was some sort

of neo-fascist element behind it, which was bull! It was just shock value, something that you used to catch somebody's eye. The fact that people talked about it showed it worked. We later changed it to Belsonic Sound. A lot of people kept the old name up even after we changed it. We must have been Belsen for about five years. I think we changed the name around 1985.

During their early days, Belsen were influenced by many of the leading names in punk. Finny admits:

> We would probably have been influenced most by The Clash and we would probably have had the ethic of The Sex Pistols more than the music. Then we got into more complex music like Killing Joke and Gang of Four and it started to change. Obviously, it progressed itself and we kind of progressed with it. But that is kind of where we started and then eventually, by the mid-1980s, we were broad-minded enough to take in various influences. We got into a lot of dub reggae stuff and we tried to fuse everything together. That was our background generally. We didn't like chart music at the time and we were never big fans of metal. It was very new wave and then The Doors got a mention and The Velvet Underground and everything came into the mix towards the end.

Belsonic Sound played regularly in Sir Henry's. While this venue remained a constant destination for gig-goers in Cork, the number of venues available to young rock bands dwindled during the early part of the 1980s. Finny says:

> There was always a shortage of venues. There are peaks and troughs when it comes to venues. The

> Underground was a great venue in its day. When The Arc closed there was a big void. I think that was 1981. We actually played the closing down gig. I think we played with Nun Attax and Microdisney. There was a Cork flavour to it closing down. Then there was a place opened for a while called The Gatsby, which was the back of The Queen's Old Castle. That was a nightclub and there was a local scene in there for a while. City Hall had the odd gig. People like Rory Gallagher and Simple Minds played there. Henry's really was the be all and end all of everything in the 1980s. Once that old dinosaur rock thing died off in Henry's, which was kind of around the middle of the 1980s, a healthy new band scene started. It was a great venue. Of all the venues I have ever played, on a good night, Sir Henry's was by far the best!

Finny describes the vibrant band scene in which he and his band-mates played during the 1980s:

> It was very healthy. There were other bands around like Real Mayonnaize and Cypress, Mine! and Burning Embers. It was all good fun. There was always the usual bitching between bands. That's a Cork trait anyway. But I don't have any bad memories about it. The music we were playing was getting a bit different. Cypress, Mine! were playing sort of REM-type stuff and Burning Embers were poptastic. We were more into our own thing, so we had a reggae influence and fused it with different things. We were a dance band when it wasn't popular to be a dance band.

In terms of material, Belsonic Sound released three singles

and an album. Finny enthuses about releasing their three independent singles:

> We released our first single, *Colour Blind* (1989), on our own. We signed a three single deal with a Dublin label called Ringsend Road Records, which is now Windmill Lane. We released a couple of singles with them. The second single came in late 1989 or early 1990. It was a cover of The Animals' tune *We Gotta Get Out Of This Place*. Then we did our own single again when we separated from Ringsend Road Records. It was called *Modern World* (1991) and it was the song that got us signed by a Dutch label.

In 1989, keyboardist Jim O'Mahony left Belsonic Sound after the Ringsend Road Records deal and the two single releases. In 1992, Belsonic Sound released their album entitled *Trouble*. The release of their long-player was followed up with two singles. One was called *Modern World Version 2* and the other was a song called *Heaven*. In 1993 Belsonic Sound parted ways. Finny recalls the events that led to the end of this Cork band:

> Jim had left the band and John McCormack from Kilkenny, the original drummer, had left too. Gene and I kept going and we had a third incarnation of the band with a guy called Emmett O'Riordan on keyboards, known to the band by his nickname Steamy Helmet and a guy called Colin McCarthy on drums. We actually got signed by a Dutch record label and then we got a guy called George Shilling, a top English producer. He worked with the Soup Dragons and Blur and he was pretty big. He came over and we did the album. We

did five weeks here and then we did two weeks in Van Morrison's studio in Beckington. Then we released the album, which we had spent a lot of money on. We went to Holland and toured it and did the usual things, but then the honeymoon period was over.

Following the end of Belsonic Sound, Finny started BPM Studios in the Cork suburb of Douglas. He also worked for The Frank And Walters for a couple of years, driving, tour managing and as a sound engineer.

Another Cork rock act that made quite a name for themselves in the 1980s was Idol Joy. Formed in October 1985, this Cork five-piece made their live debut in Cork Opera House in early February 1986. The band featured John McGuire on bass and vocals, Joe Cherry on guitar, frontman Ian Jack on vocals, Eddie Mulhare on guitar and Fionn Blake on drums.

With a sound they described as: 'pop/rock dance music', Idol Joy benefited from the availability of Elm Tree Studios. The band recorded a demo there, which contained two tracks *JFK* and *Eli*. This recording was engineered by studio boss Ger O'Leary.

Elm Tree Studios was also where they recorded a track called *Paradise Days*, which featured on a compilation album issued by Dublin-based Comet Records. Comet provided a showcase opportunity for new, unsigned rock and new wave acts. Two other Cork groups were also included on this compilation record, The 3355409s, with their track *Barbarous*, also recorded at Elm Tree Studios, and Cypress, Mine!, with a song recorded in Dublin called *Sounds Like Rain*.

Having played in local venues such as Connolly Hall, The Metropole Hotel and Sir Henry's, other career highpoints for Idol Joy were coming second in the National Carlsberg Battle of the Bands Competition and earning a place in the heats of the Carling/Hot Press Band of '87 Competition.

Idol Joy turned out to be a short-lived affair and three band members, John McGuire, guitarist Joe Cherry and drummer Fionn Blake went on to change their musical direction and form a band called The Pakt. They played venues such as Sir Henry's, and Mojo's on Sullivan's Quay, a venue that launched many Cork bands. Eventually, The Pakt too went their separate ways.

A band that should not be underestimated in the annals of Cork rock history is Cypress, Mine!. This group symbolised a changing of the guard in terms of Cork rock acts. They represented a newer, more modern sound that had emerged after groups such as Five Go Down To The Sea? had begun focusing on the British music scene, leaving Cork behind.

Ian Olney has played with a number of acclaimed Cork bands over the years. Having been exposed to music through his father's record collection, a collection that included the likes of Elvis and the great Buddy Holly, it was to be punk rock that would capture the imagination of a young Ian:

> I got a guitar quite late, when I was fourteen. With friends, the first kind of music I liked of my own accord was probably punk. We were too young to know it the first time around. But there was all this new wave music and second-generation punk music. When you first get into music, it's always the noisy stuff that you like first. Cypress, Mine! was my first band. I met Skoda, the bass player, when we were Youth CND members. The spectre of the nuclear holocaust was pretty frightening. At the time, there was quite a lot of activism generally. Initially, Skoda and I met through that, before I knew

he played the bass at all. Then I met up with Mark Healy, the drummer. He was playing with other bands in Cork such as Urban Blitz. He was into the scene a couple of years ahead of us. We were a bit daunted by meeting him. In terms of the stuff I was listening to, it was initially punk and post-punk, Joy Division, Gang of Four and that kind of music. Then The Smiths and early REM, once I started playing myself.

Cypress, Mine! consisted of lead singer Ciarán Ó Tuama, Ian Olney on guitar, bassist Denis O'Mullane (also known as Skoda) and drummer Mark Healy. The band was active from 1984 to 1989. Asked if they were influenced by any local acts, Ian replies:

> There were quite a lot of good Cork bands around at that stage. But when you're in your own band and have your girlfriend, you don't really have much time for a lot of the other bands. I do remember when we were up and going, there was a band called Without The who we thought were just outstanding. They were a Cork three-piece band and included a guy called Don Murphy. They were a great band.
>
> The kind of bands that were just before us were Nun Attax and Five Go Down To The Sea?. I was too young for The Arcadia scene. But Ciarán, our singer, was the photographer for The Arcadia. He knew all these bands. Denis and I kind of missed that place by a couple of years. But I remember seeing Microdisney and I was big into them and everything Cathal did afterwards, like Fatima Mansions. I thought they were really good. I think the kind of music that was influencing us wasn't

so much Cork bands as early Smiths and early REM.

Most noticeable was Cypress, Mine!'s decision to include punctuation in their band name. While not unheard of in Cork, with Five Go Down To The Sea? having pioneered this trend, there is no doubt that it proved a problem for local and national music journalists.

Discussing their choice of band name, Ian concedes:

> We had gone through a couple of different generic names like The Playroom. I think Cypress came from Ciarán, who was a photographer and had taken a shot of Cypress trees. That is how we got that. I don't know how they tagged Mine on to the end of it. I think putting the comma and exclamation mark into the band name was just our way of being wilfully obtuse.

Musically, this Cork band had a very contemporary sound that would probably sit well with many of today's local rock acts. Ian describes their sound. 'It was jangly, Byrdsy, Smithsy, REMy stuff. I think Ciarán as a singer and as a frontman had that kind of Michael Stipe, Morrissey, kind of thing going on. It was indie pop and a bit angular with not very obvious verse chorus songs.'

Cypress, Mine! were to become the first Cork-based rock act to release an album recorded in Cork. *Exit Trashtown* (1987) was recorded at Ger O'Leary's Elm Tree Studios and produced by Denis O'Herlihy. Asked if the name of the record was a veiled reference to Cork in the economically bleak 1980s, Olney responds:

> I guess it was but, to be honest about it, not in a major profound way. We had great fun playing around Cork.

There was no real angst there. A lot of Ciarán's lyrics were about Cork and Cork characters. It was the old traditional thing. We saw it as an opportunity to do something else and to travel. Everyone wants to be in a band to tour the world.

Having garnered real interest, Cypress, Mine! also released a number of singles during their career. Ian enthuses:

> We signed a deal with Solid Records. That was Denis Desmond from MCD and another guy. That was a one-album deal, but they released two singles. The two singles came out before the album. The first one was released in 1987 and called *Justine*, which was on the album. The second was *In The Big House* and that was also on the album. About a year later, we did another single called *Sugar Beet God*. It was partly about the piles of sugar beet that used to be on the Mallow Road. Ciarán is really the man! His lyrics are fairly impenetrable. That was the final single and that was produced by Joe O'Herlihy, who was U2's soundman. He was a great help all the way along. He produced a few different demos that we had done.

During their career, Cypress, Mine! were managed by Tony O'Donoghue, who used to write for *Hot Press*. Ian had met Tony through Youth CND. Today, Tony would be better known to readers as the Sports Editor for *RTÉ News*. Olney admits that Tony was instrumental in assisting Cypress, Mine! in getting signed:

> When we met Tony initially, he had no involvement in music at all really. It was just that he liked the band and was a mate. He was enthusiastic and quite happy to do

the stuff that none of us were able to do. He was doing freelance stuff for *Hot Press* and gradually built up his profile. We sent off demos and got no response at first. But as the manager, Tony knew a lot of people through his *Hot Press* work. We would always have our stuff reviewed, so there was a fair bit of a buzz about the band and then Solid Records said they would give us a one-album deal.

In 1989, Cypress, Mine! split up. Ian explains that the band had run its course:

> In one way we had achieved very little but, on the other hand, we did everything that it was possible to do on our small scale. We had done the singles, released the album and played in London. We had also done videos - for our first single *Justine* - and also for a track that would have been another single, but we split up before we had released it. For a Cork band, we were on TV a lot. But then again, once you've done all that once, that's kind of it really.

Towards the end of his days with Cypress, Mine!, Ian began playing alongside fellow band member Mark Healy in The Dancing Bastards From Hell. Mark, who was the drummer in Cypress, Mine!, was the lead singer and the main driving force in this group. Ian reminisces:

> That was an off-shoot of Cypress, Mine!. In that band was a guy called Niall Twomey, also Jim O'Mahony from Belsonic Sound and Graham Finn played guitar. There were loads of people who played drums. It was like a rotating drum stool, basically whoever was around. We just started it for the laugh really. We

played in Isaac Bells near the Metropole Hotel and started doing Sunday afternoon gigs there. We ended up selling out City Hall on New Year's Eve, probably in 1989.

In 1990, Ian left Cork and joined Dublin-based band Power of Dreams, who had supported Cypress, Mine! at a gig in The Baggott Inn in Dublin. Ian remembers how this came about:

> Denis O'Herlihy, who produced our album and also did our live sound, was working with Power of Dreams and it came up in conversation that Cypress, Mine! had split up. Power of Dreams had originally been a three-piece but were looking for a guitarist to broaden their sound. Basically, their management just asked Denis to get in touch with me, so he phoned me up and there was no pressure or anything. They just flew me over to London and then I met the record company. I rehearsed with the band and went to see them play, supporting The Wonder Stuff. They wined and dined me for the weekend and sent me home with an advance copy of the album and a week to make up my mind. As if I needed a week!

Life in Power of Dreams was certainly a contrast to life in Cypress, Mine!

> They were a totally different set-up to us. They had a major label deal. The publishing deal was with Sony and the recording deal was with Polydor. They had a worldwide deal and it was a big, proper, full-on deal. It definitely put Cypress, Mine! into perspective in terms of the machinery behind the band. It was a great experience. Basically, for two years we travelled all

over the world. We had three albums on Polydor and had the time of our lives. Then the usual thing with major labels: the third album doesn't sell as many as your second. It definitely beat working for a living. We literally played all over the world. We never got to Australia but ah well!

Power of Dreams split up in 1994, although they did announce two live dates in Dublin in September 2007. Due to unforeseen circumstances, these shows never took place. However, in November 2009, the band finally confirmed their reformation and subsequently toured to support the re-release of their first album *Immigrants, Emigrants and Me* (1990). In December 2010, they released their career spanning compilation *1989 – The Best of Power of Dreams*.

CHAPTER SEVEN

# SINGER'S HAMPSTEAD HOME

[Microdisney]

Thatcher's Britain was to form the backdrop for most of Microdisney's recording career. As a duo, Cathal Coughlan and Sean O'Hagan were eager to progress and this was their key motivation in moving from Cork to London. For a time, things looked promising. It was while based in London that Microdisney came to the attention of the prestigious British indie label Rough Trade.

Founded by Geoff Travis, Rough Trade was established in 1978 and went on to sign a number of seminal acts. Microdisney inked a deal with Rough Trade Records, which saw their 1984 debut album *Everybody Is Fantastic* released on the label. While the album entered the UK's fledgling indie chart, much of Rough Trade's focus and resources were diverted towards their rising stars, Manchester band The Smiths.

In London, Microdisney sought to expand their ranks by recruiting a number of new band members. Jon Fell joined on bass guitar and Tom Fenner assumed the role of drummer. Soon Nick Montgomery became the group's keyboardist, a role that was later filled by James Compton.

Bizarrely, in 1984, Microdisney embarked on a tour of Communist Poland. The volatile political climate of this era, both in Britain and globally, certainly had an influence on the group. Apartheid in South Africa became a particular focus of the band's attention. Lacking adequate support for new studio recordings, Microdisney released a long-player, which was essentially a compilation record. The controversial and terse title of this record *We Hate You South African Bastards!* (1984) was fuelled by the duo's disgust for the apartheid regime. This release featured their first two singles *Hello Rascals* and *Pink Skinned Man*, and a number of previously unreleased songs including *Love Your Enemies*. Interestingly, the album was re-issued on CD format in 1996 and was renamed *Love Your Enemies*, a somewhat appropriate move, given today's post-Apartheid South Africa.

Discussing why they chose *We Hate You South African Bastards!* as the title for this long-player, Sean O'Hagan is emphatic:

> We were hugely political. We were kids and we were political and very active during the miners' strike in 1984. *We Hate You South African Bastards!* was very much like a statement. It was almost like we were into this idea of incongruity - the cover of the book doesn't necessarily represent what's inside. I think we took delight in the idea that the band played at being dangerous. To a certain extent, we wanted to be dangerous and we actually lived slightly dangerously. But we continued putting out this gentle thing and it was almost like we were out to fool everyone. I don't think it was ever articulated. There was definitely a political aspect to the sound but I am talking about the politics of life as well - how there is no compromise and you never give up.

The decision to adopt such an aggressive and confrontational title early on in their recording career ran the very real risk of a commercial backlash. However, Microdisney certainly didn't fear such an outcome.

# CORK ROCK

Sean explains:

> We thought it was an uncompromising situation and at the time, we had people saying it has to be called 'We Hate You White South African Bastards!'. We said no because when you see *We Hate You South African Bastards!* everybody knows what it is referring to. It's not referring to a five-year-old black boy with a bullet in his head. It had to be a very distinct bold statement. At the time, Thatcher was the great apologist for the South African regime. We felt, we are going to make this record and it is going to be released in America, Japan and here and there. It made an impression. We didn't set out to make an impression. It was just an idea and we decided on that title. John Langford did the cover. Suddenly, it was on the news. It was like a big story everywhere. It was amazing. It was 1984, but that's not that long ago. It was on *The Tube* [Channel 4 music programme] and they had a big feature about it being withdrawn from the shelves and [how] it was sold in brown paper bags. There were people saying they supported the ban and other people saying they supported our right to make a bold political statement.

It was also in 1984 that Microdisney's *In The World* EP achieved success in the indie chart top ten. The lead track *Loftholdingswood* had its first airing during one of the band's performances on the John Peel radio show and soon became a favourite among fans. With its characteristically enigmatic lyrics, the song lashed both the Irish religious superstition of the time and the mindset of fake English liberalism. This EP also featured the tracks *Teddy Dogs* and *464*.

Regarded by many music critics and fans as Microdisney's

masterpiece, their third album, *The Clock Comes Down The Stairs* (1985), marked a creative high-point for the group. This release has been cited as one of Irish rock music's bona fide classic albums. Tom Dunne, former presenter of the popular weeknight radio show *Pet Sounds* on *Today FM*, rates this Microdisney album as the greatest Irish album ever. Writing in the *Sunday Tribune* on September 3, 2000, Dunne summed up why *The Clock Comes Down The Stairs* appealed to him, in a feature entitled *Pet Sounds Top 50 Irish Albums*. He enthused:

> Cathal's sonorous voice and mischievous dark lyrics found the perfect foil in O'Hagan's sweet melodies… It tops the poll because when I heard it first, I was distraught at just how good it was and when I hear it now, I feel the same way. Age does not wither them.

Dunne has indicated that his favourite track on the album is *Birthday Girl*, a song that during his days as lead singer with Something Happens, used to reduce their A&R man to tears. The award-winning DJ included *Birthday Girl* on his double CD compilation *Tom Dunne's Alternative Irish Anthems* (2005).

For Sean O'Hagan, working on *The Clock Comes Down The Stairs* remains a personal highlight of his days with Microdisney. This album gave him a real sense of achievement.

> I think making records and being absolutely proud of making a record that I never thought I would be involved in were highlights: especially making *Everybody's Fantastic* and *The Clock Comes Down The Stairs*. Those were very naïve moments of: 'I can't believe we have actually done that!' There were live moments, but I don't think any of them were the greatest moments in my life. For me, it was that massive buzz of being in

the studio with Cathal saying: 'I can't believe we have done it, that we have made this sound the way we want it to ... with guys like Johnny Fell and Tom Fenner.' Those were moments when we thought we had made really special records.

Discussing their records, Cathal discloses his personal favourite. 'I think it would be *The Clock Comes Down The Stairs*. That is the only one that I can listen to at all.' *The Clock Comes Down The Stairs* helped Microdisney secure a deal with Virgin Records. This move assisted the band financially, as they had run up a number of debts. In 1987, they released their first single on the label, the superb *Town To Town* (lyrics by Cathal Coughlan), an infectious 1980s pop song that deviated from the typical clichéd pop subject matter. Lyrically, this song was a triumph that addressed the possibility of nuclear war:

It's the guessing game with

those waves of flame and

sick winter for a thousand years.

Me and my ex-lover

will accept each other

help reap the dead harvest,

town to town.

*Town To Town* succeeded in garnering TV exposure for Microdisney and a support slot with U2. Sadly, chart success eluded Coughlan and co. as the single failed to break into the UK Top Forty. Although *Town To Town* featured on Microdisney's first album for Virgin Records, *Crooked Mile* (1987), which was produced by Lenny Kaye, they were frustrated by the production on the record. Some fans have labelled it 'overproduced'. As a result, the band ruled out releasing any further singles from the LP. Instead, they set to work on what was to be their final long-player *39 Minutes* (1988).

The opening track on *39 Minutes* was their next single. This was *Singer's Hampstead Home* and its subject matter generated controversy. The song is believed to have been a thinly veiled attack on their then label-mate, the famous 1980s singer Boy George and the media's fascination with him at the time. *Singer's Hampstead Home* was followed by their last single *Gale Force Wind*. Microdisney finally split up in 1988 and took the unusual step of using T-shirts adorned with the slogan 'Microdisney are shit' to reveal that they were parting ways.

Sean O'Hagan explains why Microdisney split up and how they felt about calling it a day:

> Creatively, we just thought that we couldn't make original records anymore. It happened around 1988. It was that classic thing. I think *Crooked Mile* was a big record and it had the hit single *Town To Town*. But it wasn't a case of, as you are about to make it you split up - it wasn't for us. It had been quite a long road and the creative drive was getting very tired!

Since Microdisney split, three compilation albums have been issued. The first was *The Peel Sessions Album* (1989). This offered different versions of songs featured on their original studio albums. Virgin Records issued their own compilation of Microdisney's material, recorded during their days with the label, entitled *Big Sleeping House: A Collection of*

*Microdisney's Finest Moments* (1995). However, the best compilation of their music is to be found on *Daunt Square To Elsewhere: Anthology 1982-88* (2007), which features twenty-eight tracks and includes an impressive inlay sleeve chronicling the band's history and records.

## THE FATIMA MANSIONS

Following the demise of Microdisney, Cathal Coughlan went on to form and front London-based band The Fatima Mansions.[32] Musically, their sound was far more intense, aggressive, in your face and even more lyrically acerbic and politically charged than Microdisney's. Cathal's choice of band name showed that he remained both fearless and uncompromising. Discussing his decision to call the group The Fatima Mansions, he is keen to downplay any suggestion that shock value may have played a role in his choice:

> We were operating in London and the name had no shock value there. But the idea of the acquisition of inappropriate things was something that had resonance for me. The idea that it was named after a holy place in Portugal and what is a Christo-fascist Catholic mysticism that is associated with that place. It was [also] attached to another one of the monuments to the callousness of de Valera's post-colonial reconstruction of Ireland. That had a nice ironic twist to it.

The only other Irishman in The Fatima Mansions was guitarist Aindrias O'Gruama from Dublin, while the rest of the group

---

[32] Fatima Mansions was built in Dublin in 1949. Situated next to the Grand Canal in Rialto, in Dublin's south-west inner city, it was originally envisaged as part of the inner city solution to tenement living. It became ravaged by extreme poverty and drug abuse. Dublin's heroin epidemic of the 1980s became rooted here.

were from England. Other band members included Hugh Bunker on bass, Nick Allum on drums and Zac Woolhouse on keyboards. The Mansions signed to Kitchenware Records and went on to release a number of albums during their colourful career. These were: *Against Nature* (1989), *Viva Dead Ponies* (1990), *Bertie's Brochures* (1991), *Valhalla Avenue* (1992), *Come Back My Children* (1992) and *Lost in the Former West* (1995). The band's prowess as a live entity earned them a prestigious support slot on the European leg of U2's Zoo TV Tour in 1992.

The Fatima Mansions did not actually split up in the conventional sense. Their dissolution was more of a gradual parting of ways. Cathal recalls:

> We never really did split up. It just kind of fizzled out. I guess it was around 1995 or even later, because we were intending to do one more album. It was written and everything, but it never got made because the person who was going to finance it got cold feet. People just drifted off.

As well as performing with The Fatima Mansions, Coughlan also had a side-project with comedian Sean Hughes. They released two albums *20 Golden Showers* (1993) and *Trance Arse Vol. 3* (1995) under the name Bubonique. Later, Cathal successfully made the transition to creditable solo artist, releasing his debut long-player *Grand Necropolitan* in 1996.

## THE HIGH LLAMAS

Following the end of Microdisney, Sean O'Hagan found it difficult to adjust to musical life outside his old band. He had to ask himself a lot of questions and remembers what it was like being at such a crossroads in his life:

> Immediately after the split, I didn't do anything for a while. I was pretty lost, very confused and I was trying to find my voice. Was I a guitar player? Was I a singer? Was I going to write on my own? Was I going to write lyrics? I struggled for several years trying to find what exactly I had to articulate through music. In Microdisney, I had a role but I started making very strange guitar music straight afterwards, which was not the right thing to do.

Sean finally found his voice around 1992, when he formed a new band called The High Llamas, named after his 1990 solo album *High Llamas*. The driving force behind both Microdisney and his new group was a sense of melody and trying to do something different with it. Musically, Sean opted to ignore what was happening in contemporary British and American music and instead looked to the 1950s for inspiration. Brian Wilson of The Beach Boys connected to a lot of 1950s performers and Sean was impressed by Wilson's harmonies. He explains:

> The High Llamas happened when I realised I was into strange chord progressions, sweet melodies supported by strange harmonies and then learning to orchestrate, rather than just using guitar, bass and drums, learning to orchestrate pop music…that was the voice I found when The High Llamas came about.

Appearing on the first record was former Microdisney bassist Jon Fell. Drummer Rob Allum and keyboardist and cellist Marcus Holdaway joined the line-up around a year later.

The High Llamas went on to release their first album proper, *Santa Barbara* (1992), on the V2 record label. This was followed by arguably their most famous long-player *Gideon Gaye* (1994). They went on to release four more albums on V2: *Hawaii* (1996), *Cold and Bouncy* (1998), the remix album *Lollo Rosso* (1998) and *Snowbug* (1999). After being dropped by V2, the group released three albums on the Chicago-based independent label Drag City. Other acts that have released material on this label include Pavement, Smog and Joanna Newsom. The High Llamas released *Buzzle Bee* (2000), *Beet, Maize and Corn* (2003), *Can Cladders* (2007) and their more recent album *Talahomi Way* (2011) all on Drag City. In addition, their period on the V2 label was anthologised on the double CD compilation *Retrospective, Rarities and Instrumentals* (2003).

While Sean continues his recording career, he also finds time to do arrangements and production work for bands such as The Super Furry Animals, Doves and Kaiser Chiefs, and has collaborated with acts such as Stereolab. Although, he has fond memories of his time with Microdisney in Cork and in London, Sean maintains that it is unlikely that the group will ever re-form in the future: 'I really don't think it is something we would consider. Cathal and I are both very forward-looking individuals. I have a real aversion to this reunion thing.'

*Rory Gallagher performing at Cork City Hall.
(Photo courtesy of Ciarán Ó Tuama)*

The Rolling Stones play The Savoy in Cork, January 8, 1965. Right to left: Keith Richards, Mick Jagger, Charlie Watts, Brian Jones and Bill Wyman.
(Picture courtesy of the Irish Examiner)

Left: The Axills. Left to right: Derek 'Doc' Green, Norman Damery, Eric Kitteringham and Peter Sanquest.
(Photo: Billy MacGill)

Right: The Krux in 1967. Clockwise from right: Barry Heffernan, Frank Mahony, Freddie White and Aidan Heffernan.

*Taste – Bellevue, Belfast, 1967. Left to right: Norman Damery, Rory Gallagher and Eric Kitteringham.*

*Len de la Cour behind his drum kit.*

*Rory Gallagher on Patrick's Hill in 1974. (Picture courtesy of the Irish Examiner)*

*Sleepy Hollow play The Savoy in Cork in the early 1970s.*

*John Woods of Polydor (Ireland) presents a gold disc to Rory Gallagher and his band at The Savoy cinema in 1974 for 250,000 sales of Rory's hit album 'Live! In Europe' (1972). (Picture courtesy of the Irish Examiner)*

*Tom O'Driscoll, Brigitte 'Bibi' Lehmann and Rory Gallagher in Blankenberge, Belgium on July 24, 1975.
(Picture courtesy of Brigitte Lehmann)*

*Rory Gallagher playing the Macroom Mountain Dew Festival in 1977.
(Picture courtesy of the Irish Examiner)*

*Nun Attax outside Cork Harbour Commissioners. Left to right: Ricky Dineen, Finbarr Donnelly, Philip O'Connell, Giordaí Ua Laoghaire and Keith 'Smelly' O'Connell.*
*(Picture courtesy of Ciarán Ó Tuama)*

*Microdisney on South Mall in Cork. Left to right: Cathal Coughlan, Sean O'Hagan, Jackie Walsh and Dave Galvin.*
*(Picture courtesy of Ciarán Ó Tuama)*

*Mick Lynch and Pat Kelleher of Mean Features on stage in The Arcadia. (Picture courtesy of Ciarán Ó Tuama)*

*Mean Features. Back row: Pat Kelleher and Mick Lynch. Front row: Steve O'Donoghue, Liam Heffernan and friend of the band Denis. (Picture courtesy of Ciarán Ó Tuama)*

*Bono performing with U2 at The Arcadia. (Picture courtesy of Ciarán Ó Tuama)*

*Belsen play The Downtown Kampus in The Arcadia in 1981. Left to right: Finny Corcoran, Paul Mealy and Con O'Donovan.*

*Real Mayonnaize. Left to right: Skully, David Rudd and Jerry Buckley.*

*Sabre. Left to right: John Spillane, Tony Buckley, Dave Murphy and Sam O'Sullivan at Coláiste an Spioraid Naoimh in Bishopstown around 1981.*

*Elvera Butler at the University College Cork Guild Ball in 1980.*

*Five Go Down To The Sea?. Left to right: Ricky Dineen, Mick Stack, Keith 'Smelly' O'Connell, Úna Ní Chanainn and Finbarr Donnelly. (Picture courtesy of Ciarán Ó Tuama)*

*Finbarr Donnelly performing in The Arcadia. (Picture courtesy of Ciarán Ó Tuama)*

*Porcelyn Tears. Left to right: Ann Redmond, Grace O'Sullivan, Gerlyn Ryan and Kay Creedon.*

*Cypress, Mine! pictured at the old Lee Baths in Cork. Left to right: Ciarán Ó Tuama, Denis O'Mullane, Ian Olney and Mark Healy.*
*(Photo: Jim McCarthy)*

*Idol Joy pictured in 1986. Left to right: Ian Jack, Joe Cherry, John McGuire, Eddie Mulhare and Fionn Blake.*

*Stump playing Glastonbury 1987. Left to right: Kevin Hopper, Rob McKahey, Mick Lynch and Chris Salmon.*

*Microdisney. Back row: Cathal Coughlan and Jon Fell. Front row: Tom Fenner and Sean O'Hagan.*

*Belsonic Sound appearing on the RTÉ television programme Visual Eyes. Left to right: Finny Corcoran, Jim O'Mahony, Gene Russell and John McCormack.*

*Princes Street in May 1990 at De Lacey House in Cork launching their single Song For You/ Speak To Me. Left to right, back row: Art Lorigan, Edel Sullivan and Martin Moylett; front row: Hank Wedel, Mick Geraghty and Brian Carroll.*

*Hot Guitars. Left to right: Bill O'Brien, Pat Lynch, Charlie Butler and Joe O'Callaghan. (Photo: Billy MacGill)*

*Paul Linehan of The Frank And Walters on stage at Glastonbury 1992.*

*The Frank And Walters in New York in 1997. Left to right: Niall Linehan, Ashley Keating and Paul Linehan.*

*Nine Wassies From Bainne. Left to right: Michael Mullen, David Murray, Peter O'Kennedy and Giordaí Ua Laoghaire. (Photo: Liam O'Callaghan)*

*The Sultans of Ping playing The Savoy in Cork. Left to right: Ian Olney, Morty McCarthy and Niall O'Flaherty. (Picture courtesy of the Irish Examiner)*

*Sultans' fans doing the Turnip Fish dance at their gig in Club One in 2005. (Photo: Mark McAvoy)*

*Rubyhorse. Left to right: Gordon Ashe, Owen Fegan, Dave Farrell, Declan Lucey and Joe Philpott. (Photo: Danny Clinch)*

The V-Necks play The Lobby Bar.

Freakscene DJs Velma Velour, Alan Fadd and Jenny Glitt.

The Sir Henry's building months before its demolition. (Photo: Mark McAvoy)

The Shanks. Left to right: Mick Hayes, Donnagh O'Shea, Stan O'Sullivan, Niall Lynch.

*Cathal Coughlan in Leadenhall Market, City of London. (Photo: Bleddyn Butcher)*

*Barry McAuliffe (centre) and the Rulers of the Planet.*

*Waiting Room. Left to right: Nigel Farrelly, Wayne Dunlea and Dave Ahern.*
*(Picture courtesy of the Irish Examiner)*

Simple Kid aka Kieran MacFeely performing live.

Stanley Super 800. Left to right, back row: Stan O'Sullivan and Dave Hackett; front row: Michael 'Tosh' O'Sullivan and Flor Rahilly.

Fred. Left to right: Jamie Hanrahan, Eibhilín O'Gorman, Justin O'Mahony, Jamin O'Donovan and Joseph O'Leary.

The Frank And Walters at the Louvre, Paris, in 2009. Left to right: Paul Linehan, Ashley Keating, Cian Corbett and Kevin Pedreschi.

# CHAPTER EIGHT

# STARING AT THE SUN

[Simple Kid]

Everything that has a beginning has an end. Cork rock music's two most inspirational figures, Rory Gallagher and Five Go Down To The Sea? frontman Finbarr Donnelly, were both unique characters with their own contradictions. Both originally came from the north of Ireland and rose to prominence in different times and against the odds. Rory's guitar hero on-stage persona was clearly at odds with his off-stage personality, while Donnelly's ability to improvise lyrically, vocally and melodically gave him an edge. Unfortunately, Cork lost both of these great performers in tragic circumstances. Their deaths occurred during the month of June, six years apart.

FINBARR DONNELLY

Despite travelling to Britain in search of further musical recognition and having played live extensively while there, Five Do Down To The Sea? eventually broke up. However, this would not be the end of the musical adventures of Finbarr Donnelly and Ricky Dineen.

Ricky recounts the events that led to the members of Five Go Down To The Sea? parting company:

> We went to England around 1983 to seek our fortune! But cellist Úna Ní Chanainn stayed behind, so we were back to a four-piece again. We played up and down

Britain in small clubs, like Dingwall's in London, and developed a very small cult following. After a while, Mick Stack wanted to move to America and he has been there ever since.

After Mick departed, Donnelly and Dineen decided to remain in London. Drummer Smelly O'Connell had had enough of playing and withdrew from live music and from life in Britain. He concedes: 'When I left the band, I left England. I left because I got disinterested in the whole thing.'

The final stage of Donnelly and Dineen's musical partnership was played out in a band called Beethoven. While no other former members of Five Go Down To The Sea? were involved in this venture, the pair did successfully recruit another Irishman into their ranks. Ricky explains how Beethoven emerged:

> We moved from one part of London to another. We moved to Shepherds Bush and met a guy called Maurice Carter, who was from Dublin, and a drummer called Daniel Strittmatter. Unfortunately, Maurice is now dead. I have a picture of myself, Maurice and Donnelly and I'm the only one still alive, so I'm watching out for myself.

Beethoven caught the eye of Setanta Records founder Keith Cullen who promptly signed the band:

> I came to know Donnelly through Maurice Carter who played bass in Beethoven. I was squatting over there and he was squatting as well. He was from Dublin and I'm from Dublin, so I knew him through a mutual acquaintance.

As a frontman, Finbarr impressed Cullen who believed he was a talented performer. He recalls: 'Finbarr was a very strong character. He was a very funny and interesting guy. As a frontman, I guess he was a lunatic, but he was charismatic.'

In 1989, Beethoven released their debut 12-inch single, *Him Goolie Goolie Man*. The single was awarded 'Single Of The Week' status in the *NME*. While Beethoven had talent, they were undermined by one key flaw – over-indulgence in alcohol. Keith Cullen considered them: 'A good band, but it was all about drinking really. Donnelly and Ricky were always drunk. It was a laugh basically. I think that's the best way to put it.'

A short time after being recognised by the *NME* for their song-writing talent, tragedy brought an end to the London-based four-piece. On June 18, 1989, an incident took place in the Serpentine Lake in London's Hyde Park, which resulted in the unfortunate death of twenty-seven-year-old Finbarr Donnelly. The circumstances surrounding Donnelly's tragic death have been the subject of much speculation within parts of Cork's music community over the years.

Fellow band member and friend Ricky Dineen remembers the day that Cork lost one of its most influential musical personalities. Present on the occasion were two female friends, a girlfriend of Ricky's and a mutual friend of both musicians:

> Well it was an accident. A load of people came up with theories about him committing suicide. But I don't think it was. I knew him better than anyone. It was just an accident. It was one of those boiling hot days that you get in London in the summer. We were in Hyde Park and it was the natural thing for Donnelly to take off his clothes down to his jocks and go for a swim.

He took off [swimming] and the lifeguard people came out on a boat and tried to get him out [of the water]. Mischievous person that Finbarr was, he tried to go under the boat and he didn't come up. I think he got caught in the undergrowth underneath the water. We had been sitting down having a few cans of whatever it was at the time, with girlfriends, shooting the breeze.

Asked what his lasting memory of Finbarr would be, Ricky responds:

It was a love-hate relationship, but as time goes on, it becomes more of a love relationship. He basically opened out the whole music scene to us. By doing that, he sort of opened up this quirkiness that Cork people have been tarred with. It all kind of started around there. I remember people saying to me that the first time they heard 'wacker' and northside words like that was from Donnelly. I think if Donnelly hadn't been around, I would have ended up playing in a rock band instead of a punk band. In other words, even if we were going to be an alternative band, I don't think there would have been any other singer able to carry it off at the time other than Donnelly.

Smelly O'Connell also has distinct memories of Finbarr Donnelly, but believes that his death may well have been inevitable:

My lasting memory would be his death was a big loss. Mick Jagger wouldn't be a patch on him. He was unique! The way his life was going, he wouldn't have been alive much longer. He was a hedonist of the highest order. Big time! He would be dead now anyway and that's my personal opinion. I reckon it was inevitable. Hedonistic in the highest degree and that was when half the things weren't around that are around now.

Following the death of Finbarr Donnelly, Ricky Dineen returned to Cork. Nowadays, Ricky is no longer actively involved in the Cork rock music scene. He did, however, use his musical skills to great effect in the Corcadorca theatrical production *Losing Steam*. Directed by Pat Kiernan, the production was staged in June 2004 as part of the Cork Midsummer Arts Festival. Written by Cork actor, writer, director and former lead singer with local group The Shades, Raymond Scannell, the production focused on Cork in the 1980s. This was a dark era for the city, when it had to contend with factory closures such as Fords and Dunlops, and an economic downturn. Discussing his involvement with the music element of this production, Ricky says: 'We played three songs. I put a band together for that. It was a play set in the early 1980s and we were supposed to be in The Arc.'

## RORY GALLAGHER

In the late 1980s, a legendary Cork rock icon broke free from the shackles of large mainstream record companies and their continuous demands. Rory Gallagher, with his ever vigilant and business savvy brother Dónal, decided to form his own independent record label and publishing company. Capo was born. As a result, Rory was to become an indie hero in the truest sense. Dónal Gallagher recounts the reasons for establishing the Capo label: 'All through Rory's career he wanted to produce himself and wanted control.' Not surprisingly, as one of the world's great rock guitarists, Rory was frustrated that companies like Polydor and Chrysalis expected him to follow their direction and were not throwing their weight behind where he wanted to go. When the contract with Chrysalis ended, a number of companies lined up with shopping lists for Rory, but he was not inclined to sign up with them.

Dónal believed it was time to move on and reassured Rory that this was the right course of action and would bring added security. He remembers advising him at the time and remembers some of Rory's frustration with the Chrysalis situation and what they learned from it:

> I told Rory: 'You know your catalogue still continues to sell and really and truly you don't need anybody's money. You have got your own operation. We have got our own offices. You call the shots anyway. Let's form a label.' He was going: 'Oh I'm not so sure!' He always felt he had to have a record company backing him. On the one hand, he wouldn't be told what to do, but liked the security of a record company. Through the experience of working through the Chrysalis situation, things like distribution came into focus. When Rory signed to Chrysalis, it was on the basis that their music was distributed in America by Warner Brothers, who wanted to sign Rory.

> Once we had signed [to record] two albums, Chrysalis moved to become an independent sales operation and it was a disaster. They wanted to be the biggest small label in America and left Warner's, which was the beginning of the end of Chrysalis as its own entity. So we learned from that. In a way, the label didn't matter. It

was who was putting the records around the place [that was important]. It was working with the sales guys. I had learned that by then, as well as all the management and road management.

Dónal analysed the situation and realised that, when you signed with a company in the UK, you could not be sure that their European or worldwide marketing was up to scratch. He explains:

> Maybe they were strong in Holland, but not in France or Germany. Whereas, we knew that Rory was huge in Germany. So my tactic was why can't we just sign with a big company in Germany that will do the best job in Germany, one in France that will do the best job in France, etc. We make the masters anyway, we cut the records and Rory would oversee every single part. So that was the idea. I just said: 'Rory all you have to worry about is giving me a name.'

The name for Rory's label stemmed from his great love of crime stories, as well as the capo on a guitar. 'Capo was a double entendre,' reveals Dónal. 'Rory's love of crime novels and Capo being the mafia boss. He is the boss of bosses. So it translates from mafia Italian to boss records and I was Don!'

Having released *Jinx* (1982), his final record for Chrysalis, Rory followed this up with *Defender* (1987), his first album to be released on the Capo label. This album featured Rory playing a variety of different guitars as well as his trademark Fender Stratocaster. Interestingly, *Defender* included a track entitled *Failsafe Day*, which boasted an anti-nuclear message typifying the world events of this era. *Defender* topped the British indie chart.

Rory's final studio album *Fresh Evidence* (1990) was also released on Capo. This last studio offering from Rory included tracks such as *Ghost Blues*, *Heaven's Gate*, *Walkin' Wounded* and *Slumming Angel*. Many fans believe that through the songs on his last album, Rory was referring to his own sense of mortality, making this a genuine swan-song record. Rory's old friend and former band-mate Oliver Tobin offers his thoughts on the themes behind *Fresh Evidence*: 'On some of the last album that Rory wrote, if you listen carefully to the words, they are all about him dying.'

The year after *Fresh Evidence* was released, Rory was to meet and jam with a rather famous fan, while on tour in America. This fan's name was Saul Hudson, better known by his stage name Slash. On March 9, 1991, Rory Gallagher and the Guns N' Roses guitarist met and jammed at Rory's gig at The Roxy Theatre on the Sunset Strip in Hollywood. Dónal recalls how they met for the first time:

> Slash just turned up at our first gig on an American tour. Rory was warming up for the rest of the tour. Before Rory went on, this guy came up to me and said: 'There is a guy here from Guns N' Roses, Slash, the guitarist. He is a fan of your brother. Is there any chance he could meet Rory and say hi to him?'

Rory was just about to go on stage when Dónal informed him that Slash was there. His response was: 'Wow! He's a great guitar player and I'm really honoured and delighted.' Dónal reminded him that he was due on stage, but Rory said: 'Send him up beforehand, because afterwards these guys can go crazy!' Rory then invited Slash up on stage. Slash immediately agreed.

Rory was to play his final live gig in Cork at the Regional

Technical College (renamed Cork Institute of Technology in 1998) in Bishopstown on November 18, 1993. On this occasion, he performed a rare acoustic show in the atrium area of the RTC, accompanied by Lou Martin on piano and Mark Feltham on harmonica. Understandably enough, Rory's setlist included *Going To My Hometown*, which always struck a chord with his Cork audience.

It was despite having poor health that Rory decided to play this show. Dónal remembers:

> He was reluctant, but he wanted to do it. He had been asked by the RTC to do a tribute to his uncle James Roche, who had been the principal and who had died suddenly. They were establishing the first Cork Arts Festival and that was the very first year. It was partly to boost the arts festival that he came back. He felt that bringing a rock band in to do something like that wasn't appropriate in a way. He was very nervous about doing it and he wasn't particularly well at the time, but he rose to the occasion.

Rory played his last concert on January 10, 1995 in Holland. Unfortunately, his poor health now took centre stage and time was running out for the acclaimed blues guitarist. Rory had resisted Dónal's requests for him to seek medical treatment, and when he finally acceded to Dónal's wishes, he was already seriously ill. On Wednesday, June 14, 1995, the world lost Rory Gallagher at the age of forty-seven. He died after contracting a virus following a liver transplant operation at London's King's College Hospital.

Rory's death touched many people. Family, friends, fans and many within the music industry, all mourned his passing. Philomena Lynott, mother of the great Thin Lizzy frontman

Phil Lynott, recalls her initial reaction upon hearing the sad news of Rory's death:

> My Philip worshipped Rory. He worshipped him! I know it's a terrible thing to say, but when Rory passed on, I thought of the sadness for his family but the joy for Philip in heaven. He would have been at the pearly gates waiting for Rory. I'm sure they would be having great [jamming] sessions up there now.

On June 17, the people of Cork lined the streets as a mark of respect, while Rory's funeral cortège made its way to the Church of the Descent of the Holy Spirit on Wilton Road. While Cork enjoyed a prolonged spell of good weather during the summer of 1995, on Monday, June 19, the day of Rory Gallagher's funeral, it was weather that all Corkonians are only too familiar with – rain.

This didn't dampen the spirits of the thousands who attended his Requiem Mass and funeral. The church was thronged with mourners eager to pay their respects to Cork's guitar hero and many were forced to remain outside during the service due to the sheer numbers wishing to say goodbye.

Among the mourners were The Edge and Adam Clayton from U2. Other big names from the music world in attendance included former Thin Lizzy guitarist Gary Moore and Ronnie Drew of The Dubliners. During the service, Lou Martin (on piano) and Mark Feltham (on harmonica) performed Rory's song *A Million Miles Away*.

When the service concluded, Ronnie Drew joined Dónal Gallagher and Rory's best friend Tom O'Driscoll and together with a number of others carried the coffin out of the church. Rory was laid to rest in St. Oliver's Cemetery just outside Ballincollig to the west of Cork city. His grave is marked by a beautiful sculpture created by uilleann piper Eoin Ó Riabhaigh.

Promoter Pat Egan, who championed Rory through his columns in *Spotlight* magazine, got to know both Rory and Dónal over the years. Pat ran four record stores in Cork, including Rainbow Records at 120 Patrick Street, and regularly sold tickets for Rory's Christmas hometown shows in Cork City Hall. Pat retains the impression that, right to the end, Rory was truly original and never succumbed to any of the rock star clichés:

> He was a very soft, gentle, friendly guy, who would talk to anyone no matter who they were. I also got a feeling that he was an extremely private and lonely kind of guy. I don't know why. It seemed that he got his freedom on stage. He got up on stage and that's when he really came alive. He absolutely loved every second of it. You knew by just watching him that he was loving it. He was loving the attention he was getting from the fans and loving what he was doing. I wouldn't have been a close friend by any means, but I knew him fairly well and you couldn't help but like the guy. Dónal and Rory were both very likeable guys. Rory wasn't a star in the sense of the attitude and personality. The new cult of personality would have been the other extreme from Rory. I don't think he was rock 'n' roll in the sense that it was sex, drugs, rock 'n' roll, leather jackets and wild women. I don't think it was that with him. He probably had his own private little world that everybody has and the things they get off on. But it certainly wasn't what the public would think.

Rory Gallagher possessed and conveyed a certain purity in his personality that was reflected in his music. Speaking about the spiritual dimension to Rory, Dónal admits:

> To be honest, I always marvelled at him, that he always seemed to have another kind of thinking. He seemed to be on a totally different plain. I really couldn't put my finger on that. Growing up, in my teenage years, I was aggressive - the way street Cork made you. Rory always seemed to be a level above violence. He almost had a Christ-like quality and would turn the other cheek. I think that is part of being an artist. It's something that you find with artists, something spiritual, because their talent is coming through from some other source.

To date, Rory Gallagher remains Cork's most prolific rock 'n' roll recording artist. He has sold in excess of twenty million records. While Rory's talent as a musician and as a songwriter are beyond question, his achievements in a national sense are far greater. Rory played a key role in shaping Ireland's live music industry. The outdoor music festival, which Irish music fans today take for granted, was pioneered in this country by Rory and Dónal. In 1977, they helped stage the Macroom Mountain Dew Festival, which featured Ireland's first ever open-air rock extravaganza.[33] Held in the grounds of Macroom Castle, County Cork, on Sunday, June 26, 1977, this concert, headlined by Rory, illustrated just what outdoor music festivals could achieve.[34]

Dónal remembers how he and Rory became involved in the festival and how local family connections came into play:

> The organisers had a marquee down there [in Macroom] and were looking for a headline act to go down and

---

[33] The first Macroom Mountain Dew Festival had taken place in June 1976.
[34] Among the gig-goers at the 1977 Macroom Mountain Dew Festival was teenager David Evans - better known to music fans today as U2 guitarist The Edge.

play. They got my mother's phone number because the Roche family originally came from Ballyvourney/ Cúil Aodha. So elements of the family knew each other. They kept ringing looking for me. And I was kind of going, 'Macroom? Playing a marquee?' I said to my mother: 'Just tell them buzz off!' My mother said that our relatives were from back there and this wouldn't be perceived to be the polite thing to do. So I spoke to someone and agreed to come down and have a look. With bands in those days, you didn't go outside the cities, you really didn't!

I got down there and they were really enthusiastic and were showing me where the marquee was. They were telling me that the next night they were going to have Joe Dolan or somebody like that. But I was thinking this was not our scene. So I said: 'It would be nice to play Macroom, but not in a marquee tent. We've just come back from an American tour, playing Shea Stadium and huge arenas. Maybe something like an open-air festival could work.' Then they suggested the sports ground down the road. So we walked down the road, through the gates of Macroom Castle, into the back, where there were football and GAA pitches. I just went: 'Wow! This is a natural amphitheatre.' Then I had to convince Rory, which was very difficult. He didn't want to do it. He was very nervous about the whole thing. This is also in the context of the time when other bands like Thin Lizzy had broken through. So there was always the threat that they were going to do a festival in Dublin. Of course, the thing was that it would be great to have this for Cork - to be the first one and in Cork. Rory agreed that we had the expertise to pull this together. So we went for it.

We built a stage and there was a lovely rise so everyone would get a view. You had natural security from the river behind. By now we had a PA company, Stage Shows. We had people like Mike Lowe and Keith Ferguson who were brilliant technical guys. I told them that the budget was limited and that I didn't want any exploitation of anybody, and Rory didn't want that, so we kept the price at a reasonable figure because these kids had to come from Cork. If they were coming from Cork, they had to come fifty miles. If they were coming from Dublin, they had to come over two hundred. So that was the key thing. It cost only IR£2.50 in old money for entry to the gig. The stage was built from three flat-bed trucks and scaffolding. We got generators from Ardmore Film Studios in Dublin. Everyone in the Macroom organising committee was brilliant and totally committed. All it really depended on was getting the weather.

Asked did they feel they had accomplished something really special when the festival was a success, Dónal responds:

Oh absolutely! There was no benchmark to say a festival has to have this many people. What you want is a big crowd. We got around 10,000 people. You also have to remember that security was different to today. I'd say there was probably over and above that 10,000 figure because another couple of thousand, I would say, managed to get in for free.

So successful was this Macroom Mountain Dew Festival that a further festival was organised for the following year, with Rory Gallagher again as the star attraction.[35]

Rory and Dónal were also intrinsically linked to the establishment of *Hot Press* magazine, which launched in June 1977.[36] This connection arose from the Gallaghers' efforts to ensure that the Macroom festival would be a success. Dónal explains:

> I had gotten to know Niall Stokes [founder and editor of *Hot Press*], who had come down to Cork for the Film Festival to review *Rory Gallagher - Irish Tour 1974*.[37] He was a journalist at that time and was reviewing the film for the *Irish Independent*. Then I got to know him and he stayed in touch. He was writing for a magazine at the end of the *Spotlight* era, a magazine called *Scene*, which he was the editor of, which was kind of a forerunner to *Hot Press*.

Dónal remembers that Niall Stokes was desperate to start his own magazine and that he asked him if he knew any potential backers. Dónal agreed to introduce Niall to some people in London. In the meantime, the Gallaghers got involved with the Macroom festival and Dónal needed some first rate PR. He realised that advertising the festival through small advertisements in a lot of newspapers would not make a big impact. So he contacted Niall Stokes hoping that he had already set up his magazine. But Stokes didn't have the finance

---

[35] Rory Gallagher's concert at the 1978 Macroom Mountain Dew Festival was the first time that former Sensational Alex Harvey Band drummer Ted McKenna performed live as a member of Rory's band.
[36] The first edition of *Hot Press* was published on June 9, 1977.
[37] British film-maker Tony Palmer's documentary about Rory entitled *Rory Gallagher – Irish Tour '74* was premiered at the Cork Film Festival in 1974.

yet. Dónal told him the size of the budget and asked how many issues that would generate. Stokes thought that the budget would stretch to four issues and Dónal indicated they would put in more money to kick-start the project. For Dónal it was 'a means to an end'.

The first edition of *Hot Press* came out in good time to advertise the gig. Rory dominated the cover. Dónal remarks it 'was really a bang and it was a free ad! Rory was the man at the time irrespective of that. In a sense, we were putting the budget that we had in - to make sure that the paper happened - so that news about Macroom would get out there.'

RORY'S LEGACY

While Rory's prolific recordings and live shows were achievements in themselves, he left another legacy in Cork. Many different events have been organised over the years on Leeside to commemorate and pay tribute to our late guitar legend. At the heart of Cork city centre lies what is arguably the most fitting tribute to Rory. In 1997, Cork Corporation renamed St. Paul's Street Square, Rory Gallagher Place. On October 25, 1997, a bronze sculpture paying tribute to Rory was unveiled at Rory Gallagher Place. The artist who created this most striking sculpture was a childhood friend of Rory's, Geraldine Creedon. The location of this sculpture is particularly fitting, as Rory Gallagher Place and the coffee bars in the surrounding streets have traditionally been very popular with Cork's young music fans.

In east Cork, in the town of Midleton, a man called Tony Moore was responsible for developing what later became known locally as 'The Rory Gallagher Bar'. Officially called The Meeting Place, it was situated on Connolly Street in the town and first opened in July 1985. While in Taste, Rory famously played a charity gig at the Midleton Arms Ballroom. The charity concerned was the local branch of the Order of Malta. This successful gig helped Rory develop quite a following in this small east Cork town.

Inspired by Rory's music, in 1988 the bar expanded and created the Rory Gallagher music room. Rory tribute bands regularly played the pub and this is why it became known as 'The Rory Gallagher Bar'. The Rory Gallagher music room was officially opened on the first anniversary of Rory's death in June 1996 by Dónal Gallagher. Rory's mother Monica accompanied Dónal, on what for both of them must have been a day of mixed emotions. Tony Moore sold his famous bar in 2004.

In Cork city, The Rory Gallagher Music Library was dedicated to Rory and inaugurated in October 2004. The music library is located within Cork City Library on Grand Parade and is a regular destination for many of the city's young music fans eager to expand their musical tastes.

Award-winning Cork musician John Spillane dedicated a song on his album *Hey Dreamer* (2005) to the legendary blues man. *A Song For Rory Gallagher* features lyrics, half in Irish, written by John's great friend, the Cork-born poet Louis de Paor. Interestingly, Louis' father used to be Rory's dentist. The Cork poet was inspired by one of Rory's acoustic tracks *Bratacha Dubha* (Black Flags), which featured on *Wheels Within Wheels* (2003).

In 2006, the Rory Gallagher *Homecoming Exhibition* was staged at the Triskel Gallery on Lavitt's Quay in Cork. This impressive exhibition was launched by Dónal Gallagher and showcased instruments used by Rory. It boasted a large collection of photographs by rock photographer and Corkman, Fin Costello. The same year, the excellent *Rory Gallagher Live At Cork Opera House* DVD was released. Featuring thirteen tracks recorded live, this DVD release also included *A Rough Guide To Rory's Cork* that showed locations, memorabilia and rare and unseen photographs.

Today on MacCurtain Street, a pub named Gallagher's marks the street where the young Rory and Dónal Gallagher used to live. A few doors down, at 29 MacCurtain Street, is the building that for years housed Crowley's Music Centre, the family-run business that sold Rory his famous trademark Fender '61 Stratocaster.[38] On the wall is a small plaque that reads: 'Rory Gallagher 1948 - 1995 musician and composer. He lived on this street.'

Nationally, a notable Rory Gallagher commemoration occurred when, in 2002, An Post immortalised Rory on a stamp they issued, featuring him as part of a four stamp series celebrating Irish rock legends.

In Paris, where his music had been very popular, a street has been named after Rory. It was in the Parisian suburb of Ris-Orangis that Dónal and his mother Monica saw the mayor of Ris-Orangis inaugurate Rue Rory Gallagher. More recently, in Dublin in 2006, a life-sized bronze statue of Rory's famed Stratocaster was erected at Rory Gallagher Corner in the Temple Bar district.

On Leeside, blues music is alive and well thanks in part to the efforts of the Lee Delta Blues Club. Formed by a group of local musicians and enthusiasts in March 2001, this club has also organised the Lee Delta Blues Festival in Cork, bringing foreign blues artists to the city. In June 2006, they brought

---

[38] In 1973, Crowley's moved from Merchants Quay to new premises on MacCurtain Street.

acts such as Carvin Jones and Florida blues man Randall 'Big Daddy' Webster to Leeside. The festival also featured a walking tour of Rory Gallagher's Cork presented by Dublin native Marcus Connaughton.

Ger Horgan of the Lee Delta Blues Club explains how the club honours Rory: 'We normally dedicate our festival to Rory Gallagher and we have done that from the start. While we don't claim to play the way Rory played, the Lee Delta Blues Club was all down to Rory Gallagher having played in Cork.' The club's headquarters are in The Corner House bar on Coburg Street and they organise a blues session every Thursday night.

Two campaigns are under way at present in Cork to further commemorate Rory. The first is calling for a statue to be erected in the city centre. One location being proposed is outside the Cork City Library on Grand Parade, as it houses the music library named in his honour. The second campaign is calling for Cork International Airport to be renamed Cork Rory Gallagher Airport and a petition to support this measure has been posted online.[39]

Finally, in discussing Rory's legacy, Cork-based musician Hank Wedel offers his thoughts on what Rory's legacy may be:

> I think his legacy is that he was the guy who was the main antenna in the same way that Van Morrison was in Belfast and in the way that The Beatles were in Liverpool. He was the guy who was born in the 1940s, who in the 1950s heard Lonnie Donegan and heard Chuck Berry. In Cork, he was the guy that got it! That is his legacy. If you look at the history of rock 'n' roll on these islands – Great Britain and the island of

---

[39] For more information on the long running campaign to rename the airport – Cork Rory Gallagher Airport, visit the campaign website: http://rorygallagherairport.com/

## CORK ROCK

Ireland - you had people that got it. They got everything from Muddy Waters to Chuck Berry to Elvis Presley. In London, you had what became The Rolling Stones, The Who and The Kinks. The Animals got it in Newcastle. Van Morrison got it in Belfast. Rory Gallagher got it in Cork. He got it! He understood what it meant! He understood its power!

# CHAPTER NINE

# WHERE'S ME JUMPER?

[The Sultans of Ping F.C.]

In the late 1980s, a young Cork band was to emerge that would have a dramatic effect on the local music scene and beyond. The Sultans of Ping F.C. brandished a refreshingly distinctive cartoon punk sound that soon garnered the attention of music fans both at home and abroad. They were led by the flamboyant Niall O'Flaherty, regarded by many as one of the best frontmen ever to come out of Cork.

Formed in 1988, the group's original line-up consisted of Niall on lead vocals, Pat O'Connell on guitar, Paul Fennelly on bass guitar and Ger Lyons on drums. However, a number of personnel changes have taken place throughout the band's career.

Although born in Brighton, England, to Irish parents, Niall O'Flaherty grew up in the Cork town of Carrigaline, just outside the city. It was there that the young Niall gravitated towards punk and indie rock music. He reflects on the groups that he was exposed to:

> I probably listened to some very embarrassing stuff. I listened to a lot of punk, The Ramones and that kind of stuff. I liked The Smiths, The Wedding Present and later on, of course, The Golden Horde. I didn't initially like The Golden Horde, but later I came to love them. Eventually, I got into the garage kind of punk music.

> I quite liked The Damned when I was younger. They came to Cork a few times. I also went to see The Pogues in Sir Henry's. That gig was a great show, but I nearly got my legs broken. I was at the front of the crowd and I caught my leg somewhere. I was screaming for help and B.P. Fallon was on the stage. I was screaming to him 'Fucking Help Me!' and he thought I was waving at him, so he waved back. Great show though and they were at their best then.

The roots of The Sultans of Ping F.C. stem from Niall O'Flaherty's school days in Rochestown College. He recalls:

> I went to school in Rochestown and there they had a tradition of finding sort of punk bands. Bands like The Redskins and The Exploited were popular and that was really strange. I got my first Ramones album from a guy in school and you could get everything there. The Sultans were originally made up of people from my school and our first gig was in the school concert. I played the concert a couple of times. We formed around the school and we didn't take it very seriously. Certain members had a habit of getting a bit drunk at the gigs. Maybe, it is always a thing with me - I always get pretty serious about bands. Eventually, the members changed and there was no animosity. I just think the [former] members couldn't be arsed putting in the hours for practice, but I liked the guys very much.

Originally from Douglas in Cork, Sultans of Ping guitarist Pat O'Connell has been with the band since its earliest incarnation. In addition, O'Connell performed alongside Niall in their short-lived, acoustic-based, side-project, Sexy Shop. Pat reveals how he was drawn musically towards Niall:

> We were in the same class in Rochestown and we shared the same interests, so we decided to start playing [together]. I was in the band because I was in school with Niall and he had the band going. It was an early version of the Sultans.

Much has been made of O'Flaherty and co's choice of band name and its similarity to British rock band Dire Straits' 1978 debut single *Sultans of Swing*. Niall insists that no great thought went into christening the renowned Cork band and admits 'it was just a drunken thought or teenage moment. I don't think any great amount of thought went into it. I'd like to say there was a deeper meaning but there just isn't.'

For nightly entertainment, Niall and his friends followed a routine that was adopted by many music conscious Corkonians. He explains that his regular haunt during this period was:

> Sir Henry's: that was it! There were a few other venues but that was the main one. Well, you know, that is where I went every Friday. That was where the night was rounded off. The Liberty bar was my local.[40] It was in there first and into Sir Henry's afterwards. That was the ritual! That is where I met all my loves. That was where everything happened. It is kind of strange that, in Ireland, that was one of the few places, I would say, where you just heard music that you wouldn't hear elsewhere. I have always thought that! I have always wondered why. I think you start to realise why the kind of bands that came from Cork came from there. You know, bands like Stump.

---

[40] The Liberty bar used to be located at 93 South Main Street in Cork. This building has since been demolished.

If the early musical influences on the Sultans of Ping included bands like The Wedding Present, The Fall, The Buzzcocks and The Ramones, their later influences would stretch to include bands like The New York Dolls and British rock group Half Man Half Biscuit.

A number of the band's anthems, such as *Where's Me Jumper?* and *Turnip Fish*, were written during the Sultans' early incarnation, which featured Rochestown natives Paul Fennelly and Ger Lyons. Fennelly was the only member of the group who did not attend Rochestown College. He went to Presentation Brothers College in Cork city centre and he and Ger Lyons were childhood friends. Paul Fennelly remembers that on occasion the band would perform live with go-go dancers:

> There were go-go dancers once upon a time. I remember getting shoved off the stage by three of them looking for their fifteen minutes of fame. They got so excited about it that I ended up going overboard off the stage in Sir Henry's. I can remember go-go dancers being at three of our gigs.

In 1990, the Sultans travelled to Fermoy in County Cork to record their debut demo EP in Studio Fiona, run by Brian O'Reilly of local band Loudest Whisper. Entitled *Confessions Of A Sellafield Sex Guru*, the EP featured three tracks: *Stupid Kid*, *Riot At The Sheep Dog Trials* and *Eamonn Andrews*. The Sultans' first release was popular around Cork and went on to sell in excess of five hundred copies.

That same year, they made their Dublin debut supporting Dublin-based band The Golden Horde. The Sultans also received an important boost when they were selected as the Leeside entry in the Eurorock festival, which took place in Cork in October of 1990. The group gained valuable exposure while playing to a receptive hometown audience. Their live set was broadcast on radio and they also came to the attention of RTÉ radio producer Ian Wilson, who produced the *Dave Fanning Show*. Impressed by their performance, Wilson offered them their first radio session.

In 1991, both Paul Fennelly and Ger Lyons departed the Sultans' ranks. They were replaced by bassist John McAuliffe and drummer Morty McCarthy. To his credit, Morty, who originally hails from Barrack Street in Cork city, has played a major role in championing Cork rock music. Before he joined the Sultans as a full-time member, McCarthy played with a number of other acts and founded local music fanzine *Sunny Days*. Fanzines like this helped promote a community spirit among musicians and drew attention to local bands and smaller venues such as The Shelter.[41] Morty recalls his time running *Sunny Days* and his involvement with an array of local niche publications:

> *Sunny Days* went for about three years. It was around in 1988, 1989 and 1990. I think I did about twelve issues. I did lots of interviews with groups like Fugazi and My Bloody Valentine. I interviewed Cork bands as well. I had a free tape. I think *Where's Me Jumper?* was one of the tracks on the tape. I've met people in Sweden who have copies of it. The magazine was also sold in England, so it got around the place. I was doing *No More Plastic Pitches* [local football fanzine dedicated to Cork City F.C.] at the same time. Then we had another publication called *Choc-A-Bloc*. *Choc-A-Bloc*

---
[41] The Shelter, located on Tuckey Street, was a small venue, which opened in 1991. It had a capacity of approximately two hundred and fifty people. Unfortunately, it lasted only a few years.

was going after *Sunny Days* for a long time. That was done with Jim Morrish. It was a monthly publication with all the gig listings and reviews. It was going for a good few years. A lot of people like Shane Fitzsimons [journalist and promoter] and Emmet Greene [local promoter] helped out. Emmet is now one of the bigger promoters in the city.

Despite the energy invested in these publications, it was Morty's formidable drumming abilities and characteristic level-headedness that were to prove major assets for the Sultans. Morty recalls the events that led to him joining the band:

> First of all, I was a fan. I saw the Sultans by accident in The Phoenix bar way back in 1988. I thought they were fantastic. They actually had a manager at the time called Darragh Breen. He was moving to England, so he said to me: 'I know you understand the Sultans. Can you manage them?' So I said yes. Managing them at that time was just a case of booking a few gigs around Cork. Then we got a part in Eurorock in 1990; it was a big festival held in Cork that was being broadcast around Europe. Dave Fanning and Ian Wilson were there and they really liked us and offered us a radio session. At that time, I still wasn't playing with the band. I was just the manager. Then, when we went up to Dublin, it was just the usual Sultans chaos and I ended up playing drums on one of the tracks because the drummer couldn't get the drum track right. So Ian Wilson said to Niall that you are much better off using him. As it happened, the other drummer, Ger Lyons, went off to Tibet, believe it or not! So Ger disappearing

off played a big part in me joining the band.[42] Then Paddy and Niall had their own sort of solo project called Sexy Shop and they were doing a show up in the UCC College Bar in 1991. I just happened to be there and there was a massive crowd and everyone was saying: 'Do some Sultans songs'. Paul Fennelly happened to be in the audience and I knew all the songs, so we just went up and played away. Then Niall basically said: 'You're the drummer, that's it!'

1991 proved to be a pivotal year for The Sultans of Ping F.C., as they were soon discovered in Cork by a representative of the record industry and promptly signed. Morty remembers the momentous night when the band came to the attention of Martin Heath:

The guy who signed us was in Cork on holiday in June 1991. We were headlining the Sunday night of the Cork Rocks festival in Sir Henry's. Out of the sixteen bands that played there, eleven ended up signing [deals]. We were signed by Martin Heath, the man behind American band The Killers. He was in Sir Henry's and he had a filofax, which we had never seen before. We signed in August of that year.

Niall O'Flaherty also has understandably fond memories of this important event in the Cork group's history. He recalls:

The organisers had us on last to close the thing. We were on after Therapy? and I think on the night we outdid them. It wouldn't have been hard because it was our home territory. So... somehow this guy was really impressed with us, Martin Heath from Rhythm King

---

[42] Nowadays, Ger Lyons is a spiritual and healing guru.

Records, and he came and spoke to us and said: 'I want to sign your band straight away!' and of course we said yes! There wasn't any hard dealing. Pretty soon they had signed us and EMI Publishing signed us.

Having joined the Sultans as their new bass player, replacing Paul Fennelly, John McAuliffe's tenure with the group was relatively brief. 'We signed the deal with John McAuliffe on bass, but he had just got into university and two weeks later he left the band,' Morty explains. 'We were really worried that we were going to lose the contract. I was threatening to firebomb his house but then we got Alan MacFeely in on bass and everything was fine.'

During the same month that The Sultans of Ping F.C. signed their record deal, three upstarts from Seattle were set to play Sir Henry's. They would soon become one of the biggest bands in the world - Nirvana. The grunge legends played Sir Henry's on Tuesday, August 20, 1991, as the support act to headliners Sonic Youth. The show was promoted by Cork promoter Des Blair with tickets for the gig priced at IR£7.00. Nirvana's performance on Leeside quickly gained legendary status in the annals of Cork rock music.

Local interest in the grunge sound had already been roused, thanks to an earlier Babes In Toyland/Therapy? concert. The Sonic Youth/Nirvana gig was a sell-out, attracting around seven hundred music fans. At the time, Sonic Youth were the main lure for the crowd. However, following Nirvana's rise to prominence, accounts of the numbers in attendance for their support slot at Sir Henry's have become greatly exaggerated over the years.

Morty McCarthy was one of the select few who did witness Kurt Cobain, bassist Krist Novoselic and drummer Dave Grohl play Cork. He remembers:

> At the time, Sonic Youth were very popular. This guy Des Blair used to put on shows in Cork and he secured them. It was just before the Reading Festival. Bands would always do a warm-up show somewhere in the UK but Sonic Youth and Nirvana decided to do one in Dublin and one in Cork, which was unusual because normally bands didn't come across to us. They would play in Oxford or somewhere nearby. No one could believe it because Sonic Youth were a very big band, so the show was sold out. It was a big deal! Niall was also at the gig. I remember being down in The Liberty at the time and Niall was buying a two-litre bottle. You know, if you finished your two-litre in time, you saw Nirvana and if you didn't, you missed them. To be honest, it was just a fluke that we saw them. The main reason I went up was because there was a guy called Joss, from a Cork band called Muffdive, he told me not to miss it. They were big into the grunge thing before it happened. Joss telling me not to miss it was why I was there.

Niall also remembers the gig in Sir Henry's, but seemingly not Nirvana. 'I saw that gig but I wasn't blown away. I think Sonic Youth were a bit arty for me. They had a few good tunes, but they were never my style really. I thought they were a bit pretentious and, possibly, I was a bit jealous of them.' Footage from Nirvana's performance in Sir Henry's can be found on the documentary *1991: The Year Punk Broke* (1992) directed by Dave Markey.

In November of 1991, the Sultans played their first UK live date with a well-received show in London. In late January 1992, the Cork band released their infectious debut single, a quirky three-minute track that would sustain its appeal far beyond its year of release. This was *Where's Me Jumper?*. It came complete with b-sides *I Said I Am I Said* and on the CD edition *Turnip Fish* was included. When *Turnip Fish* is performed live, it usually inspires a wacky bicycle dance from Sultans fans, who lie with their backs on the floor and make cycling movements with their legs in the air.

*Where's Me Jumper?* became very popular in Britain as well as at home, where it earned the impressive accolade of the biggest selling single in Ireland during 1992, even outselling Bryan Adams' alarmingly bland *(Everything I Do) I Do It For You*. Written by Niall O'Flaherty in his late teenage years, *Where's Me Jumper?* was an extremely catchy, unusual and distinctive song with an unforgettable drum intro and bizarre lyrics that even managed to name check the German philosopher and revolutionary socialist Karl Marx. This single went on to become the band's signature song and earned them an instant fan-base in Britain.

Given its title and subject matter, there has been much local speculation about where Niall lost his beloved jumper. It has been claimed that the jumper was lost in Cork indie clubnight Gigantic, which used to be held in Sir Henry's on a Friday night. However, the truth is far more disturbing!

Niall discloses that the famous jumper was actually lost in Spiders, an old nightclub just off Washington Street. 'It is about losing my jumper in … Oh God! This is going to be even more embarrassing …in Spiders! It was in there that I lost it.'

Reflecting on the early success of their debut single, Morty admits:

> It was quite a shock at the time. When we released that, it got a lot of play in England and people were

calling us from the UK saying: 'Oh you are on the radio again!' That was a shock. The demo *Confessions Of A Sellafield Sex Guru* was very popular around Cork but, nationally and internationally, it was a different story.

Niall also admits to being surprised at just how quickly their first single took off. He states:

> It was kind of a rope around our necks but at the same time, when we arrived in London, we never played an empty gig because of that song. It was played in all the clubs, so it broke the ice for us big time! At the same time, it is hard to move on from that. I can't believe how short the song is!

*Where's Me Jumper?* got to number 67 in the UK singles chart and to number 8 in the Irish singles chart. It spent a total of eight weeks in the Irish chart. Following the release of the single, the Sultans were invited to record a John Peel session for *BBC Radio 1* and, of course, they leapt at the opportunity.

The band's follow-up single, *Stupid Kid*, came out in April 1992. Like its predecessor, this second single showcased Niall's talent for humorous and bizarre lyrics. However, *Stupid Kid* was a more straightforward punk number than their debut single. Three other tracks were included with this release: *Give Him A Ball (And A Yard Of Grass)*, recorded live at The Borderline on February 28, 1992, *Football Hooligan* and *No More Nonsense*. *Stupid Kid* scaled the British indie chart to reach number 1, got to number 67 in the UK national chart and achieved a respectable number 11 in the Irish singles chart.

The year 1992 also saw The Sultans of Ping F.C. release their EP *What About Those Sultans!*, which was a 12-inch only release, on London-based label Fantastic Plastic Records. This

EP was the label's inaugural release. For fans, this is a real collector's item. It featured five tracks: *Miracles, Crash Pad Chick, Stupid Kid, Riot At The Sheep Dog Trials* and *Eamonn Andrews*.

During the summer of that year, the Sultans performed at the Fleadh festival in London's Finsbury Park, the Reading Festival and Féile 92, held in Semple Stadium in Thurles, County Tipperary. The band then embarked on an Irish tour, while also finding time to work on their debut long-player.

September saw the Sultans release their third single, entitled *Veronica*, which was a real indie pop gem that featured some impressive orchestrations. Because of its lyrics, fans have speculated that this song was in fact written about a greyhound. The single also featured two other tracks *Teenage Vampire* and *Riot At The Sheep Dog Trials*, which was a different version of the song that also appeared on *Confessions Of A Sellafield Sex Guru*. After releasing this single, the Cork band supported Carter The Unstoppable Sex Machine on a European tour. Later in the year, the Sultans inked a deal with Epic Records. Their fourth single, *U Talk Too Much*, became their first with Epic. It was accompanied by a number of other tracks. These were *Japanese Girls, Armitage Shanks* - a track honouring the UK toilet manufacturer of the same name - *I Said I Am I Said* (on the 12-inch only), *Robocop* (on the 10-inch only) and *Turnip Fish* (only on the CD release). *U Talk Too Much* entered the British singles chart at number 32 and reached number 4 in Ireland. Interestingly, to emphasise the band's love of football, this single was issued with three exclusive 'Pingini' football cards, which featured Morty, Pat and Alan. Fans could obtain a fourth football card by writing to the official Sultans fan club, Friends of Desmond.

The Sultans' debut long-player *Casual Sex In The Cineplex* was released in January 1993. Recorded at Marcus Studios in London and produced by Steve Lovell, it entered the British album chart at number 26. Featuring twelve tracks, the album included all four of the previously released singles and a number of other standout tracks, such as the album opener *Back In A Tracksuit*, the gloriously warm love song *2 Pints of Rasa*, the live favourite *Give Him A Ball (And A Yard Of Grass)* and the beautifully sentimental *Let's Go Shopping*. Lyrically, *2 Pints of Rasa* is distinctive in that it features Cork slang terminology. 'Rasa' is the Cork slang term for a raspberry cordial drink, while the phrase 'Me Daza', which also crops up in the lyrics is the Cork slang for excellent.[43]

The title of the Sultans' debut record made reference to the old Capitol Cineplex that was located on one of Cork city's main thoroughfares, Grand Parade. Discussing the name of their first album, Niall admits 'it was putting two elements of our lives together. We were from Cork. That is where we grew up: that is where most of that album was made, that is where you get the 'Cineplex' part. 'Casual Sex'? I think you can put two and two together.'

Given the album's suggestive title, the question presents itself – was there any casual sex in the Cineplex? According to Niall: 'No there wasn't! Oh, you never know. Not on my part anyway. Certainly!'

Considering the enthusiastic response of music fans to the release of *Casual Sex In The Cineplex*, Morty acknowledges that he wasn't too surprised when it took off:

> The only reason I say that is because we already had the experience of the year before with the release of

---

[43] Morty McCarthy, *Dowtcha Boy!*, pp. 49-50.

the first single *Where's Me Jumper?* and then *Stupid Kid* and *Veronica*. Thanks to the first three singles, we had already developed a good audience in the UK. So it was more of the same but with slightly bigger shows. *You Talk Too Much* came out at the same time as the album. Both charted at the same time in the Top 30. The wave was just getting bigger!

The British music press also became interested in the Sultans. However, on one occasion, a photo of the Cork four-piece that appeared in *Melody Maker* caused some confusion on the streets of Cork.

Morty recalls:

> We were up in the Shetland Islands and I had the flu. So I was dying sick and Gerry Breen, our roadie, had black hair, so he just pretended that he was the drummer in the band and we didn't say anything to *Melody Maker*. We were away for a month and *Melody Maker* appeared in Cork and people were like: 'Jesus! Morty has left the band and Gerry Breen is drumming!' That was the kind of rumour that went around.

With their star firmly in the ascendancy, the Sultans managed to sell-out the legendary London Astoria. Following this, they returned for a riotous homecoming show at Cork City Hall. The band then completed a tour of Holland before heading to Japan for a short but well-received mini-tour that included a gig in Hiroshima and sell-out shows in Tokyo.

During this period, the Sultans were also working on material for their second record. In July 1993, they began recording tracks in Marcus Studios in London. The band also took time out from recording sessions to play Féile 93 in Ireland

and the Hultsfred Festival in Sweden, while also performing at an Irish festival in Stockholm.[44]

The Sultans of Ping F.C. began putting the finishing touches to their second LP after an expected appearance at the Reading Festival failed to materialize. Entitled *Teenage Drug* (1994), this long-player would feature the standout tracks *Wake Up And Scratch Me*, *Teenage Punks*, *Michiko*, *Love And Understanding* and *Teenage Rock And Roll Girl*.

Many bands find writing their second album to be a difficult process. Part of the reason for this is that they usually have said everything they have to say on their first. Constant touring can also stifle creative energy and ideas. Looking back on the main differences between *Teenage Drug* and its predecessor, Morty reveals:

> I'm not a big fan of the second album. I like the singles; I think there are some good pop songs on it, but we just didn't get the time to write a second album. The first album was written in Cork; the conditions and the atmosphere around that [city] created the songs. That didn't exist on the second LP because we were on the road most of the time and we were in the studio. It was a bit artificial, like being forced to write a second album. When you write a first album, you are just writing songs, you have no real plan that it's actually going to be an album. So it's a better process, whereas, when you become an established band, it's like now we have to release a second album.

---

[44] A humorous documentary on The Sultans of Ping F.C. entitled *Trying To Sell Your Soul When The Devil Won't Listen* (2002) featured archive footage from their Féile 93 appearance. It also included footage shot in Dublin's Rock Garden in 1992 and from the Sultans' Sexy Love Japanese tour in 1993. It was screened at the 47th Cork Film Festival as part of the 'Made In Cork' programme of 2002.

Another change that occurred around this time was that the Sultans chose to remove the F.C. from their name and were now known simply as the Sultans of Ping. Asked what precipitated this move, Morty laughs:

> That's hilarious! The whole novelty band thing got attached. When Sony took over Rhythm King Records, I remember this big meeting with record company executives and they were saying: 'You have got to drop the F.C. or you'll remain a novelty act!' I remember bursting out laughing at the meeting.

Niall indicates that ditching the F.C. in their band name was also a defensive move:

> I guess we were a little bit sick of every review we got that said: 'Oh, for fuck sake, give up! This isn't funny!' We were trying so hard to write decent pop songs and we felt that we didn't deserve that kind of treatment all the time. We entertained the punters every time they turned up and I think we were thinking: Can we do anything in any way to get ourselves taken a little bit more seriously? Then I listened to the second album and thought: Oh my God! What are you doing all that shit for?

The new album was preceded by a number of singles; *Teenage Punks*, released in September 1993, reached number 49 in the British singles chart. Other tracks included with this single were *Indeed You Are*, *He Thought I Was Your Best Friend*, *Crash Pad Chick* and a live version of *Veronica* (on the 12-inch only). After its release, the Sultans supported Carter USM on a UK tour. They then released their next single *Michiko* and it reached number 43 in the UK singles chart. Accompanying the *Michiko* single were the tracks *Miracles*, *Xmas Bubblegum Machine*, *Japanese Girls* (acoustic party mix) and a live version of *Stupid Kid* (on the 12-inch picture disc only). The Cork group then returned to tour Japan where, strangely, they played in high schools. For the lucrative Japanese market, the Sultans released their track *Japanese Girls*. This release was complimented by three other tracks: *Armitage Shanks*, *I Said I Am I Said* and *Turnip Fish*, and a twenty-page colour booklet was also included as part of the package. The Sultans had one other Japanese only release, the *Miracle Michiko EP*. Tracks included were: *Michiko*, *Miracles*, *Do Re Mi*, *So Far So Good* (a cover of a Carter USM song), a live version of *Veronica* and *Japanese Girls* (acoustic party mix).

After recovering from a nasty bout of sinusitis that he developed while in Japan, Niall led the band out on a Christmas tour of Ireland. In January 1994, the Cork quartet commenced an extensive tour of the UK, taking in twenty-two live dates. The Sultans' next release was the single *Wake Up And Scratch Me*, which got to number 50 in the British singles chart. It also featured the tracks *Do Re Mi*, *So Far So Good*, *Everything You Do, You Do For You*, and *Let's Go Shopping*.

Having spent more than a year writing, arranging and recording, their LP *Teenage Drug* was finally released in March 1994.[45] It got to number 57 in the UK album chart. Despite releasing three singles from the album, it failed to emulate the success of *Casual Sex In The Cineplex*. A major European tour was lined up in support of the new record with live dates in Sweden, Denmark, Holland and Germany. Following this successful tour, the band departed Europe for yet another

---

[45] In a bizarre marketing move, in Japan, *Teenage Drug* was issued under the name *Teenage Planet Sexy War*. On this Japanese release, the band was still referred to as The Sultans of Ping F.C..

Japanese tour. In September, the Sultans also managed to cross the Atlantic and made their first visit to America.

Reminiscing about life while recording and touring *Teenage Drug*, Niall confesses:

> I think it was a departure from our first record. I only listened to it again recently. It took a while to write some of the songs and some just flew out. We were on a bit of a high at that stage and certainly we were starting to think: 'Oh God! This is our second album!' We were travelling all over the world and we were pretty pleased with ourselves. We started to believe that we were musicians! I don't know if some of the album proved us wrong, but I think we cut a few good songs on that [record]. I wouldn't say we sustained the quality all the way through though. I guess...it was not about Cork anymore, it was about our lives in London and the other places we were going. We were excited about it. We no longer missed home I must say. We were well on the rollercoaster and enjoying it...I can't deny that we lapped it up!

Early in 1995, former Golden Horde guitarist Sammy Steiger was recruited by the Sultans as a second guitarist. The addition of their new half-Irish, half-Swiss, guitar player would have a dramatic effect on the band's sound. Niall explains why they chose Sammy:

> We were looking for a second guitarist and we had some of the songs written. We held auditions and amazingly we had loads and loads of people audition. We were always thinking, either they weren't good enough or they were too good. Sammy was just about right. He

certainly wasn't too good, but he was a mean-looking son of a bitch!

In terms of Sammy's impact on the Sultans' sound, Morty explains how he helped them morph into a different band and how this facilitated yet another shortening of the group's name:

> I think the Sultans evolved in quite an organic way. It was a lot to do with Sam Steiger joining us. After the second album was released, we started doing some live shows and he had a heavy influence on the sound. Sam and Niall kind of moved in the same direction. I don't think it was that conscious really, but when we heard the stuff, we thought, this isn't the Sultans of Ping, so we called the band The Sultans.

At the start of 1996, The Sultans supported US punk legends The Ramones on their farewell tour. The Cork act also supported The Sex Pistols in Paris on July 4 that year. Morty enthuses about these experiences:

> When we supported The Ramones in January and February of 1996, it was incredible! Then supporting The Sex Pistols was another great buzz! I remember Johnny Rotten was throwing chicken wings at me at the after-party, so I started throwing them back.

Taken from their third album, a new single entitled *Mescaline* was released. This single was accompanied by two other tracks: *Shake* and *Bird Doggin'*.

*Mescaline* got to number 21 in the UK Indie Chart. In June 1996, The Sultans released their third album *A Good Year For Trouble*. In hindsight, this was a rather appropriate title as there was trouble ahead. The album failed to sell more than a few thousand copies and it looked like the writing was on the wall. Part of the reason for their poor fortune came from a shift within popular music, which took place in the mid-1990s. Britpop was now at its height and one of its biggest bands, Manchester five-piece, Oasis, played two sold-out dates at Páirc Uí Chaoimh in Cork during the summer of 1996.[46]

*A Good Year For Trouble* did include the standout tracks *Scar On My Face*, *Mescaline* and The Sultans' cover version of The Third Bardo's 1967 single *I'm Five Years Ahead Of My Time*, which has proved to be a live favourite with fans.[47] Morty expresses relief that this was their last album, because if they had continued releasing albums, they ran the risk of having no name to release them under:

> I'm glad we didn't release a fourth album because there would have been no title left for the band by that stage. When we became The Sultans, we were virtually a different band. We were a five-piece and we had a much harder sound. Also Sony didn't back the third album. We were back with Rhythm King Records.

In a way, The Sultans had become victims of their own success. Having first come to the attention of the record-buying public with their infectious *Where's Me Jumper?* single back in 1992, it appears that this ultimately contributed to their demise. Morty describes how this came about:

> People said that *Where's Me Jumper?* was a millstone around our necks. But we would never have been

---

[46] Oasis played Páirc Uí Chaoimh in Cork on Wednesday August 14 and Thursday August 15, 1996. The Prodigy and The Bootleg Beatles were the support acts for these shows. Oasis played Cork after their two huge concerts at Knebworth Park in England, where they reportedly played to 250,000 fans over two nights.

[47] *I'm Five Years Ahead Of My Time* is listed simply as *Five Years* on the tracklisting of *A Good Year For Trouble*.

anywhere if it wasn't for that record. As regards the third album, it definitely affected it in a way. The third album is a very good rock album, but people couldn't take it seriously because we had the song *Where's Me Jumper?* and the sound was too different for them. We did pigeonhole ourselves to a certain extent.

A number of factors contributed to The Sultans parting ways. The economics of their situation certainly played a role after the release of *A Good Year For Trouble*. Morty notes:

If you live in London, it costs a lot of money to keep a band going. It was incredible! We had reached such a high level at the start. The tours for the first two albums were sell-outs. We would be playing to between 1,000 and 3,000 people a night. When we began to go down, we didn't get much radio airplay and the crowds began to drop to a few hundred.

The Sultans' last stand took place in Sir Henry's on December 19, 1997. The two support acts on the night were Orchid, who won the UCC Battle of the Bands competition in 1996, and the band Anomie. Fronted by singer, guitarist and keyboard player Chloe Nagle, Anomie also featured lead guitarist Dave O'Mahony and his brother, drummer Justin O'Mahony, who later played with the Cork band Fred, and bass player Niall Connolly, who has since become a popular folk singer-songwriter in Cork and, more recently, in New York.

Watching The Sultans perform on the night, Niall Connolly recalls that the irony of the occasion wasn't lost on their colourful lead singer: 'I remember Niall O'Flaherty on stage telling the crowd: "It all started here, it's all ending here…it doesn't mean we like you!"'

Unfortunately, The Sultans' farewell performance was plagued by security problems, with many fans who attended the gig feeling that security staff had behaved in an overly aggressive and heavy-handed manner.

During the gig, lead singer Niall O'Flaherty ended up getting into an altercation with a fan:

> There was usually very little violence at our gigs but, at our last gig, I did jump off the stage and punch a guy. He got thrown out and I didn't mean that, but the reason I jumped was that he grabbed me by the gonads and squeezed very hard. He had been up near the stage... and he leaned over and did it. I think it was a bit of self-preservation on my account. He was only a young fella. I couldn't believe that he went down when I jumped on top of him. Later, I had to leave the place in danger of my life.

Sir Henry's was the location where The Sultans' career really took off, but it looked like this was where it was destined to end. Sadly, The Sultans split up following this chaotic gig. Morty acknowledges that it was a very emotional night for him; however, even then, he felt that it couldn't end like this. And what's more, he was right!

## CHAPTER TEN

# AFTER ALL

[The Frank And Walters]

Having become something of a Cork institution, The Frank And Walters etched their way into the public consciousness with their trademark warm, pop sensibility and jingly-jangly, guitar sound. Hailing from the Cork suburb of Bishopstown, this three-piece indie band was centred around brothers Paul and Niall Linehan.

Originally from the city's northside, the Linehan brothers moved with their family to Bishopstown in the late 1970s. The pair attended Bishopstown Community School as did the band's drummer Ashley Keating. Keating too was originally from Cork's northside. He came from Mayfield, but moved to Glencairn Park in 1976, the same street where Paul and Niall came to live.

Colloquially known simply as 'The Franks', the trio was led by lead singer and bass player Paul Linehan. Paul's first flirtation with performing came in the mid-1980s with a skiffle-styled four-piece. This led to a number of musical incarnations. He recalls:

> My first introduction to music was with two lads in school called Paul Duggan and Colin Chambers. We went jamming in Colin's house. We were about sixteen or seventeen. They were the only fellas in school who played guitar. I made a drum out of a barrel and a bit of

canvas. Another friend of mine, Leonard Cremin, made a tea-chest bass using a broomstick and a tea-chest with a bit of twine. We went jamming with the two lads, playing Beatles' songs and songs like that. I liked the sound of the bass and Leonard liked the sound of the drums, so we swapped instruments. I think we only had two jams, probably in the summer of 1985.

The boys had plans to upgrade their instruments. As Paul explains:

> That summer I went to London and Leonard went to America. The plan was to save up enough money from working, so I could buy a bass guitar and amp, and he could buy a set of drums. Then we would go back jamming with the boys. When we came back, Leonard didn't buy drums. He bought a guitar instead. So the line-up was myself, Paul Duggan, Colin Chambers and Leonard. In the meantime, Ashley Keating decided to buy a drum kit to join the band. Then there were five of us jamming in our front room in Glencairn Park. I had got my first bass - a Morris Fender Precision copy. I bought it in the swap shop in MacCurtain Street. I bought my small bass amp from a fella called Darren Boylan. He was in a Bishopstown band called Echoes In The Shallow Bay. Brendan O'Connor was in that band, believe it or not.[48] So we started jamming away. I think

---

[48] Brendan O'Connor is a Cork-born former comedian turned RTÉ television personality. He also works as a columnist for the *Sunday Independent* and edits the newspaper's *Life* magazine. Brendan is a former pupil of Coláiste an Spioraid Naoimh in Bishopstown and a graduate of University College Cork. In 2000, he tasted chart success as Father Brian And The Fun Lovin' Cardinals with the song *Who's In The House*, which peaked at number 3 in the Irish singles chart.

we had about three sessions and then split up. After a few months, Ashley, myself and my brother Niall, who had been playing acoustic guitar, started jamming. Niall had saved up enough money to buy a Satellite electric guitar. We called ourselves Sun Factory. It was just the three of us as the rest of the lads went their own way.

Surprisingly, the trio who would ultimately emerge as The Frank And Walters, failed to solidify as a performing unit on their first attempt. Paul remembers:

> We started off learning songs by Joy Division and The Cure and that is how we learned to play our instruments. We used to have to get Ashley out of bed every Sunday because he was in the Navy.[49] Eventually, I felt there wasn't enough commitment in the band and I joined another band called Judith Sunrise for a couple of months. I did a couple of gigs with them in places like Mojo's, which used to be on George's Quay, The Phoenix and in Redz supporting The Gorehounds.[50]

However, like so many young bands, Judith Sunrise soon broke up. Following their demise, Paul joined Cork band The 3355409s. His time with this group was short-lived. In fact, he only lasted about a month. Paul reflects:

> I had just left Judith Sunrise and someone told me that a band was looking for a bass player because their old bass player, who was Australian, had moved back to Australia. So I joined The 3355409s. In that band at that stage were Dave O'Connell, Ruth Beecher and I

---

[49] Drummer Ashley Keating served in the Irish navy from 1985 to 1989.
[50] The Gorehounds were a Dublin group whose musical sound has been compared to that of US band The Cramps.

think Morty McCarthy was playing drums. I remember I turned up late one day and I had a very legitimate reason for being late. I remember one band member just ignored me and tried to ostracize me, to punish me. I came out of their practice room and just never went back.

In the meantime, Bishopstown native Brendan O'Connor had entered the fray to link up with Niall Linehan and Ashley Keating - in Paul's absence - in another incarnation of Sun Factory. This band also split. Paul recalls:

> About eight or nine months after that, I was in my front room jamming with my brother Niall and we both just started making a bit of music and we thought it sounded good. So we called up to Ashley and asked: 'Do you want to start the band up again?' He did and he bought a new kit and it was cool! Brendan came in as the singer and I was the bass player. We started jamming in Sullivan's Quay with Brendan.[51] I think we called ourselves either The Believers or The Established. Then that summer, Brendan and Niall left to go to London. Brendan had said that he didn't feel he got on with Ashley and me and that we were on a different planet from him.

With Paul's younger brother and Brendan having left for London, the remaining band members were presented with a bit of a dilemma. Paul and Ashley decided to look beyond their own social circle for new recruits. They advertised looking for a new guitarist and local musician Kieran Kelleher joined them.

Around this time, the trio settled on the name The Frank And Walters. While the band now had a new lead guitarist,

---
[51] The Frank And Walters used to rehearse in a room in the Christian Brother's school on Sullivan's Quay in Cork city.

Niall Linehan would soon rejoin their ranks. Paul reveals:

> Kieran played guitar with us when we recorded our first demo tape. Then my brother came back from London and he was asking could he get into the band again. He was begging me but Ashley didn't want to bring him back because he had already left us. I managed to convince Ashley to bring him in as rhythm guitarist, while Kieran was now playing lead guitar. We became The Frank And Walters. With Kieran, and before Niall came back, we had the band name The Frank And Walters.

Like The Sultans of Ping F.C., the Franks decided to utilise Brian O'Reilly's studio skills and the demo was recorded at Studio Fiona in Fermoy. It featured three tracks: *Twenty Minutes Longer With You*, *Sleepless Nights* and *Back Beneath Your Feet*.

As a quartet, Paul and Niall Linehan together with Ashley Keating and Kieran Kelleher made their live debut at De Barras in Clonakilty. Paul and his fellow band members played this renowned west Cork venue on October 14, 1989 without any support act, to a respectable audience largely made up of friends of the band. Like many first gigs, The Frank And Walters' setlist on the night was heavily laden with cover versions including *Turquoise Days* by Echo And The Bunnymen. The band also played original material including their songs *Back Beneath Your Feet* and *Sandra Dee*. Having overcome understandable first gig nerves and gained in confidence, they soon returned for a second gig at De Barras. In these early days, the band was conscious that one of the advantages of playing in Clonakilty was that any unfortunate mishaps that may have occurred onstage could be confined to an audience made up of friends and locals.

However, the Cork live circuit beckoned. In February 1990, the Franks played The Phoenix bar on Union Quay – something of a rite of passage for many young Cork bands. They were supported by Dirty Turtles, which featured former jamming partner Leonard Cremin.

Following this performance, Kieran Kelleher decided to leave the band apparently after a disagreement with Niall Linehan. To this day, a lot of ambiguity surrounds Kelleher's departure. Suffice to say that when a disagreement arose, Paul says that he felt he had to stand by his brother. After Kieran's departure, The Frank And Walters evolved into a three-piece with Niall assuming lead guitar duties.

Inspired by post-punk bands, the Cork trio counted acts such as Joy Division, The Stranglers, The Cure and Echo And The Bunnymen among their early influences. But it was English pop group Prefab Sprout that initially drew Paul to songwriting:

> At the time, Prefab Sprout were my favourite band and the first album I ever bought was *Steve McQueen* (1985). The reason I got into music in the first place was after hearing the song *When Love Breaks Down*. When I heard that song, it was the first time that music ever touched me. I started writing music just after that.

Character-driven songs have been something of a speciality for Paul Linehan. On a number of occasions, he has written about local characters in Cork city. One of his early songs, *Michael*, was written about a good friend of the band called Mick Hurley. This psychedelic influenced song was a personal nod to a close friend who sat in on their early jamming sessions and who went on to handle the band's merchandising and manage their fan-club.

Through their early manager, Kevin O'Mahony, the Franks got gigs at both the Regional Technical College, where Niall studied mechanical engineering, and at University College Cork's Old College Bar. At the RTC, the band performed a lunchtime gig in the atrium. Remarkably, it took several meetings with the venue manager in UCC, before the band was allowed to play their first gig on campus. The venue was not usually difficult to book for a gig, so this perhaps reflected a closed-shop mentality at UCC, given that the band were not students at the university.

Getting signed has always been a bit of a challenge for Cork acts, as they don't have the luxury of having major record companies in their own backyard, unlike their Dublin counterparts. As happened with the Sultans, an element of luck played its part in The Frank And Walters' signing their record deal. Paul recounts the chain of events that led to this momentous occasion.

> We played a gig in The Hole In The Wall down in Kinsale. We were trying to sell a demo tape and I think the songs *Michael* and *Walter's Trip* might have been on it. No one would buy them, so we actually gave the tapes to people for free. One of the tapes ended up in a clothes shop in Cork called Mannix and Culhane. There was a fella working there called Philip Kennedy and he was a friend of Colm O'Callaghan from RTÉ. Colm heard the demo tape and he loved it. He rang us up and wanted to meet us. He said: 'Lads! I know this label that would be perfect for ye! They're called Setanta Records and I think I might be able to get you a deal with them. Your music is up their street!'

He also told us at the same time there was a label called Go! Discs and they would also be interested in us. At this stage, we would have given money to be signed. We would have actually paid money! We wanted a record deal. Colm O'Callaghan decided to help us out. He came in and did a bit of production with us and helped with the arrangements of our songs. We didn't know much about bridges and middle eights and the structure of songs. He taught us all about it. We made a demo tape with him down in Caroline Studios in Blackpool. He sent it off to Setanta and basically produced that demo tape with us.

Colm O'Callaghan was never actually in a band, although he has helped many Cork bands over the years, including six-piece Turner's Cross jazz/funk band Serengeti Long Walk, which featured guitarist Joe Dermody.[52] Another mid-1980s Turner's Cross band familiar to Colm was guitar band The How And Why Insects. Their drummer Keri Jones was also the drummer in Serengeti Long Walk. According to Colm, The How And Why Insects used to do a rather convincing cover version of *I Wanna Be Your Dog* by Iggy And The Stooges.

Colm had a lot of expertise and valuable experience when it came to advising and helping the Franks. He had worked on a temporary basis for the now defunct Cork radio station *Radio South* based at White's Cross, where he played records on a graveyard shift from midnight until 6 a.m., covering for an overnight DJ. Franks' drummer Ashley Keating even telephoned Colm at *Radio South*, to ask him would he play one of their demos on air. Another obvious benefit was the fact that Colm had a background in music journalism, as he used to

---

[52] Serengeti Long Walk took their band name from a track on Stewart Copeland's album *The Rhythmatist* (1985).

write for both *Hot Press* and *Melody Maker*.

Colm helped the Franks record another demo tape, which featured the tracks: *Walter's Trip, Frank's Right, Angela Cray* and *Turquoise Gardens*. He then sent the band's demo off to Setanta Records' boss Keith Cullen in London. At the time, Colm was working for Keith in an unofficial capacity. Of course, Setanta had also previously been home to Finbarr Donnelly's last band Beethoven.

Reflecting on why The Frank And Walters' music made such an impression, Colm O'Callaghan is emphatic: 'What appealed to me about their sound was what has appealed to me about every single band I have ever liked. No matter how badly recorded the tape was, the songs were magnificent!'

While Colm had forwarded recordings of the Franks' music to Keith Cullen, there was another Irish band that had caught the ear of the Dublin-born record company supremo. Limerick band The Cranberries were being enticed into the Setanta stable and this was threatening the Franks' prospects of securing their much sought-after deal.[53]

Paul Linehan explains how this predicament was eventually resolved:

> Setanta Records were just about to sign The Cranberries, but their manager changed his mind and went with Island Records, so Keith Cullen was then ready to sign us. He wasn't going to sign us. It was either us or The Cranberries and then The Cranberries went to Island. So we signed to Setanta.

Like Colm O'Callaghan, Keith Cullen recognised Linehan's

---

[53] The Cranberries played Nancy Spains on Barrack Street on December 11, 1991. Their swift rise to fame is evidenced by the fact that they played the Green Glens Arena in Millstreet County Cork on June 4, 1995. They returned to play this large venue on December 11, 1999.

great songwriting talent and it was this that compelled him to sign the Cork trio. Cullen admits: 'They had very good simple pop songs and they were a very hard-working band as well. I guess it was the catchy songs that really clinched it.'

For the Franks, getting signed was a welcome morale boost, although it came without any great financial windfall. This development ultimately saw the band relocate from Cork to London. This was a smart move, as London was a music industry hub with large record labels and a well-established music press, not to mention a diverse range of venues and a larger audience for live music. Paul enthuses:

> Getting signed was amazing! It was all we ever wanted. When we signed we didn't get any money or anything like that. There was no money involved! It was basically a distribution and recording deal. In 1991, we moved to London and we lived in the YMCA there for over a year.

Before they moved to live in the YMCA in Wimbledon, in the summer of 1991, The Frank And Walters played a number of gigs in the greater Cork area. One of these gigs still holds a particular significance to this day for some Cork rock aficionados. On Friday, January 4, 1991, the Franks supported The Sultans of Ping F.C. in one of the county's best live venues: Connolly's of Leap in west Cork.[54] Both bands knew each other from socialising in The Liberty bar in Cork. Other acts on the bill at this gig were Bedroom Convention, Ballycotton band The Stern Tubes, Suburban Rebels and Buttox.

---

[54] Owned by Eileen Connolly and Paddy McNicholl, Connolly's of Leap was a world-renowned pub and venue based in west Cork. In terms of national and international artists, Connolly's played host to the likes of Nick Cave, the Patti Smith band, Garth Hudson of The Band, Shellac, Dirty Three, The Frames and Damien Rice.

Sultans' drummer Morty McCarthy describes what this gig meant to him and, in the process, offers an interesting overview of the Cork rock music scene:

> Cork tends to go in waves. It kind of had a wave around 1985/86 with bands like Belsonic Sound and Cypress, Mine!. A lot of Cork bands were doing well nationally. But after that, they kind of faded away. Then there was nothing coming through and it was a bit grim. Then when the Sultans started to get going around Cork and The Frank and Walters, you had a lot of new bands coming out at the same time. The culmination of this was a gig down in Connolly's of Leap, where six bands played. We had a bus trip down and there must have been at least two hundred people that came to the gig. A new scene came out of that. That was the beginnings of it. That was the first time everyone was together. I don't know would you call it the key players of the next four to five years, but the main bands sprang from there.

Other gigs which the Franks played during this period included a show at De Lacy House in Cork supported by The How And Why Insects. The Franks also supported The Sultans of Ping F.C. at the Baggot Inn in Dublin and in late February they played a 'Stop The Slaughter In The Gulf' gig in Sir Henry's. The line-up for this concert protesting against the first Gulf War also featured the Hank Wedel Band.

Before departing for the British capital, the Franks found time to record a session for the *Dave Fanning Show*. A very popular radio show at the time, recording a session was something of a rite of passage for Ireland's new bands.

Local author Jack Lyons recalls in his book *A Renewed Interest In Reading* (2007) that the Franks played a farewell gig in Sir Henry's on April 17 before heading for London.

Shortly after arriving in London, they released their debut 12-inch EP on Setanta in July 1991. Simply entitled *The Frank And Walters EP1*, it featured four tracks: *Walter's Trip*, *Frank's Right*, *Michael* and *Never Ending Staircase*. The colourful artwork that accompanied this release came courtesy of artist Donncha Wilkie, who, like the band, had attended the Bishopstown Community School in Cork. This first EP was produced by Dave Couse, who would oversee production for the band on a number of occasions later in their career. Coinciding with this release, the Franks made their UK live debut at The Underworld in London's Camden Town, on July 4, 1991, to an audience of six hundred people, while their first headline gig took place in the White Horse pub in Hampstead supported by P.J. Harvey.[55]

The Frank And Walters released their second 12-inch EP in October 1991. In keeping with the title of their first Setanta Records release, this was called *The Frank And Walters EP 2*. Again this featured four tracks: *Fashion Crisis Hits New York*, *Rasputin*, *Daisy Chain* and *Angela Cray*.

Both releases met with enthusiastic responses from the British music press. However, life in London did prove a bit of a culture shock for the Cork band. Paul Linehan explains:

> At the time, everything seemed to escalate with the success. First of all, we did a gig supporting Carter USM in the Mean Fiddler. That was amazing! At the time, we just couldn't put a foot wrong. For our first EP, we got 'Single Of The Week' in the *NME* and *Melody Maker* in the same week. Everything was happening with everything we did. We would do a gig and we

---

[55] Jack Lyons, *A Renewed Interest In Reading*, p.41.

would get amazing reviews for it. Then we released the *Fashion Crisis EP* and that too was 'Single Of The Week' in *Melody Maker* and the *NME*.

Setanta issued the songs from the Franks' first two EPs together on a combined mini-album CD in 1991. This was followed by the release of a 7-inch flexi-disc single *We Are The Frank And Walters*, which was accompanied by the b-side *Humphrey*. Importantly, on November 3, 1991, the Franks followed in the footsteps of Cork acts like Microdisney, when they recorded tracks for John Peel's radio show at the BBC. Paul Linehan and his band-mates recorded *Fashion Crisis Hits New York*, *Happy Busman* and *The World Carries On* for their Peel session.

With a rising profile in Britain, the Franks secured a record deal with London-based label Go! Discs. On this label's books were acts such as The Beautiful South and the great English songwriter Billy Bragg. After signing to Go! Discs, The Frank And Walters were afforded the opportunity to tour, supporting popular British indie band the Inspiral Carpets. On this tour, the Cork group met a young roadie for the Inspiral Carpets, Noel Gallagher. Noel ended up working as a roadie on a temporary basis for the Franks on this tour after they became short-staffed. Of course, Noel later rose to prominence as lead guitarist and chief songwriter for Oasis.

During this period, the Franks took the unusual step of selling band T-shirts adorned with strange slogans. This illustrated the band's quirky sense of humour. In a strange twist of fate, one of these slogans would be adopted by Oasis as the title for their sixth studio album *Don't Believe The Truth* (2005). Paul Linehan recalls:

'Don't Believe The Truth' was on the back of one of

our T-shirts.[56] It was our kind of slogan. We had a load of them. We had a 'Who's The Langer In The Franks T-Shirt?'[57] That was another one. Most of England at the time would be asking: 'What's a langer?' We were just messing! The only thing that we took seriously was the music!

In March 1992, the Franks released another 12-inch EP. The release of *Happy Busman* also marked their first release on Go! Discs, whom they signed to in November 1991. As well as the title track, this EP, produced by Edwyn Collins, also featured the songs *Humphrey*, *The World Carries On* and *If You're Still Waiting*.

The lead track, *Happy Busman*, an uplifting guitar-driven indie tune, was actually written about a Cork bus driver who drove the number 5 bus to Bishopstown. In the lyrics, Paul Linehan disguised the identity of the busman referring to him in the song as Andy James. He explains who exactly the song was written about:

> It's about a busman called Frank Brett. That was the real name of the bus driver. He drove the bus to Bishopstown and he was just this very happy fella. You would be getting on the bus on a Monday morning with a hangover and he would be all smiles. It was just a really good start to the day.

---

[56] In the early part of the music video for The Frank And Walters' single *After All*, released in 1992 and directed by Tim Smith, you can see the slogan 'Don't Believe The Truth' being constructed by Niall Linehan, using children's plastic alphabet letters.

[57] The word 'langer' has a variety of meanings including idiot or fool. One suggestion is that it derives from the Langur monkey and the term was brought to Cork by the Munster Fusiliers returning from service in India. (Beecher, A Dictionary of Cork Slang, p.56.)

The Franks' song *Humphrey*, which was released along with *Happy Busman*, is written about a very unusual topic. Jack Lyons recounts an interview between *NME*'s Steve Lamacq and the band in Blackpool in England. The group admitted:

> *Humphrey* is all about when people kind of say things like…they say tea is bad for you or they say that butter is good for you…We first noticed this when we came to London…we asked each other 'Well who's "THEY"?' And we kind of thought up this idea that they are all in a room somewhere and this character called Humphrey goes into the room and gets a job as 'THEY'. So he goes around telling people that they can fly and do all sorts of crazy things because 'THEY' (Humphrey) says they can.[58]

The release of their third EP garnered rave reviews and more critical acclaim from the British music press who appeared smitten by the Franks refreshingly light-hearted songwriting style. *Melody Maker* and the *NME* rewarded them with 'EP of the Week' status. As well as receiving such impressive accolades, the Franks kept up a hectic touring schedule mixed with promotional duties in the media. Appearances on both BBC2's cult TV show *Rapido* and Channel 4's *The Word* were later followed by an extensive UK tour supported by Radiohead.

In late June 1992, The Frank And Walters fulfilled the dream of many a young band when they became one of the select few Cork acts to play the legendary Glastonbury music festival. They took their place on a line-up that included Blur, Lou Reed, James and Primal Scream. A live version of their song *Walter's Trip* recorded at Glastonbury was included on an

---

[58] Jack Lyons, *A Renewed Interest In Reading*, p.59.

*NME* double CD compilation entitled *In A Field Of Their Own – Highlights of Glastonbury 1992*. All profits from this release were donated to the charity Greenpeace.

The band's next proper release came in the form of the *This Is Not A Song* EP, which was released in September 1992. To promote the lead track from this EP, the group were flown to Salzburg in Austria where they filmed a rather lush music video complete with sweeping landscape shots. The centrepiece of this video featured the Cork trio in a rowing boat on an Austrian lake.

Included on this release, were three other tracks *Laurence Olivier*, *Davy Chase* and a live recording of *Happy Busman* from their March performance on the Channel 4 show *The Word*. To coincide with this release, The Frank And Walters graced the front cover of the *NME*'s September 12 edition, which also carried a two-page feature on the band.

The following month, the Franks made their triumphant return to Sir Henry's in Cork for a headline show. Here they treated Leesiders to material from their soon to be released debut album. On this occasion, they were supported by the bizarrely named local band LMNO Pelican. Hailing from Ballincollig, this Cork four-piece was previously known as Fred and under that name had supported The Sultans of Ping F.C. a number of times both at home and abroad. This group should not be confused with the five-piece Cork indie band Fred discussed in Chapter 12.

Released in late October 1992, the Franks first long-player was entitled *Trains, Boats And Planes*. They named their debut album after a Cork toy store that was located on Princes Street, which specialised in model aeroplanes. The album artwork came courtesy of British artist Bow Watkinson whose work the band had taken quite a shine to while in London.

Featuring eleven carefully-crafted tracks, *Trains, Boats And Planes* was a blissfully warm and enchanting indie record that bubbled with emotion and optimism. A number of talented producers were involved in producing this record. Edwyn Collins, Dave Couse, Ian Broudie of The Lightning Seeds and Nick Robbins all produced songs on *Trains, Boats And Planes*. Standout tracks included: *This Is Not A Song*, *Happy Busman* and *Fashion Crisis Hits New York*. However, the album's fourth track, *After All*, released as a single in December 1992, was to become the band's anthem. Upon release, *After All* peaked at number 11 in the British singles chart.

This single also boasted artwork from the artist Bow Watkinson. It was issued in two different CD packages. One CD featured the tracks *The Day Before The World Ended*, *The Turquoise Gardens* and a live version of their early song *Michael*. The second CD also featured *The Day Before The World Ended* and *The Turquoise Gardens* but instead of *Michael*, it featured a cover version of the Tone Loc song, *Funky Cold Medina*, which to this day remains a live favourite.

Lyrically, *After All* is an example of superb songwriting. Rather than crudely exploiting clichéd images and scenarios, like many contemporary pop love songs do, *After All* paints a more balanced and realistic portrait of love and its many different forms. This is the secret of the song's lasting appeal, with audiences in Ireland and abroad.

With the release of *After All*, The Frank And Walters made their first and only appearance on the BBC's iconic TV show *Top Of The Pops*, where on January 7, 1993, they performed their infectious new single. That same night, The Sultans of Ping F.C. had the video for their punk rock inspired hit *U Talk*

*Too Much* featured on the show. That week *U Talk Too Much* debuted at number 32 in the UK singles chart.

Such was the local interest in the Franks' *Top Of The Pops* adventure, that Cork's *Evening Echo* newspaper sent journalist David O'Connell and photographer Dan Linehan over to London to cover the band's experience. This resulted in a two-page feature on the band, much to the delight of their Cork fans.

That night, the Franks also shared the bill with former Beatle Paul McCartney and got to meet him. Understandably, this was a big bonus for Paul Linehan:

> It was brilliant! It was something that you always wanted to do when you were a young-fella. His dressing room was directly across from ours. We've got pictures taken with Paul. Linda McCartney was trying to make us become vegetarians. I think it worked on my brother Niall because he has since become a vegetarian. But it didn't work with us. I remember at the time she was saying: 'You know that a cow has to die every time you eat a burger!' I was looking at her and I said: 'What about those shoes you're wearing. Did a cow have to die for them?' She got all embarrassed and said: 'Oh my God!' I said: 'They're leather aren't they?' She said: 'Oh my God, they are! I'll have to get on to my wardrobe.'

*Evening Echo* scribe and Cork rock champion Shane Fitzsimons noted the significance of two of Cork's leading bands being in the British Top 40 simultaneously in his *Rockfile* column. However, some overzealous journalists in the Dublin media, eager to pigeonhole the emerging Cork bands, attempted to brand this triumph as 'Corkchester', a term that carried no resonance for any of the musicians involved.

To support their new album and single, The Frank And Walters went on a nationwide tour, which culminated in a gig at Cork City Hall on February 21, 1993. Support on the night came from Cork bands Treehouse and the amusingly named Spacecake.

Having already been on the cover of *NME*, the Franks obliged the other leading British music bible *Melody Maker* by appearing on its front cover on April 10. This was in support of their next single *Fashion Crisis Hits New York*, which was produced by Ian Broudie.

Like its predecessor, *Fashion Crisis Hits New York* was issued in a two CD single format. CD one also included the tracks *Time* (acoustic version), *Frank's Right* and *Never Ending Staircase*, while the second CD boasted additional tracks *Rasputin*, *Daisy Chain* and *Angela Cray*.

Unfortunately, this single failed to live up to expectation and chart success eluded the Franks on this occasion. However, the band persevered and kept touring with live dates in Britain and France. In May, they returned for a show at Connolly's of Leap in west Cork. Then, in June, they played Great Xpectations in London's Finsbury Park alongside acts like The Cure and Carter USM. The Frank And Walters played Féile 93 in Thurles before playing the Reading Festival in Britain that August.

Paul Linehan now began to turn his attention towards writing their second album. The band went on hiatus and enjoyed some welcome down time, before finally re-emerging in 1996 with new material. The Franks road-tested their new songs with a number of relatively low-key gigs, including one at Connolly's of Leap and a number of support slots with their Setanta label mates The Divine Comedy.

# CORK ROCK

Lead singer with The Divine Comedy, Neil Hannon, admits to being a big fan of Cork rock acts like The Frank And Walters and The Sultans of Ping:

> Two great Cork bands that I personally love are The Sultans of Ping and The Frank And Walters. They are great pop bands with a wonderful sense of humour and great, great tunes! From the early 1990s, I've been a fan of theirs ... When I was label mates with the Franks on Setanta, they enjoyed royally taking the piss out of me at the early stages basically because I was terribly middle class.

Both The Divine Comedy and The Frank And Walters featured on a tribute album to seminal English indie band The Smiths. Released in 1996, *The Smiths Is Dead* (a play on The Smiths' 1986 album *The Queen Is Dead*) included The Frank And Walters' cover version of *Cemetery Gates* and The Divine Comedy's cover of *There Is A Light That Never Goes Out*. It also boasted a track from former Microdisney guitarist Sean O'Hagan's new band The High Llamas, who offered their take on *Frankly, Mr Shankly*.

The first fruits of the Franks creative hiatus were revealed on a single called *Indian Ocean* released in June of 1996. This was a breezy, happy-go-lucky, cheerful summertime song. Three other tracks, *Pathways*, *You Can't Take Too Much Notice* and *Restraint* also accompanied this single. An *Indian Ocean EP* was also issued outside of Ireland in 1997 by Setanta and Go! Discs through Red Distribution in America. It featured six tracks: *Indian Ocean, Restraint, Pathways, Last Train Home, Fast Anthony* (a faster, more rock 'n' roll sounding version of their song *Tony Cochrane*) and *Little Dolls* (acoustic version).

The *Indian Ocean* single was soon followed up by another,

this time entitled *Colours*. This uplifting, slice of guitar-driven indie pop was served up to Franks' fans to keep their spirits up as they headed into the winter months and long dark evenings. The other tracks that accompanied this release were *Surrender To Win*, *You Asked Me* and *Last Train Home*.

Around this time, The Frank And Walters' label, Go! Discs, was absorbed by its parent company Polygram Records and essentially dissolved. This meant that the *Colours* single was their last release on Go! Discs and, from now on, the band were going to release their music through Keith Cullen's Setanta Records. Being signed to Go! Discs had not been without its problems, as the label wanted to market the Franks as being part of the Britpop phenomenon of the 1990s. This had been a source of friction between the label and the band.

It was through Setanta that the Cork trio released their second album *Grand Parade* (1997). Named after one of Cork city's main thoroughfares, this album made reference to Cork lyrically, but also contained subtle melancholic undertones. A positive vibe and sense of resolve are also projected through the songs on *Grand Parade*. Standout tracks included: *Colours*, their emotive ballad *How Can I Exist* and *Tony Cochrane*, a song that lyrically acknowledges Cork's Barrack Street Band.

During the latter part of the 1990s, the Franks temporarily relocated to New York with a view to making inroads into the lucrative American music market. Here they played venues such as the legendary CBGB's and also moved beyond New York to play venues in Boston, San Francisco, San Diego and Los Angeles. They also played the famous music showcase festival South By Southwest in Austin, Texas.

The Frank And Walters maintained their profile in Cork during the year with a gig in Sir Henry's on May 30, 1997, and a further live show as part of the Millstreet Music Fair '97. Held on the August bank holiday weekend in the north Cork town of Millstreet, and plagued by heavy rain, this event featured artists such as headliner Christy Moore, Steve Earle, The Divine Comedy and Suzanne Vega to name but a few.

The Franks rounded off the year with a sold-out Christmas gig in Sir Henry's on Sunday, December 28. Here the Franks treated the full to capacity Sir Henry's Main Room audience to a lengthy live set with two encores. Their set-list that evening was composed of classic Franks' songs such as *Indian Ocean*, *Colours* and of course their signature hit *After All*. The support slot for the night was filled by local rock act The Shanks.

Hailing from Newmarket in north Cork, The Shanks were originally a school band called The Sick who changed their name after moving to Cork city in 1991. The Shanks featured guitarist and singer Tim Murphy who left around 1992, and the other band members, lead guitarist Eoin 'Stan' O'Sullivan, bass player Mick Hayes and drummer Niall 'Daish' Lynch then reverted to a three-piece. Their band name was inspired by toilet manufacturer Armitage Shanks. Musically, The Shanks' sound could be described as melodic punk rock. During a career stretching from 1991 until they split in 1999, The Shanks released two albums *The Prawn Lawn* (1995) and *Brang* (1999) and a number of singles and EPs. They also toured with The Sultans of Ping F.C. and supported British indie band Suede in Cork City Hall in 1994. Suede had also supported The Frank And Walters in their early days.

Promotional opportunities for *Grand Parade* beckoned in France and Spain during 1998, as the Franks had inked a deal with Spanish-based label Elefant Records, who began releasing their music. While living in New York, Paul had also started writing songs for what would become their third record, *Beauty Becomes More Than Life* (1999).

The band set about recording this album at a studio in Wrexham in Wales. It was produced by Rob Kirwan. With the record largely complete, the Franks returned to Leeside to play what, by then, had become their annual Christmas gig. That year, it took place on Friday, December 18, in Sir Henry's, where they previewed new material to local fans. Support on the night was provided by local indie band Trampoline. Led by Paul's younger brother, Leo Linehan Jnr., Trampoline frequently acted as a support act for the Franks. Fronted by Leo, the band also featured drummer David Forde, Stephen Byrne on guitar and Gerard Murphy on bass. This local indie outfit was active in the Cork rock scene between 1996 and 2000.

The Frank And Walters recruited a new member in 1999 in the form of Manchester keyboardist Sarah de Courcy. She joined after the recording of the band's third album and made her Cork debut with the Franks at a show on June 4, 1999. Released in the summer of 1999, *Beauty Becomes More Than Life* featured thirteen tracks and was something of an experimental album for the band in terms of its dance rhythms and production. Standout tracks included *Plenty Times*, *Something Happened To Me* and *Time We Said Goodnight*.

Again this album was well-received by critics with the *NME* branding it 'One of the lost classics for the twenty-first century', while in Ireland, *Hot Press* described the record as 'this year's first essential slice of guitar pop'. Buoyed by a warm critical response, the Franks set about touring, taking in destinations in France and Spain.

In November, the band lifted *Plenty Times* as a single, which was released with two b-sides, *Open Up* and a cover version of *Falling Out Of Love*, which was originally a song written by American singer-songwriter Stephin Merritt. In December, the Franks played their traditional Christmas concert at the Old Oak in Cork to a full capacity crowd.

Early in 2000, the Franks released their second single from *Beauty Becomes More Than Life*. *Something Happened To Me* was an eerily infectious song, which remains popular among many of their local fans. This single release included two other tracks: *Take Me Through This Life* (remixed by Kevin Shields of My Bloody Valentine fame) and *An Elegant Chaos*.

The band's next long-player was to prove their final album of new material on Setanta Records. In late 2000, The Frank And Walters released *Glass*. Recorded in Cork, and again produced by Rob Kirwan, this album was a genuine departure from their previous output. Sonically, the album was a fusion of influences such as New Order and Joy Division, and more modern electro acts such as Ladytron. *Glass* incorporated elements of downbeat electronica and a variety of dance music styled rhythms.

After recording had been completed, keyboardist Sarah de Courcy departed the band. Her only contribution to the record can be found on the opening track *Underground*.

Unlike its predecessor, their fourth album acquired mixed reviews from critics, although it was awarded 'Pop CD Of The Week' by well-respected British newspaper *The Guardian*.

Standout tracks on *Glass* included *Underground*, *New York* and *Talking About You*. Sadly, *Glass* met with a negative reaction from the record-buying public and risked alienating fans of the Franks who had expected their trademark happy guitar-based indie anthems.

In January 2001, The Frank And Walters released *Underground* as a single. It was accompanied by a video for the title track, the b-side *Pistons* and a remix of *Simple Times*. Despite the fact that *Underground* was mixed by Flood, whose previous production credits included U2 and Nick Cave And The Bad Seeds, its release failed to make an impact on the charts.

The Cork band continued to tour in 2001, playing Berlin on St Patrick's Day and later in the year supporting Paul Weller in Waterford. They played their traditional Christmas gig in The Savoy Theatre in Cork supported by the Cork indie act Fred.

Clearly affected by the commercial failure of *Glass*, Franks' gigs became fewer and fewer as they receded from the live circuit. In 2002, a glimmer of hope came when a 'Best of' compilation record was issued by Setanta, which was well-received and reminded music fans of former glories.

However, in 2003, Niall Linehan informed his fellow band members that he was departing The Frank And Walters to focus on the Linehan family restaurant.[59] This event brought the band, as a live and recording entity, to a halt and it looked like the only thing left to write about the Franks was a suitable epitaph. Yet, all was not lost!

---

[59] The Linehan family restaurant is Currans Restaurant, located at 6 Adelaide Street in Cork.

## CHAPTER ELEVEN

# HOW CAN I EXIST

[The Frank And Walters]

MÉTISSE

Former Real Mayonnaize lynchpin Skully and ex-Porcelyn Tears frontwoman Ann Redmond had worked hard with their Cork-based band The Chapter House during the latter part of the 1980s. However, they came to a crossroads that many musicians reach - whether to continue their music careers or settle into routine nine-to-five jobs.

The Chapter House also featured drummer Paul Moore who joined Real Mayonnaize following the untimely death of original drummer Dave Rudd. In Ireland, the group had achieved a good measure of success. Looking back on their career, Skully admits:

> We were the *2FM Hot Press* band of 1986, but we just released singles and never released an album. We should have had an album out, but we were always aspiring to get a record deal and get a record company to pay for it. We appeared on every single [Irish] TV programme including *The Late Late Show* and the only thing that didn't happen for us was that we didn't get a deal. We went as far as we could in Ireland. So, like a lot of other bands, we just folded and went our separate ways.

Today a band can release an album relatively easily in Ireland with the cottage industry that is now so prevalent, but for The Chapter House it was much harder. Back then, national radio would not play an album unless it was handed to them by an established record company. This prevented many bands from forging lengthy careers and made it hard to break out of Ireland before the arrival of the Internet.

While there had been plenty of highlights for Ann Redmond during her time with The Chapter House, she decided to leave Cork after they split. Ann recalls:

> The highlight was probably winning the *Hot Press* Battle of the Bands. I got voted the 'Best Irish Female Singer' by *Hot Press*. That was alright! But I left Cork in about 1989. I went to London and did a lot of session work and worked with Paul Weller.

Skully too decided to leave Leeside. He turned his back on a career in music to pursue teaching. Ultimately, this career change failed to satisfy the Corkman, as he reflects:

> I ran away to France with a French woman and started teaching English. I was living the life of Riley there, but I got fed up with it and felt there must be more to life than teaching. I got on a train in a really bad mood. I went through Paris in the middle of the night and I was sitting on the train looking out the window at all these millions and millions of lives flashing past. I really didn't want to be insignificant in this world. I just thought to myself, 'How can I touch every single one of these people in every single one of those little windows?' The only way I could think of doing that was with music. So I decided to go home to Ireland. When I got back, I just took out my synthesizer for the first time in six or seven years and went back to work.

Skully achieved greater success with his next musical incarnation, Métisse, a unique musical partnership, which he formed in 1997. Having begun his musical journey at a time when punk rock was becoming a major force in Cork rock circles, Skully now gravitated towards world music and potentially a more lucrative existence. Discussing this pivotal moment in his career, he reveals:

> I got the money to make some decent noises. It started to work and I was getting guidance from people in London. Then I met Aïda Bredou in Toulouse in France and we put Métisse together and we went off to London. Basically, the first time I ever got a positive reaction from a record company was when Aïda and I came together.

As Aïda was born in the Ivory Coast and was of African extraction, the pair devised the name Métisse for their duo. 'It means mixture in French. When you describe somebody who is a mixture between a black person and a white person in French, it is this beautiful word métisse,' explains Skully.

Métisse made their live debut playing a gig in Connolly's of Leap. Through the fusion of Skully's electronic studio wizardry and Aïda's versatile yet haunting vocal talent, the pair impressed many within the echelons of the international music industry. A big confidence boost came before they had even acquired a record deal, when they signed a worldwide publishing deal with Sony Music Publishing. They later signed a record deal with Telstar Records. This provided Métisse with the necessary financial support to establish an international profile. The group enjoyed both exposure and success and rose to international prominence through the dance music scene. Their debut single *Sousoundé* reached number 4 in the UK dance chart. A Freq Nasty re-mixed version of *Sousoundé* was used on New Year's Eve in Dublin's Point Depot to welcome the arrival of the new Millennium.

The involvement of a major record company, however, brought added pressures. Telstar and Métisse had conflicting views regarding how best to market the group and this ultimately resulted in both parties going their separate ways. Skully and Aïda then made the brave decision to buy back their debut album *My Fault* from Telstar. Upon release, the duo dedicated the title track of their album, which was also released as a single, to anyone who had suffered from domestic violence.

Buying back their debut record proved to be an intelligent move, which led to greater success. Madonna selected the Métisse song *Boom Boom Ba*, from this album, for the soundtrack to her film *The Next Best Thing* (2000), which reached number 1 in the USA Billboard soundtrack album chart. In France, *Boom Boom Ba* made it to number 2 in the French singles chart. This was followed by multiple high-profile soundtrack offers, which allowed the pair to have their music featured in a wide range of television programmes including *ER* and *The Bill*, and also on compilation records. Métisse made the shrewd decision to license their first album in individual territories around the world. This move yielded real dividends for the group allowing them greater control over their long-player.

In 2007, Métisse released their second album entitled *Nomah's Land*. They had two tracks, *Boom Boom Ba* and *Nomah's Land*, featured in the hit US television series *Dead Like Me* after they were selected by Police drummer and soundtrack composer Stewart Copeland. *Boom Boom Ba* was also featured in a film version of *Dead Like Me* called *Life After Death* (2009).

While Métisse were on hiatus, Skully released his eagerly awaited solo album *Without A Voice* (2007) and this was soon followed by his album *Irish Makeover* (2008), which saw the Crosshaven-based producer recruit and collaborate with emerging talent in an effort to bravely reinterpret and revamp classic Irish folk songs. Musicians who featured on this record included Cork troubadour and rising star Mick Flannery, Cork songstress Annette Buckley and Dubliner Myles O'Reilly from the band Juno Falls. In 2009, Métisse began work on their third album and the next phase of their career.

## NINE WASSIES FROM BAINNE

Giordaí Ua Laoghaire, another veteran of the punk rock era in Cork returned to the fold in the early 1990s with a new group called Nine Wassies From Bainne.[60] During the 1980s, Ua Laoghaire had travelled to Central America on a voyage of discovery. This had a profound effect on him and his musical output. Giordaí remembers:

> I was working in the Cork County Council and I got stuck in that loop for a while. Musically, I did some stuff with Roger Gregg; he's a playwright and director. He was American but he was based in Cork. So I got a few jobs doing music for plays, which I liked and then I did a bit of stuff with a guy called Stano. He was this unusual Dublin character who made these strange records and I ended up playing on a few tracks on his first few albums. Then I went to Central America - Mexico down to Nicaragua and all those countries - in

---

[60] Wassie is a Cork slang word meaning wasp.

the mid-1980s and came back somewhat culturally and politically out of step with my previous persona. Central America at the time was a linguistic and political hot house. You had the Contras, the whole business with Nicaragua, Guatemala and El Salvador, the varying juntas. There were a lot of Europeans living there who were working in Nicaragua, who were questioning me about Ireland. These people were far more politically aware and were asking me loads of questions about Ireland, the north of Ireland, politics, culture, music and language. I came out of the same culture as everybody else and I didn't know anything about it really, except for the intuitive things you soak up. So when I came back, I literarily acquainted myself with everything I could on all matters of Irish culture, like Irish literature, the Irish language and everything else.

Returning to Leeside, Giordaí found it difficult to readjust after his adventures and experiences abroad:

I suffered a culture shock when I came back to Cork. In my naïvety, I thought that I would suffer a culture shock when I got to Mexico, but what happens is you actually start adapting to the new environment and, very quickly, you start getting into the vibe of it and don't realise that you are changing and that you have changed phenomenally.

In Cork, Giordaí returned to music and formed a very unusual band called Soon along with fellow musicians Martin Vallely, Tony O'Sullivan and Art Lorrigan. Giordaí recalls:

It produced five or six really bizarre songs. We went to Sulán Studios in Baile Bhúirne [Ballyvourney] and recorded a demo there. The singer was very gifted. I mean he was a stunning talent called Tony O'Sullivan. He had the most amazing voice! The band was fairly good musically but it was a bit odd. We had a song called *Fadó, Fadó* and it could be construed to be minimalist, African, Philip Glass type stuff. We played at a *Hot Press* Battle of the Bands competition, where people either loved it or hated it. Tony had an operatic voice. He really had a stunning voice, but Soon was a difficult environment to work in. It was very much in that spadgy tradition, but it was operatic.

However, Soon was not to last and Giordaí pursued his music through another act with an equally odd name. He came up with the name for his avant-garde band Nine Wassies From Bainne during a chance conversation in The Long Valley bar on Cork's Winthrop Street. He explains:

Occasionally, people thought that the name was a conscious effort to be wacky. But it actually happened very naturally. I was inside in The Long Valley with a guy called Paul Drohan who is a very good visual artist from Waterford and has a very droll, dour sense of humour. He is well into his music. I would say this was 1992. We were with this young guy from Tramore who definitely loved his heavy metal. There was a great slagging going on. It was one of those wacky conversations: 'Did you know that there are nine lovely lassies from Bandon?' "I was in Bandon and that can't be true." 'There was nine lovely wassies from Bandon alright.' I was walking down the street and thought 'nine lovely wassies from Bandon' that would be a mad name for a band. That's how it happened. I just changed

Bandon to bainne. And when I said nine lovely wassies from bainne, I fell around laughing. Nine lovely wassies from bainne and then Nine Wassies From Bainne. It doesn't mean anything and it means something. That's bizarre! It doesn't mean anything in English or in Irish. It doesn't mean anything!

Nine Wassies From Bainne formed in 1993 and contrary to public perception the band were based in Dublin. Giordaí explains:

> Occasionally, when we would get a bit of press, the lie that we were from Cork was repeated over and over again. The Dublin media used to say we were from Cork but in Cork they didn't know who we were. I was living in Dorset Street in Dublin when I formed the band. There was a bass player called Enda Doyle who was actually a guitarist. I couldn't get anybody to play bass with me in Dublin. It wasn't very easy to say, 'Well I kind of want to start a band called Nine Wassies From Bainne and sing strange songs in Irish and be influenced by Frank Zappa and John Zorn!' Later, Enda was replaced by Eddie Lee on bass guitar and then Michael Mullen was our final bass player. Our drummer was Peter O'Kennedy who played with The Golden Horde. His connection with Ireland was only tenuous and he had no connection with Cork. But he liked it because he used to play in Cork with The Golden Horde. He thought it was mad! But the singer with the Wassies at the time was called Dave Murray and he was also from Cork. He's actually an actor now.

Giordaí linked up with his friend and former Microdisney

bandmate Cathal Coughlan when the Wassies toured with him. Giordaí recalls they 'were sailing away pretty well in terms of energy levels. But Cathal was going through a bad period just after Fatima Mansions failed to take off as a commercial entity. We were friendly with Cathal and I suggested that he come over and stay in my place and we could do a bunch of gigs together.'

Cathal needed to find a piano player before he could commit to touring, so Giordaí helped him recruit a suitable pianist. Giordaí recalls:

> I knew a piano player called Dawn Kenny, so I asked her. She had never heard of Cathal before that. Dawn was from Limerick, but I met her in Dublin. She is a gifted musician and songwriter in her own right. So Cathal sent her over his music with all his chords written out. When he came over, he moved into our rehearsal room and we rehearsed his songs for two weeks.

When the tour took place, the Wassies and Cathal played Cobh, the Kino cinema in Cork and two gigs in Whelan's in Dublin. Reflecting on how the tour went, Giordaí says:

> The Cobh and the Whelan's gigs were amazing. The Kino gig was desperate, but I think none of us have ever been happy about playing in Cork. I personally never felt good about playing there because I'm too nervous. I might do an amazing gig in Dublin and Cathal would definitely be like that. You would come to Cork and feel nervous and do a bad gig because it's almost like there are too many people willing you to play a bad one. You have a lot of history there. During the course of the gig in Cobh, Dawn was blown away by Cathal's

chord progressions and the quality of the song-writing. The way he puts chords and melodies and harmonies together is genuinely stunning. Dawn couldn't get over how good the stuff was. I mean the quality is there!

The Wassies released their first and only album *Ciddy Hall* in 1998 on Numnum Records before going their separate ways that same year. This highly original genre-defying album featured a number of standout tracks such as *Fan, Mr & Mrs Lapsipah* and *The Wassie In Me*.

*Ciddy Hall* received critical acclaim. *Hot Press* journalist Peter Murphy awarded it nine out of ten in a December 9, 1998 review. Remarking that 'the group are coming from a long and perfectly disrespectful lineage', he called it a 'gloriously audacious record'. Murphy commented that the song *Mr & Mrs Lapsipah* evoked 'those sadly missed Lee monkeys Stump, while the unquiet spirit of Cathal Coughlan haunts the more sabre-toothed moments' and added that 'characters like the Wassies invariably create their own reality, wherever they lay their hi-hats. We're lucky to have 'em.'

'The Wassies thing nearly killed me!' reflects Giordaí. 'When a project ends and unless it takes off and becomes this big success, there is an anti-climax.' The Nine Wassies From Bainne song *The Day Mustrad Got Death* currently features as the theme music to the satirical *Langerland TV* programme on RTÉ Two.

## THE CORK MUSIC RESOURCE CO-OP

Traditionally, resources and adequate support for young musicians and bands has been an issue in Cork. In the 1990s, the Cork Music Resource Co-op was established by a group of like-minded individuals to try and rectify this. One of the key people involved in this worthy cause was Cork rock enthusiast and local printer Jim Morrish. Before helping to set-up the Cork Music Resource Co-op, Jim had already worked to produce a number of local music fanzines including *Choc-A-Bloc* with Morty McCarthy.

In 1994, the Cork Music Resource Co-op was officially founded and provided a number of support services, while also helping to create opportunities for bands and musicians on Leeside. It was originally based at Thompson House on MacCurtain Street, but later moved to offices above Singer's Corner on Washington Street. Jim Morrish recounts how the co-op first came into being:

> Morty McCarthy, Emmet Greene and myself put money away each week to build two band rooms in Gerald Griffin Street in a disused butcher's abattoir. Quiet man Paul the carpenter built them for us for free but we paid for the materials and soundproofing. I think Morty lent us one of his old drum kits and an amp, while other folk donated various bits and pieces. Our idea was to eventually have something going along the lines of the Nerve Centre in Derry or the Warzone Centre in Belfast.
>
> Emmet and I went to Northern Ireland to a meeting of co-ops and groups from around the country. People like Sean O'Neill [of The Undertones] from Derry and numerous others were there. Angela Dorgan worked in the Triskel Arts Centre at the time and was au fait with all the arts scene lingo and the administration side of things that we'd be crap at, so I asked her would she be interested in coming on board to look into setting up

a FÁS scheme to help the co-op get some funding and provide employment. Eventually, we got funding, so we had between fourteen and seventeen people involved: giving music lessons, working in administration, working in graphic design and looking after the band rooms etc.

Among the people involved on the FÁS scheme were Paul McDermott (now on the board of *Dublin City FM*), Paul Rudden from local rock band Treehouse, Emmet Greene of Bandicoot Promotions, Brian O'Shaughnessy from Dotdotdot Records and the band Philip K. Dick, Jim Clancy, manager of The Shanks and Roy O'Driscoll from the Cork group The Orange Fettishes.

The band rooms at Gerald Griffin Street on the city's northside were important assets for the music community and helped sustain many young local rock acts. One band that were regular users of this facility were The V-Necks, later renamed The Young Offenders. Lead singer with The V-Necks, Kieran MacFeely (brother of Sultans of Ping bass player Alan MacFeely) explains the origins of the band:

> We formed while sitting on a very cold wall in Douglas in Cork. It feels like we spent our whole teenage existence sitting on cold walls....waiting. We formed in about 1993, in our heads, but we didn't actually play for a while after that....maybe 1995. I formed the band with my friend Steve Hackett and school friends Ian Hurley and Brian Dunlea.

Kieran describes his band's musical influences as being: '*Ziggy Stardust* era Bowie, *Parklife* era Blur, Buzzcocks and 1950s musicals. Standard teenage boy stuff really!' The V-Necks were famously offered a record deal by major label Columbia Records in the latter part of the 1990s and this news spread like wildfire through the local music community. However, upon moving to London, they changed their name from The V-Necks to The Young Offenders. Kieran explains why this happened:

> I think there was another band in London called The V-Necks but ....the real reason was that the MD of Sony UK suggested the name. He was offering us an awful lot of money but he hinted that he would 'very much like it' if we changed our name to The Young Offenders. We had a song called The Ballad Of The Young Offenders and that's where he got the idea. We really wanted to get out of Cork, so we didn't agonise over it for too long. It was one of many lessons I learned about the music industry at that time....never listen to anyone. They are always wrong and you are always right.

Arguably the most successful new Cork rock act to emerge in the late 1990s, The Young Offenders released a number of singles and performed at the Glastonbury 1998 music festival, as well as the V98 and T In The Park music festivals in Britain. They made their TV debut when they performed their song *That's Why We Lose Control* on the British television programme *TFI Friday*, which was broadcast on Channel 4 and hosted by Chris Evans.

The band released *That's Why We Lose Control* as their debut single, which was followed by the *Science Fiction* EP and the single *Pink And Blue*, which was included on the *Melody Maker* compilation *1998 The Album*. While The Young Offenders did record an album, it was later shelved and soon the band just disintegrated.

Looking back on his time as frontman with the group, Kieran reflects on one unfortunate incident that deprived him of meeting two big names from the world of rock 'n' roll. He recalls:

> We were invited to a party by Aerosmith. The night before, I went to my local and got very drunk indeed whilst doing the pub quiz. The next day, I was so ill that I was bedridden, so I couldn't go to the party. Steve Hackett went and was chatting to Aerosmith's Steven Tyler and Joe Perry all night, while I was at home sick as a pike. A beautiful story that I think sums up my ability to snatch defeat from the jaws of victory whenever given half a chance... didn't win the pub quiz either.

Another supportive gesture made by the Cork Music Resource Co-op was the release of a ten-track CD, *Ten By Ten: Volume One* (1995), featuring the best local unsigned bands of the time. These included Manhole, Inhaler and The Orange Fettishes. One co-op member, Paul McDermott, remembers its launch:

> The co-op CD was a pretty big deal at the time. There was a big buzz around town with all the bands trying to record demos to get chosen for it. There was free recording time for all the bands to record for the CD and a big launch gig in both Sir Henry's and Whelan's in Dublin. I remember The Orange Fettishes played support to Squeeze in a sold-out Connolly Hall and then had to rush over to Henry's to play at the launch.

A number of musicians worked for the co-op providing valuable services to the Cork music community. According to Paul, other people on the original Community Employment scheme included:

# CORK ROCK

Kieran Curtin guitarist with Flywheel, a cork band that got a deal in Sweden and went off to Stockholm to record an album and quite good it was too; and Tim O'Connell, a drummer with various bands around town. He was a very decent guy, who once played drums for The Buzzards [a UCC garage rock band] supporting Dublin band The Mary Janes in The Forum and spent the entire Mary Janes' set standing behind them disassembling his ridiculously large drum kit. Mic Christopher of The Mary Janes was not impressed and the crowd were nearly on the floor laughing away at the scene. Another really nice guy who worked on the scheme was Alan Murphy - guitarist with the late 1980s Cork band The How And Why Insects.

The co-op had ambitious plans to expand and wanted to establish fully equipped band rooms in a more central location on MacCurtain Street. Unfortunately, this failed to materialise. Jim Morrish explains:

> We applied and were approved for a grant of IR£50,000 from the Enterprise Board to build proper band rooms on MacCurtain Street. However, the way these grants work is that we had to put up IR£50,000 of our own money too. My dad passed away around that particular time, so I had to put all my savings and time into the family business, so we were never able to draw down the grant, one of my biggest regrets in life. My accountant was going to sell us a building on MacCurtain Street for a discounted price as he was a very good friend of my dad's and then we were going to move the co-op offices in there and have band rooms, etc. Now every time I drive past it, I feel ill! We came so close to getting it.

There were also personnel changes in the co-op. Paul McDermott explains:

> Angela Dorgan left the co-op to move to Dublin and establish the FMC-The Federation of Music Collectives. This was a federation of all the music co-ops from around the country. Basically, it was funded by the Arts Council to try and create a network of music centres and foster a sense of community between different scenes in different cities. This was very much what Jim, Morty, Emmet and everyone had originally intended. It has subsequently become First Music Contact (FMC). When Angela left, the co-op was run by a girl called Leslie Ryan.

In early 1996, the co-op opted for a name change, restyling itself The Cork Music Resource Centre. This corresponded with the physical move of the organisation to the appropriately named Singer's Corner. Their new location was right in the heart of the city centre and very accessible to most young local musicians. Discussing their rebranding, Leslie Ryan maintains that: 'The renaming wasn't a big deal. The reason was that it was set up as a co-op in theory but legally it wasn't a cooperative. So we changed it to Resource Centre because that is what it was essentially.'

The Cork Music Resource Centre organised showcase gigs in The Lobby Bar on Union Quay on Monday nights for unsigned local bands. These also provided the centre with an income. The bands would play for free with admission set at a reasonable IR£2.00, which would go towards the centre. Leslie reveals:

> We did Monday nights in The Lobby for a good couple

of years and we also branched off and did Tuesday nights in The Hairy Lemon [formerly on Oliver Plunkett Street]. I think it was Annette Buckley who set up the Tuesday singer-songwriter night in The Hairy Lemon. So we were running two gig nights a week - one specifically for singer-songwriters and the other for guitar bands.

Having a facility such as the Resource Centre made a huge difference locally, as it helped to level the playing-field for bands in the city. Providing access to resources was a key factor that improved the health of the local rock music scene and also encouraged musicians to co-operate with one another. Leslie explains:

> The centre helped by giving access to practice rooms, gigs and national organisations. It also helped with the representation of musicians. At that time, there were a lot of really interesting bands around Cork. The Music Resource Centre became a one-stop shop for all the A&R people from record companies in England and Europe. That was really important. They liked the non-industry setting of the Resource Centre and the home-grown feel to it.

Some of the local bands that the Music Resource Centre had helped took part in the *Evening Echo's Downtown* Battle of the Bands competition, which ran between April 2 and May 21, 1998, at The Brewery Tap's Attic Bar on Leitrim Street in Cork. While the surprise winner of the contest was a band called Monster On A Bus, other acts that took part included the Britpop and U2 influenced Rakastan; The Herbivores, fronted by Sean Murphy; Backtrack from Mahon; And The Rest In

Jellies, winners of the Crazyhorse Band of the Year competition 1997; and Trampoline, who won the CIT vs. UCC Battle of the Bands competition earlier that year.[61]

In late 1998, the Cork Music Resource Centre was forced to close after funding from a state agency was cut. Leslie recalls:

> It was primarily funded by FÁS through a community employment scheme. That is where it got all of its revenue funding. I suppose you had the beginnings of the Celtic Tiger when FÁS were changing their policies on what they were funding and how they were funding them. The arts organisations were probably the first to really get hit by that. Unfortunately, the Music Resource Centre was one of the first to get cut. So it suffered from a change of policy by FÁS. The music co-op/centre had been running for over four years. Unfortunately, the centre was too dependent on FÁS as an institution for funding to be able to sustain itself after funding was withdrawn.

CYCLEFLY

While the Cork Music Resource Co-op was helping the vibrant rock music scene in the city, a band in Cork county was creating quite a stir. Based in the Midleton area of east Cork, and originally called Dogabone, Cyclefly was a five-piece alternative rock band that formed in 1995 and harboured influences such as Black Sabbath, Tool and David Bowie. Musically, this group blended elements of metal and grunge and has been compared to US band Smashing Pumpkins. Cyclefly was centred around brothers Ciaran and Declan O'Shea, Ciaran being the guitarist and Declan the vocalist. It

---

[61] The band name Rakastan is the Finnish word for love.

also featured the all-French rhythm section of bassist Christian Montagne and drummer Jean Michel Cavallo, with Italian born guitarist Nono Presta completing the line-up. During their career, the band released two EPs: *Dogabone* (1995) and *Cyclefly* (1998). Having played a series of showcase gigs in London, the group signed to Radioactive Records. Cyclefly decamped to California for the recording of their eleven-track debut album *Generation Sap* (1999), produced and mixed by former Skunk Anansie producer Sylvia Massey. *Generation Sap* was followed by a second album entitled *Crave* (2002). *Crave* featured a track called *Karma Killer*, which included vocals from Chester Bennington of American rock band Linkin Park. In 2003, Cyclefly broke up. The following year, Declan and Ciaran O'Shea formed a short-lived group called Hueman with guitarist Aidan Lee, drummer Kieran O'Neill and former Cyclefly bassist Christian Montagne. After Hueman split, Declan O'Shea and Christian Montagne formed Mako. They released their fourteen-track debut LP, *Living On Air*, on Drive Records in 2007.

RUBYHORSE

Over the years, many Cork rock acts opted for a strategy of first trying to develop a large following at home in Cork and then, through touring and recording, they would attempt to attract the attention of the record industry in the hope of getting their 'big break'. This approach tended to be flawed, as many performers ended up playing to audiences heavily laden with their friends and associates and thus avoided getting objective feedback from the public.

In the 1990s, Bishopstown rock band Rubyhorse decided to break this mould by moving to Boston and leaving their comfort zone behind.[62] While this approach brought obvious risks, it was to yield dividends.

Taking their name from a song by The Wonder Stuff, Rubyhorse were a five-piece rock band, which featured guitarist Joe Philpott, lead singer Dave Farrell, bass player Declan Lucey, keyboardist Owen Fegan and drummer Gordon Ashe. Ashe also played drums with local group Burning Embers.

Like so many other acts, Rubyhorse had its roots in Bishopstown secondary school Coláiste an Spioraid Naoimh. It was here that the group first formed. Guitarist Joe Philpott recalls:

> We were all originally from Bishopstown. I moved out to Ballincollig when I was about ten. But I went to school in Bishopstown. We met in Coláiste an Spioraid Naoimh as we were in the same class. I was in Rubyhorse since I was thirteen, as we formed when we were in first or second year in secondary school.

Like musician John Spillane, Joe praises the efforts made by Coláiste an Spioraid Naoimh teacher Tony Doherty, who supported live music in the school:

> We had a really cool teacher in Tony Doherty. He encouraged the arts. There was a lot of acting as well as music. This was in the 1980s. There was a little stage with lights and everything. Our very first gig as Rubyhorse was in the school gym. It was packed and it was fecking mental. I met Paul Linehan and Ashley Keating from The Frank And Walters who were in the audience going: 'Jesus this is massive!' It was a good school and they provided for us, in the sense that we could rehearse there and do shows.

[62] In the early part of their career, Rubyhorse were known locally as Ruby Horse *(two words)*.

Having established themselves locally, Rubyhorse released their debut album *A Lifetime In One Day* (1995). Standout tracks on the album included *Devil And The Deep Blue Sea*, *Horses* and the song *Radio Daze*. An interesting dimension to this album was how it was financed. 'Ger Kiely from The Old Oak is a great supporter of local music,' explains Joe. 'When Rubyhorse started out, he was brilliant to us. He helped us out with our first album. It was literarily Ger Kiely, The Washington Inn, Gorby's nightclub and The Maltings Bar that paid for it at the time.'

The songs on Rubyhorse's debut album were certainly warm and catchy. However, mainstream success still eluded them. One possible reason for Rubyhorse failing to take off in Ireland during this period was that their music veered more towards American influences and was at odds with the then dominant force in music, which was Britpop. In the summer of 1995, Cork played host to the three-day music festival Féile '95, which was dominated by Britpop groups.[63]

A perception has existed in the record industry that Cork is a great place to find quirky rock acts but, musically, Rubyhorse did not come from that tradition. Joe admits:

> We just weren't those kind of quirky individuals. You can't fake what you are. If you do, you will be found out. We were what we were. We got slated in Ireland for being who we were. I look at some people in bands and I've absolutely nothing in common with them. To me,

---

[63] Féile '95 was staged at Páirc Uí Chaoimh in Cork city by promoters MCD. This summer music festival took place on a bank holiday weekend from Friday, August 4 until Sunday, August 6. The line-up included The Prodigy, Blur, The Stone Roses, Elastica and Kylie Minogue. Interestingly, The Verve were announced as part of the bill but never actually played Cork as they split up shortly before Féile '95.

it is like whatever blows your hair back. We were just a bunch of mates who loved to play music. We didn't really know what our music was. We had no idea if it was quirky or not. I think we just loved the adventure of music and what it could do for you. I think that was always our thing. Where could we take this? What we listened to musically changed almost every two years.

Rubyhorse made the decision to look to America in the hope of furthering their career. 'It's funny actually because we couldn't get arrested in Cork, but we got massive attention in America,' says Joe. They played their farewell gig in Cork at the Crazy Horse Saloon on Washington Street on New Year's Eve 1996 and left for the USA on January 13, 1997. This decision proved to be the right one and the band were about to go on a rock 'n' roll rollercoaster ride. Joe explains:

We were very young at the time, in our early twenties, and we were just going for a bit of adventure with no real plans. Our album in Ireland did fine but we were either going to pack the whole thing in or just try something absolutely ridiculous and mad! So we decided to head off with no real plan. They say the Irish conquered the world with a piece of paper and a phone number, so that is kind of what we did when we landed in Boston. There, we were overwhelmed with the reaction to the band. It was actually very hard for us to keep up with what was going on. We arrived in January 1997 and by January 1998, we had secured the biggest record deal for a debut band in America and a manager called Tim Collins who had managed Aerosmith.

Rubyhorse gigged relentlessly and toured America and beyond

in an effort to bring their own brand of indie rock to the masses. The band was strong in spirit and determination, and their big departure across the Atlantic mimicked the old well-trodden Irish immigrant trail; but this was entirely unplanned. In Boston, the group had to work hard, but quickly built-up a solid fanbase after gaining a residency at the Irish bar The Burren, where they played every Thursday night for sixty weeks. The relative stability that this residency brought provided an opportunity to branch out. In 1998, they released a four-track EP entitled *Mini Hummer*. Within a year of arriving, Rubyhorse had picked up three Boston Music Awards and a contest soon ensued between record companies to sign the Cork ex-pats.

Understandably, this was a welcome scenario for the band members. 'Obviously, the record deal was a big thing for us,' Joe enthuses. 'At the time, there were sixteen labels in existence, though I think there are only three now. We were courted by pretty much all of them.' The band attracted the attention of Interscope Records and a deal was struck. They moved to Los Angeles and recorded a big-budget album with producer Paul Fox. However, this was to prove fruitless, as the record was not released.

Rubyhorse's next release was an independent LP aptly named *How Far Have You Come?* (2000), which the band toured across America. With a new-found status, the group signed to Island Records and released *Rise* in 2002, which came complete with a cameo slide-guitar solo by the late ex-Beatle George Harrison on the song *Punchdrunk*.

Getting Harrison was quite a coup for the band. Joe explains: 'That really was such a fluke. We wrote a song and felt it had a Beatles flavour to it. So we sent his management company a copy and they passed it on to him.' Harrison took to the tune in a big way - whistling it around his house - and he offered to play his legendary slide guitar on the song. Having George Harrison play on your album would be a serious achievement for anyone, but Rubyhorse didn't publicise this fact too much. Joe Philpott explains the reason why:

> People often ask us why we didn't capitalise on it in a more obvious way. The truth of the matter is George actually died around the time the album came out and we just felt it would be a bit cheap to put it out in that way. It would have been the obvious thing to do at the time and it was suggested to us by the label as a possibility, but we just felt it was such a special thing for him to do. He actually did it for union fees. I think we paid him twenty-five dollars. We had to pay him something to make it legitimate. So he only took a union fee and he didn't ask for any royalties or anything like that. It was a really nice thing for him to do, so I suppose, out of respect, we decided not to release it [as a single].

*Rise* also included the single *Sparkle*, which charted at a very respectable twelve on the American Billboard chart. The group took to American TV screens with appearances on the *David Letterman Show*, *Late Night With Conan O'Brien* and *Good Morning America*. Joe has vivid memories of the Letterman appearance, recalling:

> We were in the middle of a whirlwind tour, on our way from Chicago to Milwaukee, when we got a telephone call saying go back to Chicago and get on a plane, you are on Letterman tomorrow night. Out of all our appearances, Letterman was definitely the best buzz. Filmed in the Ed Sullivan Theatre, you just see photos

of everyone who has played there in the past, like The Beatles, who played their first performance in America there, so from that point of view, it was a bit nerve-wrecking. Being on Conan O'Brien was much easier. His parents are Irish and talking to him was like talking to a Corkman.

The fortunes of Rubyhorse took a dive when they parted company with Island Records and were faced with some tough soul-searching regarding their future. Joe's view of major labels is that:

> They can sign you and then screw it up for you and they can have serious difficulties with letting bands grow. All they care about is the next pay cheque. Smaller labels are great because they give bands more breathing space to mature. I think the days of major labels making and breaking bands are over.

During this period, keyboardist Owen Fegan decided to hang up his spurs. Joe admits:

> It is a real commitment being in a band as you are away from home a lot and it involves an enormous amount of travel. I guess he just wanted to do other things. We had moved in a more guitar-driven direction and this might also have had a bearing on Owen's decision.

Never short of determination, the band regrouped and rose above the chaos that threatened to engulf them. In 2003, they released their next album, appropriately named *Goodbye To All That*, the title possibly hinting at their shaky relationship with Island Records. This album was released on the Brash Music label based in Atlanta. The record garnered critical acclaim and featured the standout tracks *Fell On Bad Days* and *Long Time Coming*. After extensive touring in support of the album, the band parted ways. Although, Rubyhorse never officially confirmed that they had split up, the evidence suggests that they have. Joe says:

> To be honest about it, it was a bit mad! It was great and we have very, very fond memories. Who knows what the future holds for Rubyhorse? At this point, we are all just happy doing what we're doing. We all just have a chuckle every Christmas when we meet and look at each other and go, 'Jesus! That was mad wasn't it!'

In 2005, Joe Philpott formed a new band called Jodavino with brother and sister duo Joe and Aoibheann Carey and fellow musicians Humphrey Murphy and Dave Ryan. They released their debut album *Deep End* in 2006 and a follow-up long-player *Say It Like It Is* in 2009.

## FREAKSCENE

Cork has produced some of the most popular and unique club nights in Ireland. Local institutions such as Sweat, in Sir Henry's on a Saturday night, and Mór Disco on a Tuesday night in Zoes (formerly of Caroline Street), caught the imagination of clubbers far beyond Leeside.

However, fans of rock music and its various subgenres were also well catered for thanks to the establishment of the seminal indie alternative club night known as Freakscene. Originally based in Sir Henry's, the first Freakscene was held on Wednesday, January 26, 1994, and, since its inception, it remained a regular fixture of Wednesday nights on Leeside.

Founded by John O'Leary, aka DJ Alan Fadd, who hails

from the Lough area of the city, and his friend Bill Twomey, aka DJ Chicken, Freakscene surpassed their early expectations and became the longest running alternative club night in the country.

John O'Leary explains that they started Freakscene out of real necessity. Both John and Bill had been regulars at Tight, a previous indie club night in Sir Henry's. Held on a Friday night, Tight was run by Philip Healy and lasted for a number of years. After this finished, John and his friend Bill were left in a predicament:

> Tight was a great night. It was gone well over a year before we started Freakscene. Chicken and I definitely got ideas from Philip. I suppose we were going to Tight for about two years. When we set up our club night, it was as a New Year's resolution. Basically, we had nowhere to go and we were getting a bit sick of that. The idea was very simplistic in that we had no long-term plans or great marketing plan. It was basically that I was meant to DJ one week and Chicken would go with our other friends and vice versa. So, when we started, we wanted Friday nights. We didn't want Wednesdays. We were both working. We were basically trying to continue where Tight left off, so as to have somewhere to go ourselves.

Their decision to name their popular club night Freakscene seems to have been an inspired choice, which played a role in its longevity. John admits:

> I can remember walking up South Mall with Chicken and I just suggested that the Dinosaur Jnr song *Freak Scene* would be a good name. We both really loved the

song and we were huge fans of Dinosaur Jnr at the time. Had it been three months later, the club could have been called Cannonball after The Breeders' song or something else. We didn't realise just how marketable a name it was. So it was a bit of good luck. *Freak Scene* was possibly our favourite song at the time and it was a song that used to be played in Tight.

Discussing the early days when they were trying to market their new club night, John indicates that he and Bill managed to incorporate a real DIY aesthetic into the promotional side of Freakscene. 'I can remember the first flyers because ... they were hand drawn and hand written and hand cut.'

Unfortunately, DJ Chicken's involvement in the DJing side of the club night was short-lived, as John O'Leary explains: 'Chicken was working in Limerick when we set it up and he found the travelling hard going. So he pulled out after about six months.'

As well as playing indie/alternative music to the masses in Sir Henry's Main Room, Freakscene later incorporated Danascene, which saw DJ Jenny Glitt and DJ Shirley Sparkle play retro disco tunes in Sir Henry's Back Bar. This element of the club developed a considerable following.

After running Freakscene for a few of years, John established a sister club night on Friday nights called Gigantic, which began in Sir Henry's in 1997. Named after The Pixies' song *Gigantic*, this proved to be a very popular night. As part of Gigantic, Sir Henry's Back Bar played hip-hop music courtesy of John's brother Kevin O'Leary aka DJ Fadd Jnr and DJ Keith Synnott. It also featured a third room where DJ Shirley Sparkle played disco anthems. A number of years later, Gigantic was renamed Planet of Sound after another song by The Pixies.

One big advantage Sir Henry's had over other nightclubs in the city centre was that it had three rooms and therefore could provide more choice than its competitors. This also meant that it could appeal to different audiences simultaneously.

In May 1997, Fadd Promotions made its first foray into live music when they hosted The Frank And Walters for an early gig at Sir Henry's on Friday, May 30. Over the years, John O'Leary has been involved in running gigs in Cork under the moniker of Fadd Promotions. These have included bringing English post-punk band The Fall to Sir Henry's for what was to be an ill-fated gig in the 1990s and Welsh band Super Furry Animals to The Savoy in June 2003. John reflects:

> We brought The Fall to Sir Henry's. They didn't quite break up on stage. Mark E. Smith walked off [the stage] a lot and there was a lot of fighting between the band. The guitarist was literarily kicked out of the band, as in they stopped the bus and threw him out the next day. The Fall gig was our first big gig and our first big loss. It's something we are very proud of.

As well as filling a gap in the market, John O'Leary has to be credited for turning many Leesiders on to the sound of many bands over the years. His DJ sets in Sir Henry's were heavily laden with tracks by groups such as The Pixies, The Stone Roses, Nirvana and Blur, as well as local heroes like The Frank And Walters and The Sultans of Ping.

In the entertainment industry, nothing stays static and the late 1990s was a period of inevitable change. After disagreements between the DJs and the owners of Sir Henry's, there was a mass exodus of DJs, from which the venue never recovered. Freakscene and Planet of Sound departed Sir Henry's, with Freakscene moving to the newly refurbished Savoy on Patrick

Street and Planet of Sound later re-launching in Club FX on Lynch's Street, near the Mardyke.

After a couple of successful years in The Savoy, Freakscene found a new home in Club One on Phoenix Street (now the location of The Crane Lane Theatre) and later in The Qube on Oliver Plunkett Street, which eventually reverted to its original name of Gorby's.

Having wound up Planet of Sound, John launched the Goldsoundz club night on Fridays. It also had a succession of homes, including The Bodega on Cornmarket Street, The Savoy on Patrick's Street and later it took place on Saturday nights at the Liquid Lounge on Marlboro Street.

To help foster a sense of community among his long list of regulars, John established a website, www.freakscene.com, which helped him promote events and communicate with patrons of all his club nights. He also made the generous gesture of promoting local gigs through his website and has assisted many Cork bands through the years.

Discussing the Freakscene website, John stresses just how important it proved to be:

> I'd say it saved the club night. It can be a tough enough old business because it's very cut-throat and there can be a lot of arguing with nightclub owners. Every now and then, I felt that we needed something that would invigorate and challenge us. I had no background in computers and neither did Chicken and again this is where Chicken comes in. He went away and taught himself *HTML* just for something to do. His first project was the Freakscene website. I remember him mentioning that he was thinking of doing a website and asking what did I think and I was like: 'Oh yeah, grand.

Work away!' Next thing it was up and running. Then I thought, God! If he can learn how to do it, I can! Then I took it over and I loved it. I really threw myself into the website and saw the potential of it. It has been a huge help to the club and if we hadn't set up the website, I'm not sure if we would still be going to this day.

Freakscene also went out of its way to organise special events and brought out CDs. John recalls:

We had a photography competition/exhibition called Beautiful Rebels. We did a band photography competition and we brought out two CDs. One was to celebrate our tenth birthday, which was a free CD, and the other was our first commercial release called *Happy Birthday Jesus: The Freakscene Christmas Album* (2006), which featured original Christmas songs by Cork bands.

This release showcased acts such as Niall Connolly, The Girls of Summer, My Evil Ex and The Grunts.

Traditionally, Freakscene's annual birthday celebrations have always been big events with multiple local bands performing on these occasions. John has also organised annual one-off nights, such as the Freakscene Halloween Ball, the Freakscene Christmas Party, the Freakscene New Year's Eve Masquerade Ball and their Sixties/Seventies Night.

Through the years, Freakscene saw off many competitors and remained a constant presence in Cork nightlife. Having respect for their patrons is a key reason why the club night survived for so long. Discussing his own personal highlights, John enthuses:

There were loads and loads of small moments. But

one night that I can remember just feeling really proud was during 2005, when we did our band photography competition. For us, to get involved in something like band photography was well outside our remit. An Bróg were clever, as they picked our launch [date] to be the Monday night of the May bank holiday weekend, when they would be really quiet. Four hundred people turned up and seven bands that had photographs [displayed] played. It was an achievement. There was just a brilliant, brilliant atmosphere in there. It was an offshoot project of Freakscene and Freakscene wasn't even on that night. There was just a brilliant vibe and I remember being really proud of the whole thing that night.

## FREAK FM

While Freakscene flew the flag for alternative music on the dance floors of Cork, a pirate radio station with a name not dissimilar to John O'Leary's famous club night, took to the airwaves in 2000. *Freak FM* was not actually connected to the alternative club, although this has been the source of much speculation in some quarters.

Originally based in Mallow, this pirate radio station broadcast on a number of frequencies such as 107.6, but was mainly on 105.2. *Freak FM* began broadcasting in Mallow in 2000 and moved to Cork in 2001, where it broadcast for a year. It re-emerged in 2004 and broadcast until 2006. Aimee Setter, who worked for the station explains how the name came about. 'It was a lash back at all the names metallers were called such as 'freak' and 'hippie', etc. We thought the name *Freak FM* was appropriate.'

Aimee explains the music policy of *Freak FM*:

> The station started off as a rock, metal, punk station and, in later years, it became more diverse with various genres including rock, metal, punk, drum 'n' bass, soul, hip-hop, psychedelic and various subgenres. We also had some chat shows where people could ring in with personal problems or funny stories. We had a number of DJs in the later years and we had twenty-eight DJs on the go before we were shut down.

Reflecting on how such a venture was funded and what sort of ethos the station espoused, Aimee says:

> The station ran on donations from the DJs. Each DJ paid €5.00 towards maintaining the station and this paid for the rent. We also did some fundraiser gigs, where we involved the under-eighteens. The listeners had great delight in putting a face to the voice and some DJs had huge followings. We all enjoyed the station, though it was hard work! We saw the station as having a vital role in the alternative music community. It was providing a community service. The rewards were the endless texts and listeners and being able to play what you wanted - for us and for the people.

## SIR HENRY'S RIP

Sir Henry's was the centre of gravity around which many Cork bands, music fans, clubbing aficionados and DJs orbited. It was the city's most famous clubbing and live music venue. It had served as a Mecca for music lovers of all tastes and genres, as well as being a focal point for youth culture in the city.

Over the years and through several incarnations, Sir Henry's had played host to many world-renowned rock acts including Nirvana, Sonic Youth, Phil Lynott, Echo And The Bunnymen, My Bloody Valentine, Pavement, Ian Brown, Mercury Rev and Cork bands The Frank and Walters and The Sultans of Ping F.C.

Sir Henry's also showcased some of the best artists from the world of dance music including Laurent Garnier, Goldie, David Holmes, Carl Cox, and Kerri Chandler, to name but a few. The venue's most renowned club night, Sweat, launched in 1988 by Greg Dowling and Shane Johnson, quickly established a cult following both in Cork and far beyond for its superb selection of house music, served up in an eclectic, anything goes atmosphere. Indeed, it was Sweat that established Sir Henry's as one of the nation's premier dance venues.

Two short independent documentaries were made, which focused on the Sir Henry's dance era. *The Cork That House Built* (2006) examined the early days of influential Cork DJs and veterans of Sir Henry's, Stevie G, Greg Dowling, and Shane Johnson, while *Sir Henry's - 120 BPM* (2007) featured interviews with, among others, DJs Jim X Comet, Stevie G and former Sir Henry's manager Seán O'Neill.

While many Cork nightclubs offered standard nights out to a soundtrack of bland cheesy chart music (and, of course, there is nothing wrong with that), Sir Henry's always managed to offer something more. In doing so, it attracted a more distinctive, adventurous and sometimes creative crowd.

After Sir Henry's lost all its big name DJs in late 2000, the club entered a downward spiral and died a slow death. When the DJs left, they took most of the regular customers with them and the club suffered the fatal blow of losing both of its acclaimed club nights. Later, the downstairs area, formerly known as

Rattlesnake Annie's bar, was expanded and converted into The Bakery Bar – a bright but ultimately soulless super-pub. In the long run, this only served to further alienate the previous clientele and ended up drawing a less desirable crowd. The writing was on the wall.

The venue finally closed in late 2002. When this happened, it had an interesting effect on the local rock music scene. Ironically, while Sir Henry's had served as a magnet for many bands to socialise in and play, its demise appeared to actually expand the band scene in the city, making it more progressive. Perhaps this could be attributed to the less cliquey atmosphere that soon asserted itself in the overall Cork rock music community.

The Sir Henry's building was demolished in 2004 to make way for 'luxury apartments'. A decade later, however, it remains a vacant site at the heart of Cork city. While the club is gone, its spirit lives on in the memories of all those who were part of the Sir Henry's experience.

CHAPTER TWELVE

# BACK IN A TRACKSUIT

[The Sultans of Ping F.C.]

## CROSS-POLLINATION

Entering a new century, the number of active Cork rock acts decreased, with many bands that formed in the 1990s having either broken up or ceased performing. This reflected an evolutionary cycle, evident for some time on Leeside, where bands broke up and members from different groups later came together to form new ones.

A prime example of this was Cork rock act Rulers of the Planet, who formed in 2003. This five-piece included frontman and lead singer Barry McAuliffe, previously a member of Cork alternative rock group Semi.[64] In Rulers of the Planet, McAuliffe was joined by former members of The Shanks, Niall 'Daish' Lynch and Mick Hayes. This sort of cross-pollination between bands is relatively common in Cork due to the size and nature of the rock music scene.

In keeping with their aggressive punk sound, early on in their career, Rulers of the Planet displayed a notable talent for devising provocative names for their various releases. Their debut EP was entitled *No-One Understands The Devil's Music Better Than The Rulers of the Planet* (2003) and this was

---

[64] Semi featured ex-members of Cork bands LMNO Pelican and A Cow In The Water. This group released one album during their career entitled *Mervyn In Toronto* (1999) and also appeared on the Cork-based RTÉ music show *No Disco*.

later followed up with a second EP called *We Are The Late Night Terror Death Squad* (2004). Their debut album *In 30 Minutes We Destroy The Earth* (2005) featured the standout tracks *Backbencher* and *Dimension X*. It was released on Sofa Records and enjoyed positive reviews in both the local and national media - including an impressive review in *Hot Press*. After agreeing a worldwide publishing contract with Jewel DC Publishing in 2005, Rulers of the Planet secured a record deal with leading German record label ZYX Music. They released their second album *Disco Boogie For Death Rockers* in 2007. In addition to their recording career, the band played many high profile gigs such as the Oxegen music festival in 2004, The Spiegeltent in Cork as part of the Cork Midsummer Festival 2008, as well as numerous live shows abroad.

Born out of the ashes of Cork drum 'n' bass collective Bass Odyssey, Sylvia Saint was a four-piece Cork band who were also drawn to heavy rock 'n' roll sounds and acts such as Black Sabbath. Frontman with the group, Graham Finn was a veteran of the Cork music scene, having previously been the guitarist with Emperor of Ice Cream and later a member of Bass Odyssey. Music ran deep in Graham's family, as his father John Finn had been the drummer with Cork band Chapter Five, who had supported Rory Gallagher on occasion.

Graham's first proper introduction to the music industry came via early 1990s Cork rock outfit Emperor of Ice Cream:

> We formed Emperor of Ice Cream in 1992. I was seventeen when we signed with Sony. We moved to London in 1993. I suppose we were signed for two and a half years, then we came back home and were together for about another year. It all happened over a three-and-a-half year period.

Emperor of Ice Cream also included lead singer John 'Haggis' Hegarty, who now runs Sofa Records, drummer John Lynch and bass player Edward Butt. Later, drummer Colm Young replaced John Lynch when the band moved to London. They released a debut EP entitled *Overflow* (1993) and, later, a second EP entitled *William* (1993).

In 1996, Graham Finn formed dance outfit Bass Odyssey with Alan O'Keeffe and Colm Young. Later, MC Strict, also known as Chris O'Driscoll, joined the group. Their first single *Twilight* (1997) won an award for best Irish track at the first Irish Dance Music Awards in 1998. In 1999, they released the *Remote Control Soul EP* and gained widespread national recognition. Bass Odyssey split up in 2003.

Taking their name from porn star Sylvia Saint, Bass Odyssey soon evolved into a new group. Graham explains:

> Sylvia Saint came together when myself, Alan O'Keeffe and Ian Walsh were playing in Bass Odyssey. When that group came to an end, we didn't want to stop making music, so we just started making rock music. I took up the role of singing some songs for a change and we got John Kavanagh in on bass around the end of 2003.

Sylvia Saint released their debut EP *9 Bars of Fury* (2005) on Cork-based ROK Records and they also played the Oxegen music festival in 2005. The Cork band moved to New York in February of 2006 with the intention of recording an album. Since leaving Cork they have maintained a low profile and their debut album has yet to be released.

WAITING ROOM

One of the most accomplished and talented Cork indie bands to emerge in the noughties was Waiting Room. Formed in 2001, while band members Nigel Farrelly and Dave Ahern attended the Music, Management and Sound course at Coláiste Stiofáin Naofa, their line-up was completed by drummer Wayne Dunlea. This trio remained the nucleus of the band throughout their career although, when playing live, Waiting Room often included additional guitarist Rory O'Brien from the Cork-based instrumental act Ten Past Seven.

The Coláiste Stiofáin Naofa course, founded by musician and songwriter Chris Ahern, has provided an important outlet for those seeking to pursue a career in music. Former students of this course include Cork troubadour Niall Connolly, Meteor award-winner Mick Flannery and the talented and successful folk singer-songwriter Sinéad Lohan, who released the hit albums *Who Do You Think I Am* (1995) and *No Mermaid* (1998).

Chris Ahern believes that Waiting Room's Nigel Farrelly is an exceptional songwriter. 'I still think Nigel is one of the best male writers around. Waiting Room are just fantastic!'

Confusion has sometimes surrounded the origin of the group's name but, Carrigaline native and Waiting Room frontman, Nigel Farrelly explains that they 'were just trying to think of names. I came up with that and everyone liked it. It's not from the Fugazi song, as everyone thinks, because I hadn't even heard Fugazi at the time.'

In 2002, they released their debut mini-album *Losing Patience*. This was an indie rock affair and although the band played a number of gigs to promote the release, they were not happy with it and decided not to push the record.

Life was rarely uneventful for Waiting Room. In 2003, the band lost their musical equipment in a devastating fire, which engulfed rehearsal space at the Sunbeam Industrial Estate in

Blackpool, on Cork's northside. In the aftermath of the fire, the local music community rallied together and a benefit gig at the Half Moon Theatre was organised. The instruments were eventually replaced.

With a penchant for intelligent song-writing, haunting melodies and musical vision, Waiting Room stood out from the crowd when they released their self-financed album *Catering For Headphones* (2004) on Out On A Limb Records. Recorded with sound engineer and producer Ross O'Donovan, this long-player received near universal acclaim from music critics. On February 26, 2004, in the *Irish Times* supplement *The Ticket*, journalist Kevin Courtney wrote: 'True to its title, this record caters nicely to those who like to kick back, put on the headphones, and float into the heart of darkness.' Courtney awarded the album four out of five.

On March 10, 2004, *Hot Press* also praised the Cork trio for their efforts, with journalist John Walshe writing:

> It's fantastic to see a young band unafraid to take risks, diverting from the mainstream musical motorway onto a series of less direct but far more beguiling byroads. *Catering For Headphones* beats with an experimental heart, backed up by superb musicianship and genuinely moving songs of real artistic and musical merit. Refreshingly inventive, often magical and consistently brilliant.

He awarded the album nine out of ten in *Hot Press*.

*Catering For Headphones* boasted a number of standout tracks such as the dream-like *Another Take* and the softly plucked lullaby *Return My Rabbits*. The critical success of Waiting Room's first album proper marked something of a watershed locally. Sonically, the group differed from almost all of their contemporaries and this encouraged a shift of emphasis among younger bands. Waiting Room had proved that sometimes 'less is more' and an increased emphasis was now put on production values. It was also noticeable that the influence of British rock began to wane considerably within the local music scene during the early noughties, in direct contrast to the previous decade.

While 2004 proved to be a hectic year for the band with touring and live dates, including the inaugural Oxegen music festival, at Punchestown in County Kildare, and an appearance on RTÉ Two's *Other Voices* music programme, 2005 was more low-key with Waiting Room opting to work on demos for their second album.

The follow-up to *Catering For Headphones* was recorded in 2006 at Black Box Studios in France with Dave Odlum, a former member of The Frames, on production duties. Soon after they completed the recording, however, Waiting Room split up. Both Dave Ahern and Wayne Dunlea later resurfaced in the Cork band Hooray For Humans, while Farrelly teamed up with guitarist Jamie Fennessy – a duo that played just one gig.

In April 2008, Waiting Room reunited for one gig only at Cork's Cyprus Avenue to launch their last album, *Battle Lines Are Gently Drawn* (2008). While their earlier influences had included Sparklehorse, Mercury Rev, Low and Fugazi, their final release counted American rock group Blonde Redhead as its biggest influence. Although the songs on *Battle Lines Are Gently Drawn* were well written and recorded, and in some respects continued where *Catering For Headphones* left off, the record lacked the emotional punch of its predecessor. It did, however, include the standout tracks *Denis* and *Fire Hoops*.

## SIMPLE KID

One musician who reinvented himself in the early noughties was former Young Offenders' frontman Kieran MacFeely. Following the demise of The Young Offenders, MacFeely withdrew from the music business feeling disgruntled and disillusioned, but he made a comeback in 2003 as Simple Kid. He recounts how listening to New York band Mercury Rev inspired his reconnection with music, albeit in a different way from before. Kieran acknowledges:

> After The Young Offenders broke up, I was sitting one morning in total squalor in a bed-sit in north London. I put on the then brand new Mercury Rev album *Deserter's Songs* (1998) and heard the song *Holes* for the first time. It was so beautiful! It wasn't 'fun' and it wasn't jokey, it took itself seriously. In that four minute period, I realised just how uninterested I was in The Young Offenders and our whole 'glam' scene. I started listening to country music soon after and that's probably been the biggest influence on me since. So was it a natural progression? More like a personality transplant in the space of four minutes. It's funny how a good song can affect you.

Interestingly, around this time, on January 8, 1999, Mercury Rev had the opportunity to inspire other Cork musicians and music fans when they played Sir Henry's. They were supported on the night by local act Hooky. Guitarist with Mercury Rev, Sean 'Grasshopper' Mackowiak, remembers that his band had heard of Sir Henry's from photographer Steve Gullick before they came to Ireland. While on tour, the band specifically asked if there would be a gig in Cork. Grasshopper also provides an insight into the enthusiasm of the Cork audience that night:

> The Sir Henry's show was crazy! The crowd was nuts and so enthusiastic after the show that they tried to mob our bus. They were trying to tip the bus over. It was rocking back and forth and we were all laughing. It was really crazy because the bus was ready to tip and the driver was just like: 'I'm getting out of here!'

The Mercury Rev song *Holes* had a profound effect on Kieran MacFeely and his career. Having been christened Simple Kid by a homeless man while in the US, he re-emerged with his debut solo album *Simple Kid 1* (2003), more commonly referred to as *SK1*, which was released on the 2m label. It was a confident and well-honed debut LP, rich in social commentary and displaying a new depth to his song-writing that had been lacking in The Young Offenders' output. Discussing his new recording methodology and influences, in keeping with his new moniker, Kieran admits:

> There was a profound sense of keeping it simple. No producers, no fancy studios, no record [company] executive meetings about music etc. I had nothing to lose and felt very excited about having a new computer. I had literally just started to programme about one month before I started the album. You can hear it too…. everything is chopped within an inch of its life. It was like my new toy, so I had to use it on nearly every track. I felt really liberated by recording on my own too, as I could write, record and finish a song in an afternoon. It all felt easy and quick and uncomplicated. So there was no pressure.

Unfortunately, just as the album was released, Simple Kid's

record company went bust, leaving *SK1* in limbo and depriving MacFeely of the support necessary to promote it. This was a pity, as the quality of his song-writing shone through on the album especially on tracks such as *Truck On*, *Staring At The Sun* and the immensely well-crafted songs *The Average Man* and *Drugs* - in which he questions various societal addictions including religion and television. Perhaps unfairly, Simple Kid was later branded 'the Irish Beck' for his efforts, a reference he is keen to distance himself from.

Based in London, MacFeely released his second solo album entitled *Simple Kid 2* (2006), also known as *SK2*, on Country Gentleman Recordings, to much critical acclaim, both at home and abroad. Compared to his previous LP, *SK2* was a triumph of home recording and a more rounded affair with each track flowing effortlessly. A personal yet ambitious record, *SK2* revealed that a Corkman's propensity for conjuring up quirky rock music was still very much alive in the twenty-first century. *SK2* was heavily laden with infectious songs: the groove infused opener *Lil' King Kong*; the amusing lyrical advice of *Self-Help Book*; the lo-fi ballad *Old Domestic Cat*; the spacey epic *Serotonin*, which dissects the true nature of happiness; and the closing track *Love's An Enigma (ptII)*.

Reflecting on making *SK2*, MacFeely, who has described his musical sound as 'country music for city people', says he recognised that by creating a record that was a genuine departure from his last, he ran the risk of alienating the fan-base that *SK1* had given him:

> This album was more country and less complicated with no computers and no beats 'n' blips. It was very spontaneous with all the mistakes left in. My computer was stolen on tour and I think that affected the music

quite considerably. I got back into just leaving things alone on tape and letting them be what they are. I suppose it could have alienated everyone that liked the first album but, hey, I felt good changing.

Following the release of *SK2*, which was later released in America by Yep Roc Records in 2007, Simple Kid was afforded greater recognition. His sophomore album received rave reviews in the media. It was included in *Mojo* magazine's top 50 albums of the year and Simple Kid was recognised by *Rolling Stone* as a breakthrough act. Furthermore, MacFeely acquired some impressive support slots with Kings of Leon in America. He also supported acts such as REM, Spiritualized and Richard Ashcroft and performed at major festivals like Glastonbury and Oxegen. In addition, the song *Mommy n Daddy* from *SK2* was used in an Eircom commercial in Ireland, while *Lil' King Kong* was included on the soundtrack for the Hollywood film *Jumper* (2008).

In a live setting, Simple Kid gigs frequently enthralled audiences due to MacFeely's use of technology and unusual approaches to performing. For instance, he was known to duet with Kermit The Frog on occasion, thanks to the incorporation of a projector in his live shows.

WHERE'S ME CULTURE?

While Cork ex-pats like Kieran MacFeely carved out careers abroad, Cork was set to transform in 2005 after being designated a European Capital of Culture. Although the year proved successful in marketing Cork as a cultural hub, it fostered cynicism in many quarters. Communications at local level regarding the Cork 2005 message appeared problematic and this led many in the Cork arts community, and in particular, the local music community, to feel a degree of alienation from the Cork 2005 organisation. The spectacular opening ceremony, featuring the Waterford theatre group Spraoi and Cork hurling legend Seán Óg Ó hAilpín, was a success that attracted 80,000 people to Leeside. However, many of the other events throughout the year seemed to take place relatively unnoticed by the local community. The festivities did suffer from a lack of large inclusive set-piece events such as open-air concerts - accessible to the average Corkonian. Such was the level of despondency among the city's arts community that an alternative, voluntary, independent group called Where's Me Culture? was founded in advance of 2005. The name was an adaptation of the Sultans' song title *Where's Me Jumper?*. A central figure in Where's Me Culture? was Seán O'Neill who came from a music background, having fronted 1980s local pop band Burning Embers and managed Sir Henry's from 1988 until 1996:

> I think the Cork 2005 organisation missed the boat on so many things. There is a rich history of music and poetry in Cork. There was a lot of discontent around at the time and I think it was proven to be well founded because Cork 2005 was a bit highbrow. I think they suffered from a lack of communication, so there were a few missed opportunities. I don't think they engaged properly at the start and they had their set ideas before they even came to the public. It was as if they said: 'Okay, we're doing one bit from the arts and we're doing one bit from music etc.' They could have asked: 'What's most important in Cork?' I think music is important in Cork, music is absolutely central. It's everywhere!

The group behind Where's Me Culture? decided to focus on Cork's indigenous culture and to hold events featuring local bands, DJs, comedians and artists. Its first event, The Where's Me Culture Big Party, was held on January 8, 2005. The line-up of this sold-out event included many local rock acts such as Rulers of the Planet, Fred and Rest (a Ballincollig instrumental four-piece), as well as acts from other genres and popular local DJs like Jim X Comet and Mike D'Arcy.

Further events included The Big Picnic in Fota, which attracted 5,000 people during the summer. Where's Me Culture? also established a website, www.wheresmeculture.com, a Speaker's Corner and a short-lived newspaper.

Paradoxically, in the year when Cork was European Capital of Culture, The Lobby Bar on Union Quay was forced to close. This centrally located venue had served audiences and musicians from a variety of genres. Its loss was widely felt, not only because it was positioned to play a key role in that year's events, but also because it only charged for using a sound engineer, rather than imposing a venue charge, something that made it accessible for younger up-and-coming bands. The Lobby was immortalised in award-winning musician John Spillane's song *Magic Nights in the Lobby Bar* (from his 2002 album *Will We Be Magic or What?*).

Similarly disappointing was the fact that in 2005 the Cork School of Music was still operating in hotel rooms and scattered venues in the city. Failure to have their new premises ready for the 'Year of Culture' was a debacle that fuelled cynicism about the commitment of politicians to the arts, as it was back in 1999 (a local and European election year) that the then Cork-based Fianna Fáil Minister for Education and Science, Micheál Martin, had announced that the school would have a new home. The new school was eventually opened in September of 2007. One politician with an interest in this was Green Party Senator Dan Boyle, a Cork TD during 2005. Unusually for an Irish politician, he has a background in music having played with Blueprint, a local band named after a 1973 Rory Gallagher album. They were active during Cork's punk era playing venues like The Arc and UCC College Bar.[65] Dan thinks the attitudes of politicians to music:

> ...could have something to do with age but the usual instinct is to protect the public interest by keeping noise levels down. Generally, they don't look at the wider interest like that young people are inconvenienced. Meeting their social needs is the last thing that most politicians tend to think about.

As part of the Capital of Culture celebrations, former Microdisney and Fatima Mansions frontman Cathal Coughlan was commissioned to compose a new work. Premiered at Fr. Matthew Hall on September 16, 2005, his song-cycle *Flannery's Mounted Head* followed the derailed, aimless life of its anti-hero.

Long considered an anti-establishment 'outsider', Coughlan now found himself on the other side of the fence. The irony of being part of the official Cork 2005 celebrations was not lost on him:

> The whole thing was so ripe with ironies that it was just impossible to think about them to be honest, because it was just terrifying to contemplate. My overriding feeling was I didn't want to accept the budget and then deliver something that was po-faced or childish. So I

---
[65] Blueprint supported the group Mama's Boys (hard rock/heavy metal act) from County Fermanagh in The Arc.

didn't dwell too much on any of it to be honest.

After the demise of The Fatima Mansions, Cathal pursued a solo career that yielded the albums *Grand Necropolitan* (1996), *Black River Falls* (2000) and arguably his most accomplished solo album, *The Sky's Awful Blue* (2002). Cathal's 2006 long-player *Foburg* was derived from *Flannery's Mounted Head*. Filmed and directed by Irish filmmaker Johnny Gogan, a documentary called *The Adventures of Flannery* (2007) was later premiered at the 2007 Cork Film Festival. It explored the musical theatre presentation of *Flannery's Mounted Head* in 2005 as well as the life and work of Cathal Coughlan.

## THE RENEWAL OF THE FRANK AND WALTERS

While the Microdisney frontman made a welcome return to Cork in 2005, another famous Cork act was blazing the comeback trail, albeit with a new line-up. The future of The Frank And Walters had been thrown into doubt following the departure of their original guitarist Niall Linehan. This led to a period of soul-searching for the remaining band members. Lead singer Paul Linehan recalls: 'I had a chat with Ashley and he was saying that he wanted to keep going. We never really gave up. It was just nothing happened for maybe a year or two, although I was always writing songs.'

While the Franks were dormant, Paul divided his time between carpentry (he had worked in furniture restoration before his music career) and doing a limited amount of music production for bands. Paul believes returning to carpentry helped his song-writing:

> It kind of keeps you in touch with the real world. If you are going to write songs from the point of view

of a musician, you could be a bit isolated and I think people might not be able to relate to you as much. But if you are like everybody else, you can write a song about working or the circle of trying to make ends meet and pay your electricity bill.

Soon the Franks recruited a new guitarist, Wicklow native Kevin Pedreschi. They adopted an unusual recruitment strategy to secure his services. Paul confesses:

> We prefer to stumble across people rather than go looking for them. We never really wanted to put an ad out looking for a guitarist. This time we just got lucky. At the time, I was living in Wicklow and I was out in a nightclub there. Kevin knew I was in The Frank And Walters and he had just come back from Australia. He told me that he was looking for some session work and asked could I help him out. I was looking at him funny and I just said to myself: 'God! This is a guitarist and we kind of need one!' I didn't know him that well at the time, so I asked a few of the lads in the town what he was like as a person, as to me that was more important than his abilities. They said he was a very nice chap and very easy-going. It turned out that he was all that and he worked out fantastic!

With Kevin on board, the Franks eased themselves back on to the live circuit by playing a handful of shows in venues like Whelan's in Dublin and An Crúiscín Lán in Cork. It was at their Cork show that they met Cillin O'Flynn and Pat Doyle, a chance encounter that led to the resurrection of their recording career. Paul explains: 'Cillin loved some of the new songs. He said that he would love to put out a record for us.'

The following year, the independent Irish record label FIFA Records was founded.[66] Run by Cillin O'Flynn, it was on this label that The Frank And Walters would release new material. O'Flynn also became the Franks' new manager, assisted by Pat Doyle. Paul Linehan and his band-mates now became far more visible on the live front, incorporating a strong work ethic that would propel them to new heights.

To test the water, the band released a single called *You Asked Me* in 2005. This release also included an alternative version of their classic track *How Can I Exist* and the song *Pathways*. Having managed to buy their back catalogue from their former label Setanta Records, the Franks released a collection of b-sides and rarities called *Souvenirs* (2005) later that year on FIFA Records.

A new interest in the band had been generated and the Franks were now selling out most of their gigs. With this momentum behind them, the group prepared to record a new album, their first in six years. To help them, they recruited keyboardist Cian Corbett, who began performing live with the band in the second half of 2005.

In December of that year and in a move reminiscent of the late Johnny Cash, the Franks played a gig for prisoners in Dublin's Wheatfield Prison. While entertaining the inmates, they also recorded the vocals for a song called *Fight*, which would eventually appear on their next album. They felt recording in Wheatfield added atmosphere to the song, which seemed appropriate, as the track was intended as a metaphor for not giving up in the face of adversity.

While the Franks pursued a hectic schedule of live gigs across Europe, they also found time for an appearance at The Spiegeltent as part of the Cork Midsummer Festival and a

---

[66] FIFA Records stands for Fresh Indie Frontal Attack Records.

headline slot at the inaugural Mitchelstown Indie-Pendence Music Festival in north Cork. In late September 2006, The Frank And Walters released *Miles And Miles*, the lead single from their forthcoming new long-player, which was accompanied by the b-side *Summertime*.

The release of the band's comeback album *A Renewed Interest In Happiness* (2006) followed in October. Produced by Dave Couse, this twelve-track album showcased a diverse collection of reassuringly upbeat, infectious jingly-jangly guitar-laden indie rock songs. The Franks' new album, which had a harder rock sound than their previous LPs, received some glowing reviews in the media and helped the band establish their credentials with a new generation of indie rock fans. Highlights of the album included *Fight*, *Miles And Miles*, *City Lights* and *Johnny Cash*.

Reviewing *A Renewed Interest In Happiness* in the October 26 edition of *Hot Press*, Mark Keane stated: 'There is an audible swagger on this recording; confidence bleeds from one song to the next. ... It's impossible to hold the Franks in anything but the fondest of regard and now, just to reinforce that point, they have made their most complete album to date.' Keane awarded the album a respectable eight out of ten.

*Fight* was the next single to be lifted from the LP and this was backed up by b-sides *Changed My Way Of Thinking* and *Summer Evenings*. The striking video for this single, directed by American film student Brian McElhaney, featured predominantly black and white clips of random people, filmed around Dublin, intertwined with footage of the band playing on a rooftop in true Irish rock tradition.

The final single from *A Renewed Interest In Happiness* was *City Lights*. This was accompanied by a reworking of The

Undertones' punk classic *Teenage Kicks*. The colourful music video for *City Lights* was filmed in the Crane Lane Theatre in Cork and featured a large cast of locals dancing to a live performance from the band. Recognising their increasing popularity, the Franks also released the DVD *The Frank And Walters: Live At The Spiegeltent in Cork City* in 2007.

## THE RETURN OF THE SULTANS OF PING

While The Frank And Walters had wrestled self-doubt and overcome adversity to rekindle their career, another famous Cork group made an unexpected, yet triumphant, return to Leeside in the noughties. Early in 2005, *Today FM* DJ Ian Dempsey held a contest to identify the best Irish song of the last twenty-five years. Listeners were asked to vote. Predictably, U2 topped the poll with their rock ballad *One*, but only narrowly beat Cork's own Sultans of Ping who came second with their anthem *Where's Me Jumper?*. The high placing in such a prestigious poll took the band by surprise and demonstrated that the Irish public had not forgotten them.

Sultans' drummer Morty McCarthy recalls being a bit bemused by the whole affair: 'The *Today FM* poll result was very odd. I was working in France with REM at the time. That result came out of nowhere.' By contrast, outspoken lead singer Niall O'Flaherty claims, in his typical tongue-in-cheek fashion, that he was a bit disgruntled to have been thwarted by U2. He acknowledges that: 'It was a bit disappointing but a massive amount of people did vote for us. It was quite amazing that they would choose that song.'

The Sultans of Ping had been mulling over a possible reunion for a while and their new-found recognition seemed to give them confidence. For their comeback, they had a new recruit. As bass player Alan MacFeely had moved on to play with a new London-based band called Sister, alongside former Young Offenders' bassist Steve Hackett, he was not participating in the reunion. MacFeely's place was taken by former Cypress, Mine! guitarist Ian Olney, who had played in a band called Pharmacy with Morty McCarthy after the demise of the Sultans.

A five-date tour was announced for December 2005, which included shows in Dundalk, Dublin, Belfast and Cork. Ahead of this tour, a warm-up show at a venue called The Fat Surfer in Essex, in England, was announced for October. This would be the band's first live date since 1997 and was essentially a practice gig before they played larger venues. The Fat Surfer gig was a sell-out and a huge success. In Cork, Sultans' dates in Club One and The Savoy completely sold out. With arguably their best line-up, it was not surprising that interest in the band had re-ignited and a third Leeside gig was soon added.

On Tuesday, December 20, 2005, the Sultans of Ping performed an explosive set to a full to capacity Club One. Their opening song *Back In A Tracksuit* sounded like it had been written especially for the occasion with the crowd responding enthusiastically. The audience was a mix of older fans and younger people who had never seen the band before, but who had heard of them through word of mouth endorsements. During the show, the stage actually began to move, such was the pressure from the sea of bodies directly in front of it. To ensure there was no repeat of the violence that had marred their final gig in Sir Henry's, the band appeared to have brought their own security. The Sultans' played two encores, the last featuring the song *Turnip Fish* to which the crowd responded by embarking on the trademark *Turnip Fish* bicycle dance.

At The Savoy, the following night, there was an even larger audience of over 1,000 people. They included Cork City F.C. players George O'Callaghan and Joe Gamble, whom Niall invited on-stage, complete with the championship trophy, to celebrate Cork City winning the League of Ireland in 2005. Given the number of football references in the Sultans' music and Morty's devotion to the club, this seemed fitting. The next night the band rounded off their Cork comeback with a well-attended final show at Club One.

In 2006, the Sultans of Ping released their first live DVD, *U Talk 2 Much: Live At The Cork Savoy Theatre* on Cherry Red Records. So great was demand, that it quickly sold out in the UK. That year they also delivered a number of incendiary performances, including two homecoming shows in Cork at Christmas.

A good indicator of how alive a band really is, is whether or not they are still creating new music. Plenty of musical corpses have toured up and down the country all in the name of nostalgia and easy money. Niall O'Flaherty and his band were not in this category. In 2007, the Sultans of Ping released their first new single in eleven years, *Girlwatchin'*. This self-released sharp rockabilly number was accompanied by two other new tracks, *Kick That Dirty Job* and *Ladybug Boy*. Since its release, *Girlwatchin'* has become a live favourite among Sultans fans.

In 2008, the band continued to tour and to sell-out shows with live dates in Amsterdam, Dublin and on Leeside, where they played one of Cork's newer venues, The Pavilion, on Carey's Lane. Niall continues to write. He says:

The future plans are to put out some new material...
at least a single or a mini LP. I have written some new

songs. One of them is a punk-pop number called *Same Old A Holes* and the other tune is called *Not As Pretty As You Think You Are*. Hopefully, there is a single there. Those songs are ready to arrange while the other songs that I have been working on are less developed. To be honest, I don't want to play unless we are playing new stuff.

## THE FUTURE - POST 2009?

While the re-formation of rock acts like the Sultans of Ping gave younger music fans an opportunity to see and hear classic Cork rock music, this should not overshadow the accomplishments of a new generation of talented Leesiders. In fact, one added advantage of having acts like the Sultans return is that they often offer support slots to younger bands and in some cases take them out on tour, thus providing newer acts with the possibility of winning over larger audiences. Given the thriving live scene on Leeside, a new glossy magazine called *Backstage Traffic* emerged in the middle of the noughties and for a period gave great exposure to the local rock music scene. During 2006, the Mitchelstown Indie-Pendence Festival was launched with many Cork city musicians and music fans making the short journey to this north Cork town. Over the years, this successful festival has gone from strength to strength and featured impressive performances from both established and less established artists. The Sultans, Franks and Scottish band The Proclaimers headlined the 2006 event, while the festival has also given experience and exposure to local acts like Hooray For Humans and Bishopstown guitarist Cian Walsh.

So what of the future? At the forefront of the current crop of talented Cork indie acts are Fred. Regarded as one of the most hard-working bands in the local music scene, they have also been one of the most resilient. Technically, Fred formed in Tralee in the mid-1990s, under the name Fred The Purple Haired Ninja, and later shortened their name, but the only remaining member from this period is guitarist Jamie Hanrahan. Active as a five-piece since 1999, Fred's most consistent line-up has been: Joseph O'Leary (vocals/guitar), Jamie Hanrahan (guitar), Jamin O'Donovan (bass), Éibhlín O'Gorman (piano), and Justin O'Mahony (drums). Éibhlín O'Gorman departed the band in 2008 and was replaced by Carolyn Goodwin, who joined Fred for a three-year period before leaving to focus on jazz and classical music.

Brandishing a sound that leaned more towards the lighter side of indie rock, Fred continued the lineage of positivity and unrestrained enthusiasm pursued by The Frank And Walters. In a way, Fred offered the perfect soundtrack to the madness which engulfed Ireland during the Celtic Tiger years. However, their willingness to experiment musically by incorporating instruments not routinely associated with the rock genre, e.g. cello, trumpet and saxophone, allowed them to create their own variation – a local rock-pop hybrid.

Fred have also been productive in terms of releasing material. Since the *Fred EP* (2000), they have managed to release a number of albums including: *Can't Stop, I'm Being Timed* (2002); *Making Music So You Don't Have To* (2005), which they launched with a date at Cork Opera House; and *Go God Go* (2008). The pop-sensibilities of their 2008 long-player garnered considerable airplay and attention both nationally and internationally, as well as critical acclaim. *Go God Go* was voted 'Album of the Year' in a listener's poll on *96FM*'s *The Green Room* radio show. It received the same accolade from the Dublin daily free-sheet *Herald AM*. In 2009, the band was nominated for a Meteor Music Award in the '2FM Hope For 2009' category. While fulfilling their touring commitments, Fred consolidated a fan-base in Canada and signed to Canadian independent record label Sparks Music.

Cork's Stanley Super 800 are another key act who have been a regular fixture on the Leeside live circuit. The brain-child of Stan O'Sullivan, formerly of The Shanks, Stanley Super 800 first emerged at the end of the 1990s. Initially, a solo project, Stan later developed this into a band consisting of Michael 'Tosh' O'Sullivan, Flor Rahilly and Dave Hackett (former drummer in Cork metal band Ten Point Rule). Frontman Stan O'Sullivan explains how the group evolved:

> I started doing favours for people like support slots. Then I began making electronic tracks all the time and was kind of moving more in that direction from 1998/1999. It took about two years for the Stanley Super 800 group to start playing gigs. But the band only settled on a line-up in January 2003.

Reflecting on what influences their sound, Stan admits to liking 'odd music. I like bands like Pram [a band from Birmingham] and I still like The Stranglers, and Jonathan Richman and The Modern Lovers. I think we sound a lot like them, but not intentionally, people just seem to think we sound like that.' To date, Stanley Super 800 have released two studio albums, *Stanley Super 800* (2004) and *Louder And Clearer* (2007). The latter was nominated for the Choice Music Prize in 2008.

Macroom-based band Remma are another Cork group who may have a promising future. Armed with a more conventional rock sound, they famously caught the attention of former Smiths' frontman Morrissey, who signed the young band to his Attack label. This saw their debut EP *Worry Young* (2004) released in Europe and the US. The Cork rockers supported Morrissey at London's Earls Court and Dublin's Point Theatre in late 2004. However, their career was essentially put on hold after frontman Shane O'Herlihy became seriously ill. He has now recovered and according to their online blog, Remma are working with Limerick producer Noel Hogan (formerly of The Cranberries) on a debut album.

Local performer Áine Duffy, from Bandon, was highlighted by Tony Clayton-Lea in a November 2008 review in the *Irish Times* supplement *The Ticket*. Clayton-Lea insisted that Duffy is in the lineage of Nun Attax, Stump and Microdisney and definitely in the category of those Cork bands that 'made the word "nutter" a byword for creative genius'. As Clayton-Lea suggested, she is also one to watch.

The economic upturn generated by the Celtic Tiger has now been followed by more uncertain times, which some have speculated could lead to a golden era in Irish music. How this plays out remains to be seen, but there are some performers outside the realm of rock music who may be well placed for success in these difficult times. One of these is Meteor award-winning Cork songwriter and folk musician Mick Flannery.

## THE POWER OF THE OUTSIDER

There is no doubting that the musical landscape of Cork city has changed since the days of Rory Gallagher. Styles, trends and performers have come and gone, but the power of his music remains. Local DJ John Byrne sums this up by saying: 'There are Rory Gallagher cover bands everywhere now, particularly since he died, but it was cranking up even before then.' Musically, Cork has an affinity for the rebellious 'outsider'. Rory was not born in Cork, but his outsider status came not from this, but from his outstanding skill as a guitarist. This skill was first recognised in the showband era, during which he emerged as a musical force on Leeside, then in the international arena and finally, and most importantly, it was acknowledged amongst his peers. Rory's accomplishments have been preserved, not only on his many records, which are still available today, but also through Cork city landmarks and commemorative events.

By contrast, Finbarr Donnelly's music is no longer readily available though, in his time, he too was inspirational. One of his peers, Cathal Coughlan, describes how the influence of a performer like Donnelly can be lost within a generation:

> I have gone through various phases of music making and seen people appear and disappear without trace. Finbarr Donnelly died before people had a chance to appreciate what he did. I will always remember it because it was through Nun Attax that I first thought the whole music thing might be possible to enter. But even his work can just vanish. Don't expect people to know about you or remember you.

John Spillane suggests that it would have been good to see how a performer like Donnelly would have matured, but hints that he was also an 'outsider':

> It's such a pity that Donnelly died so young because it would have been interesting to see what he would have done. He was a mad looking guy with a shaved head. He used a lot of scary tactics and he was outrageous, but I got the impression that he was a really lovely sensitive kind of a guy and a lot of it was just a mad front. I think he was a bit of a refugee.

# CORK ROCK

John Byrne theorises that there is a paradox about attitudes to rock music in Cork. He says there is a kind of 'parochial patriotism' that means fans continue to support local acts, while being victims of 'a kind of under-confidence trick'. He reflects that this 'leads people to really believe that stuff from America is better. I think that holds for musicians as well to be honest. So you have inspired versions of things that came from elsewhere and sometimes there was a tiny little bit of individuality that rose to the top and gave it a little bit of a cut above.'

In a city like Cork, the rock music scene has constantly evolved and it is not possible to do justice to all those who have contributed to this phenomenon over five decades. Even in the 1960s, American and British rock music inspired musicians on Leeside and across Ireland. Since then, with television, the Internet and globalisation, the cultures and trends that Irish people identify with are hugely more complex. This is, however, not necessarily a bad thing and may yield greater diversity and even greater choice in the future. What role Cork rock music will play in this will be determined by future generations but, as Rory Gallagher, the Sultans of Ping, The Frank And Walters and others have proved – Cork rock travels!

# BIBLIOGRAPHY

Beecher, Seán, *A Dictionary of Cork Slang* (The Collins Press, Cork, 2004)

Campbell, Sean, & Smyth, Gerry, *Beautiful Day: Forty Years of Irish Rock* (Atrium, Cork University Press, Cork, 2005)

Coghe, Jean-Noël, (translated by Lorna Carson & Brian Steer), *Rory Gallagher A Biography* (Mercier Press, Cork, 2002)

Harper, Colin, & Hodgett, Trevor, *Irish Folk, Trad & Blues: A Secret History* (The Collins Press, Cork, 2005)

Lyons, Jack, *The Frank And Walters: A Renewed Interested In Reading* (Max Elyan Publishing, Cork, 2007)

McAvoy, Gerry, & Chrisp, Pete, *Riding Shotgun* (SPG Triumph, Maidstone, 2005)

McCarthy, Morty, *Dowtcha Boy! An Anthology of Cork Slang* (The Collins Press, Cork, 2004)

McDermott, P., Hurley, K., & O'Toole, C., *Get That Monster Off The Stage* (Cork Campus Radio, 2002)

O'Callaghan, Antóin, *The Lord Mayors of Cork 1900 to 2000* (Inversnaid Publications, Cork, 2000)

O'Halloran, Daragh, *Green Beat: The Forgotten Era of Irish Rock* (The Brehon Press, Belfast, 2006)

Power, Vincent, *Send 'Em Home Sweatin': The Showbands' Story* (Kildanore Press, Dublin, 1990)

Smyth, Gerry, *Noisy Island: A Short History of Irish Popular Music* (Cork University Press, Cork, 2005)

**Newspapers & Magazines:**
*Backstage Traffic*
*Choc-A-Bloc*
*Cork Independent*
*Evening Echo*
*Hot Press*
*Irish Examiner*
*Irish Times*
*Melody Maker*
*NME*
*Sunny Days*
*Village*
*Zeitgeist*

# USEFUL WEBSITES FOR CORK ROCK MUSIC FANS

**Bands:**

- The official Frank And Walters website: www.facebook.com/frankandwalters
- The official Fred website: www.fredtheband.com
- The Hank Wedel and Open Kitchen website: www.myspace.com/hankwedelandopenkitchen
- The High Llamas website: www.highllamas.com
- The official Hot Guitars website: www.hotguitarsband.com
- The official Loudest Whisper website: www.loudestwhisper.com
- The official Métisse website: www.facebook.com/metissemusic
- The official Real Mayonnaize website: www.myspace.com/realmayonnaize
- The official Remma website: www.myspace.com/remmamusic
- The official Rubyhorse website: www.rubyhorse.com
- The official Rulers of the Planet website: www.myspace.com/rulersoftheplanet
- Kev Hopper's Stump website: http://www.spoombung.co.uk/Stump.html
- Sister official website: https://myspace.com/sistermusic
- The official Stanley Super 800 website: http://ss800.org/
- The official Sultans of Ping website: www.sultansofping.com
- The official Waiting Room website: https://myspace.com/waitingroomirl

# CORK ROCK

**Solo Performers:**
- The official Cathal Coughlan website: www.cathalcoughlan.com
- The official Niall Connolly website: www.niallconnolly.com
- The official Áine Duffy website: www.aineduffy.ie
- The official Rory Gallagher website: www.rorygallagher.com
- The official John Spillane website: www.johnspillane.com
- The official Freddie White website: www.freddiewhite.com

**Fansites:**
- The official Frank And Walters fansite: www.frankandwalters.net
- Get That Monster Off The Stage – website that accompanies the radio documentary on Finbarr Donnelly and his bands: www.getthatmonsteroffthestage.com
- The official Jack Lyons website: www.thewho.net/irishjack
- The Microdisney fansite: http://www.bubbyworld.com/microdisney/microdisneyindex.htm
- The Sultans of Ping unofficial website: http://ping.fishtank.org.uk

**Venues, Clubs and Listings Websites:**
- Connolly's of Leap website: www.facebook.com/ConnollysOfLeap
- Cork Gig Listing website: www.corkgigs.com
- Cork Opera House website: www.corkoperahouse.ie
- The Crane Lane Theatre: www.cranelanetheatre.ie
- Cyprus Avenue website: www.cyprusavenue.ie
- De Barras of Clonakilty website: www.debarra.ie
- The Everyman Palace Theatre website: www.everymanpalace.com
- Freakscene (Cork indie club night): www.freakscene.com
- The Lee Delta Blues Club website: www.leedeltablues.com
- The Pavilion website: www.pavilioncork.com
- The Savoy website: http://savoytheatre.ie

MARK MCAVOY

# CORK ROCK AND RELATED ACTS DISCOVERED WHILE RESEARCHING THIS BOOK

Above The Maple
A Cow In The Water
Adolf Grunt
Alice In Wonderband
And The Rest In Jellies
Anomie
Anthony & De Confidence
Antibodies
Arm The Elderly
Asylum
Bacchus And The Pards
Bacuzzi
Bedroom Convention
Beethoven
Belsen
Belsonic Sound
Benny's Head
Berserk
Beveren's Toy
Blenderhead

Blueprint
Blunt
Boa Morte
Bootlace
Box Camera
Annette Buckley
Burning Embers
Buttox
Carbon Copy
Carnun Rising
Caroline Shout
Cathal Coughlan
Cavalcade
Censored Vision
Ceremony
Chapter Five
Charlie Don't Surf
Citizen Elmo
Coil
Collapse

# CORK ROCK

Richard Collins
Niall Connolly
Crowd Control
Crystal
Cyclefly
Cypress, Mine!
Dead Babies Don't Vomit
Death By Voltage
Defect
Denis And The Dinmakers
Dirty Face Kids
Dirty Turtles
Driveshaft
Áine Duffy
Duped
Dust
Dwight
Earthquake
Echoes In The Shallow Bay
Echogram
El Bastardo
Emperor Of Ice Cream
Empty Space
Eve Of Mind
Exit: Pursued By A Bear

Exit The Street
Expresso Mambo
Factor Fiction
Five Go Down To The Sea?
Mick Flannery
Flatline
Flex And The Fastweather
Fred
Freefall
Rory Gallagher
Goldfish Syndrome
Grand
Hidden Fears
Hogmoths
Honey Badger
Hooky
Hooray For Humans
Hope Is Noise
Hot Guitars
Houlinboi
Hubble
Hueman
Ideal End
Idol Joy
If

Ignition
Impact
Inhaler
Jezery
Jinx
Jodavino
Judith Sunrise
Junkyard
Keroscene
Kilterr
Kitsch
Kryteria
Lerner
Lift
LMNO Pelican
Sinéad Lohan
Loko Parentis
Loose
Los Langeros
Loudest Whisper
Lunatic Fringe
Manhole
Max Von Rap
Mean Features
Medication Blues Band

Métisse
Microdisney
Mr Not So Famous
Muffdive
My Corduroy
My Evil Ex
Nassau
Nine Wassies From Bainne
No Sangoma
Nun Attax
Stephen O'Brien
Open Kitchen
Opium For The Masses
Oswego
Painting By Numbers
Paradox
Paragon
Patrick Street
Paul And The Bulbs
Perfidia
Philip K Dick
Porcelyn Tears
Prague Over Here
Princes Street
Psychotic Reaction

# CORK ROCK

Pontius Pilot And The Naildrivers
Pure Meanness
Queen Kong
Racer
Rakastan
Real Mayonnaize
Remma
Rest
Revere
Romeo Butcher
Room 101
Rubyhorse
Rulers Of The Planet
Sabre
Scullion
Semi
Serengeti Long Walk
Sexy Shop
Short Circuit
Sideproject
Silo
Simple Kid
Sindikat
Sleepy Hollow
Sludgehook
Small Change
Snowman
Sonic Icons
Soon
Southpaw
Spacecake
John Spillane
Stanley Super 800
Stump
Subsonic
Suburban Rebels
Sun Factory
Swipe
Sylvia Saint
Syndikat
Tacapuna
Taste
T&T
Ten Point Rule
The Axills
The Banditz
The Berries
The Black Spots
The Boo Bees

# MARK MCAVOY

| | |
|---|---|
| The Buds | The Lotion |
| The Buzzards | The Lynch Mob |
| The Chapter House | The Martels |
| The Citadels | The Nellies |
| The Constant Reminders | The Orange Fettishes |
| The Dancing Bastards From Hell | The Pakt |
| The Dardanelles | The Perry Fans |
| The Dixies | The Red Sea Pedestrians |
| The Fontana Showband | The Rose Garden |
| The Frank And Walters | The Shades |
| The Gems | The Shanks |
| The Girls Of Summer | The Slaamacs |
| The Grunts | The Sneakies |
| The Herbivores | The Stern Tubes |
| The How And Why Insects | The Streets |
| The Impact | The Sultans Of Ping F.C. |
| The K-9s | The Sun Kings |
| The Khymer Rouge | The Thin Band |
| The Kidz | The 3355409s |
| The Kitsch Collective | The 5 O'Clock Heroes |
| The Krux | The Vards |
| The Laminators | The Village Idiots |
| The Last Call | The Vital Spark |
| The Lee Valley String Band | The V-Necks |
| The Little Death | The Wasters |

# CORK ROCK

| | |
|---|---|
| The Wizards | Unknown Wrecks |
| The Yaks | Violent Phobia |
| The Young Offenders | Waiting Room |
| This Is Not A Telephone | Cian Walsh |
| This Year's Models | Hank Wedel |
| Tidal Suns | Weevil |
| Too Much | Freddie White |
| Trampoline | Without The |
| Treehouse | XX Telex |
| Ugly Beautiful | 1990 |
| Urban Blitz | 24 Hour Doggs |

www.ingramcontent.com/pod-product-compliance
Lightning Source LLC
Chambersburg PA
CBHW050529300426
44113CB00012B/2018